BARKLEY FUNCTIONAL IMPAIRMENT SCALE—CHILDREN AND ADOLESCENTS (BFIS-CA)

Selected Works by Russell A. Barkley

For more information, visit the author's website: *www.russellbarkley.org*

FOR PROFESSIONALS

ADHD in Adults: What the Science Says
Russell A. Barkley, Kevin R. Murphy, and Mariellen Fischer

Executive Functions:
What They Are, How They Work, and Why They Evolved
Russell A. Barkley

FOR GENERAL READERS

Taking Charge of ADHD, Revised Edition:
The Complete, Authoritative Guide for Parents
Russell A. Barkley

Your Defiant Child: Eight Steps to Better Behavior
Russell A. Barkley

Your Defiant Teen:
10 Steps to Resolve Conflict and Rebuild Your Relationship
Russell A. Barkley and Arthur L. Robin with Christine M. Benton

ADULT ASSESSMENT SCALES

Barkley Adult ADHD Rating Scale–IV (BAARS-IV)
Russell A. Barkley

Barkley Deficits in Executive Functioning Scale (BDEFS for Adults)
Russell A. Barkley

Barkley Functional Impairment Scale (BFIS for Adults)
Russell A. Barkley

CHILD ASSESSMENT SCALE

Barkley Deficits in Executive Functioning Scale—
Children and Adolescents (BDEFS-CA)
Russell A. Barkley

Barkley Functional Impairment Scale—Children and Adolescents (BFIS-CA)

Russell A. Barkley

THE GUILFORD PRESS
New York London

A Division of Guilford Publications, Inc.
72 Spring Street, New York, NY 10012
www.guilford.com

Printed in the United States of America

This book is printed on acid-free paper.

Last digit is print number: 9 8 7 6 5 4 3 2 1

Library of Congress Cataloging-in-Publication Data

Barkley, Russell A., 1949–
Barkley functional impairment scale—children and adolescents (BFIS-CA) / Russell A. Barkley.
p. cm.
Includes bibliographical references and index.
ISBN 978-1-4625-0395-7 (pbk.)
1. Psychiatric rating scales. 2. Psychological tests for children. 3. Life skills—Testing. I. Title.
RC473.P78B372 2012
616.89′075—dc23

2011050064

For Ken

About the Author

Russell A. Barkley, PhD, ABPP, is Clinical Professor of Psychiatry and Pediatrics at the Medical University of South Carolina. Dr. Barkley has published numerous books and more than 260 scientific articles and book chapters on ADHD, executive functioning, and childhood defiance. He is also the editor of the newsletter *The ADHD Report*. Dr. Barkley is well known for his pioneering research on ADHD in both children and adults. His rating scales are based on more than 16 years of research using prototypes of the scales, and are normed on large samples representative of the U.S. population.

Acknowledgments

I wish to express my sincere appreciation to Wendy Mansfield and Sergei Rodkin of Knowledge Networks (Menlo Park, California) for their assistance with the collection of the normative sample of parents and their children used to create the norms for the Barkley Functional Impairment Scale—Children and Adolescents (BFIS-CA) in this manual. I am particularly appreciative of Laura Specht Patchkofsky of The Guilford Press for her superlative production editing of the original manuscript. And I remain indebted as always to my friends and colleagues at The Guilford Press, especially Kitty Moore, Seymour Weingarten, and Robert Matloff, for their acceptance of, support of, and assistance with the normative project behind this scale and the publication of this manual.

RUSSELL A. BARKLEY, PhD

Contents

	Introduction	1
CHAPTER 1.	Defining Psychosocial Impairment	5
CHAPTER 2.	Development of the BFIS-CA	20
CHAPTER 3.	Factor Analysis, Scale Construction, and Item Frequencies	31
CHAPTER 4.	Relationship of BFIS-CA Scores to Demographic Factors in the Normative Sample	37
CHAPTER 5.	Reliability	48
CHAPTER 6.	Validity	51
CHAPTER 7.	Relationship of BFIS-CA Scores to Disorders	64
CHAPTER 8.	Relationship of BFIS-CA Scores to Treatments	110
CHAPTER 9.	Scoring and Interpretation of the BFIS-CA Forms	119
APPENDIX.	BFIS-CA Forms, Score Sheet, and Impairment Profiles	137
	BFIS-CA Parent Rating Scale	139
	BFIS-CA Parent Interview	142

BFIS-CA Score Sheet 145
BFIS-CA Impairment Profile (Ages 6–11, Males Only) 146
BFIS-CA Impairment Profile (Ages 12–17, Males Only) 148
BFIS-CA Impairment Profile (Ages 6–11, Females Only) 150
BFIS-CA Impairment Profile (Ages 12–17, Females Only) 152

References 155

Index 163

Introduction

The fourth edition (text rev.) of the *Diagnostic and Statistical Manual of Mental Disorders* (DSM-IV-TR; American Psychiatric Association, 2000) requires that significant psychosocial impairment in major life activities be established as a separate criterion from the presence of significant symptoms to render a diagnosis for the vast majority of mental disorders, including those of childhood and adolescence. The establishment of functional impairment in the major life activities of children is also a significant component of the evaluation of a child's disability status. For instance, it is included in evaluations under the Individuals with Disabilities in Education Act (IDEA), under the Social Security Administration, and in other legal or official evaluations in which determination of functional impairment in psychosocial domains is important. The definition of impairment, however, especially in psychosocial functioning, is often vague and varied. What few measures of childhood or adolescent impairment have been developed have typically focused on just a few domains, such as family and peer relationships and school functioning. Yet children are expected to function effectively in more domains of major life activities than just these three, important as they may be. Most of these instruments are often limited to research studies and lack basic normative or psychometric information that would permit their use by clinicians; less than a handful are reliable and well validated, have norms on a representative sample of the U.S. general population of children and teens, and are commercially available for convenient use by clinicians, researchers, and others, such as professionals working in such areas as educational psychology, special education, or social services. Some widely used instruments available to the clinician are generally crude single-dimension ratings, such as the Global Assessment of Functioning (GAF) Scale in DSM-IV-TR (American Psychiatric Association, 2000) and others similar to it (e.g., the Children's Global Assessment Scale [CGAS]; Shaffer et al., 1983). They involve the rendering of a numerical judgment from 1 to 100 of psychosocial functioning, thereby collapsing impairment into a single overall rating. This is in contrast to the need in many clinical cases for evaluating far more specific domains in which children and adolescents must function effectively. These methods also are lacking in norms on a large sample representative of the general population that would allow them to be used routinely to determine the degree to which impairment is statistically deviant or abnormal relative to other children of the same age and sex. Several of the most commonly used rating systems are discussed briefly in Chapter 1, but most are limited by this absence of normative information, limited coverage of psychosocial domains, and lack of availability for widespread clinical, research, educational, and organizational use. The Barkley Functional Impairment Scale—Children and Adolescents (BFIS-CA) was developed to address this important need for a rating scale of more numerous and explicit domains of childhood and adolescent impairment for which there are nationally representative norms for children ages 6–17 years.

The BFIS-CA has benefited from more than 30 years of research with its predecessor scale, the Home Situations Questionnaire (HSQ; Barkley, 1981). It has also benefited from the development of a comparable rating scale for assessing impairment in adults, the Barkley Functional Impairment Scale (BFIS-CA; Barkley, 2011b). The BFIS-CA is an *empirically developed* scale directly based on careful consideration of its domain content, on statistical analyses identifying its underlying dimensional nature, and on a large representative sample of children and adolescents in the United States (relative to 2000 Census information) that spans the age range from 6 to 17 years.

Not only is the BFIS-CA empirically based, reliable, and valid, but it is also exceptionally convenient to use. That is in large part due to the willingness of the publisher to grant limited permission to the individual purchaser to reproduce the scales and score sheets for use in his/her clinical or research practice. It is commonplace in the scale-publishing industry to require purchasers to continually reorder rating scales and their scoring sheets. Not so here. The publisher has saved the user an incredible amount of time, inconvenience, and money associated with the need to reorder rating scales and scoring sheets by granting this limited license to photocopy the scales, score sheets, and interview forms.

A brief discourse on the nature of the concept of psychosocial impairment in children is provided in Chapter 1. Thereafter, this manual describes the developmental history, normative data, psychometric properties, and scoring and interpretation of the BFIS-CA scales. The Appendix to this manual contains the BFIS-CA Parent Rating Scale, which evaluates impairment in 15 domains of major life activities with 8 additional questions related to social, community, sports, and academic impairment. The scale is accompanied by four score sheets, termed Impairment Profiles, with one for each sex within each of two age groups—6–11 years and 12–17 years. There is also a BFIS-CA Parent Interview that is very useful in conducting a recommended follow-up interview with parents after they have completed the scales to obtain specific reasons that the parent or other informant may have rated a domain as at least moderately impaired. The Impairment Profiles contain tables of norms (percentiles) representative of the U.S. population. Normative data were not collected for the interview form. A form for obtaining teacher ratings of impairment is currently under development.

Much more research on the psychometric properties and utility of the BFIS-CA scores is desirable. Nevertheless, what information is currently available suggests that the scale scores have excellent reliability, validity, and clinical utility for use in a variety of circumstances. Those situations may include clinical practice settings in which concerns about impairment exist in a child or adolescent, in research settings in which the evaluation of impairment in children ages 6–17 years is of interest, in treatment trials as a measure of response to intervention, or in educational or social service settings in which the screening of children for possible impairment is an important objective. I hope that you will find the BFIS-CA rating scale to be useful in the screening and evaluation of potential psychosocial impairment in major domains of life activities in children and adolescents.

CHAPTER 1

Defining Psychosocial Impairment

As noted in the Introduction, impairment in psychosocial functioning is usually a requirement for the definition of the vast majority of mental disorders of childhood and adolescence, as well as for the determination of some disabilities in this age range that arise from both medical and mental disorders. As was discussed in the manual for the adult version of the BFIS (Barkley, 2011a), the term "to impair" or "impairment" has been variously defined as:

- "To cause to diminish, as in strength, value, or quality" (*American Heritage Dictionary of the English Language,* 2000).
- "A disability, any loss of physiological, psychological, or anatomical structure or function" (*wikipedia.org*).
- "Weakening, damage, or deterioration, especially as a result of injury or disease (*American Heritage Medical Dictionary,* 2009).
- "To make or cause to become worse; diminish in ability, value, excellence, etc.; weaken or damage" (*dictionary.reference.com*).
- "To damage or make worse by or as if by diminishing in some material respect" (*Merriam-Webster's Medical Dictionary,* 2007).
- "A disorder in structure or function resulting from anatomic, physiologic, or psychologic abnormalities that interfere with normal activities" (*Mosby's Medical Dictionary,* 2009).
- "A significant deviation, loss, or loss of use of any body structure or function in an individual with a health condition, disorder or disease" (American Medical Association, 2008).

Surprisingly, although psychosocial impairment is a criterion for the diagnosis of the vast majority of Axis I mental disorders for children and adolescents in DSM-IV-TR (American Psychiatric Association, 2000), the term itself is undefined in the manual. Instead, one finds the phrase "causes clinically significant distress or impairment in social, occupational, or other important areas of functioning" (p. 7) appended to the discussion of the term "disorder."

Explicit in most definitions of "impairment" is that it represents diminished functioning in important psychosocial domains of human life. It is useful to contrast this idea with the meaning of the term "symptoms," which are:

- "Any sensation or change in bodily function that is experienced by a patient and is associated with a particular disease" (*www.wordnetweb.princeton.edu*).
- "A departure from normal function or feeling which is noticed by a patient, indicating the presence of disease or abnormality" (*www.wikipedia.org*).
- "Something that a patient experiences in his or her body that is different from what is normal, and that may be the result of a disease or its treatment" (*www.gemzar.com*).
- "A sign of a disease or dysfunction (or illness)" (*American Heritage Dictionary*, 2000).
- "A feeling, sensation, or experience associated with or resulting from a physical or mental disorder and noticeable by the patient" (*Mosby's Medical Dictionary*, 2009).

A "symptom" is therefore a physical, cognitive, or behavioral manifestation of a disorder. By contrast, "impairment" refers to the *consequences* that arise from the expression of the disorder, usually through its symptoms. These consequences usually include functional ineffectiveness in one or more major psychosocial domains of human life.

I previously noted (Barkley, 2011b) that a useful view of impairment could be found in the widely regarded definition of "disorder" by Wakefield (1992, 1997) in which a disorder is defined as a "harmful dysfunction" in an evolved mental or physical mechanism. "Impairment" in this definition is the harm that can result to an individual due to some such dysfunction. Such a mechanism is actually the concept of an adaptation as adopted from the field of biology; thus, disorders are dysfunctional adaptations that are harmful to the individual. Medical disorders are failures of or reduced functioning in physical adaptations (such as organ systems), and mental disorders represent failures of or diminution in psychological functions (such as intelligence, memory, thinking/reasoning, visual–spatial abilities, language) or psychosocial functions (e.g., mobility, self-care, self-sufficiency/independence, social exchange/reciprocity, mating/pair bonding, child rearing, and receptiveness to pedagogy/education). Adaptations are functional mechanisms that serve a purpose (solve a problem in the adaptive niche of that organism). Evolved adaptations are not trivial features or characteristics of an organism. They are biologically costly for the organism to develop and maintain and so must serve some useful purpose—that is, the benefits of the adaptation must outweigh the costs to that individual for possessing that mechanism. The loss of, failure in, or reduction in functional effectiveness of an adaptation therefore often results in serious consequences (harm) for the individual: a reduced or lack of ability to continue to effectively address the adaptive problem(s) that mechanism evolved to solve. When the mechanism can no longer effectively solve the problems it evolved to address, the adaptive problems return, and the environment reacts with adverse consequences for that organism. Those consequences constitute the harm that may arise in response to such functional ineffectiveness. And that effectiveness and its attendant harms are what is meant here by the term "impairment."

As discussed previously (Barkley, 2011b), the terms "impairment," "deficiency," "symptoms," "disability," and "disorder" are often used interchangeably both in everyday conversation and in the medical, psychiatric, and psychological literatures. It is important not to confuse them. The concepts of disorder, symptoms, and impairment can be thought of as separate components in the triadic sequence of events in reality—from the disorder to its symptoms (manifestations) to the functional impairment that ensues (ineffective performance that results in harm). That symptoms of psychiatric disorders, for instance, are to be thought of as being distinct from impairment is obvious in DSM-IV-TR (American Psychiatric Association, 2000), which makes the requirement of impairment in major psychosocial activities a separate criterion for establishing the presence of a psychiatric disorder apart from establishing the presence of symptoms that result from or constitute that disorder. In short, impairment and symptoms are not identical, either in their conceptualization or in reality. The severity of symptoms is only partially coupled to or correlated with the degree of impairment, sharing less than 50%—often less than 25%—of its variance (Barkley, 2011b; Gordon et al., 2006; Lewandowski, Lovett, & Gordon, 2009). The severity of symptoms therefore does not show a perfect or direct relationship to the severity of impairment. Other factors obviously must contribute to the eventual level of psychosocial impairment an individual may experience beyond just symptoms alone. In short, psychosocial symptoms are behaviors or cognitions, whereas impairments are consequences. To be inattentive often during classwork in school is a symptom; to turn in an incomplete worksheet and so receive a failing grade on the assignment is a consequence.

Impairment therefore represents both functional ineffectiveness—the inability to perform effectively in major domains of human life (adaptive problems)—and the harmful consequences that may result. When an individual no longer functions effectively in addressing the everyday major adaptive problems of human life, the environment kicks back in ways that are costly or harmful to the individual. Functional ineffectiveness in major life activities (adaptive problem domains) resulting in adverse consequences is therefore at the heart of the concept of impairment. A reduction in functional effectiveness that leads to no harm whatsoever in the absence of any accommodations, treatment, or habilitation is a trivial if not nonexistent form of impairment. In short, "no harm, no foul" (no disorder).

But what sorts of harm can be viewed as reflecting impairment? "Harm" in Wakefield's definition typically refers to (1) increased risk of death, (2) increased morbidity (physical injury), or (3) a significant decline in functioning in a particular *major* human life activity that itself can result in greater morbidity, mortality, or suffering. Such major life activities are self-care, self-protection, and personal safety; self-sufficiency; peer and family relationships; education or receptiveness to pedagogy; and many others. A "major life activity" in this perspective refers to those important adaptive domains that are largely or entirely universal to all humans of that age and are necessary to their ability to sustain their survival and see to their welfare and hence their long-term happiness (freedom from want or dissatisfaction). When the degree of dysfunction in an adaptation reaches a certain level, the individual may not be able to perform a major activity of daily life as well as the average, typical, or normal human—he/she has become significantly less effective. This ineffectiveness begins to have adverse consequences for the individual. Harm begins to accrue. As noted, both the reduction in functional effectiveness and the attendant consequences or harms that are coupled to it can be regarded as the essence of the concept of impairment. Those consequences can even serve as a gauge to the degree of functional ineffectiveness—the degree of one's impairment.

Especially important to understand in these views of impairment is the stipulation that the "normal" or average person is to serve as the standard against which the degree of functional ineffectiveness and attendant harm is to be judged (Gordon & Keiser, 1998). This is implied, if not explicitly stated, in the foregoing definitions of the terms "disorder" and "impairment." It has been made explicit in the U.S. government's definition of the term "disability"; a term often used synonymously with "impairment." For instance, the Americans with Disabilities Act (ADA) states that a disability is "an inability to function normally, physically or mentally." It is an "inability to engage in any substantial gainful activity by reason of any medically determinable physical or mental impairment which can be expected to last or has lasted for a continuous period of not less than 12 months." Under the ADA, the term "disability" means, with respect to an individual, "a physical or mental impairment that substantially limits one or more of the major life activities of [an] individual, a record of such an impairment, or being regarded as having such an impairment" (Americans with Disabilities Act, 1990). This definition was further clarified in the Equal Employment Opportunity Commission (EEOC) regulations regarding the ADA: "An individual is not substantially limited in a major life activity if the limitation does not amount to a significant restriction when *compared with the abilities of the average person*" (emphasis added). Impairment or disability is therefore "the inability to function in the normal or usual manner" (*Mosby's Medical Dictionary*, 2009). The normal or typical human (average person in the general population), not some highly intelligent, highly functioning, highly specialized, or highly educated peer group, is the standard against which impairment is judged.

In this manual, "impairment" means a loss or diminution in the functional effectiveness of human physical or mental adaptations. It views such functional ineffectiveness as typically being dimensional, not categorical, in nature. There can be degrees of diminution in the functioning of most physical or mental adaptations as opposed to all-or-none effectiveness. When the ineffective functioning reaches such a magnitude that it begins to result in an inability to adapt to (solve) the problems that arise in any major domain of human life for the individual, adverse consequences arise for that individual (harm ensues). At that point or threshold, the person may be said to be impaired.

Impairment is often construed in a trilevel hierarchical arrangement: (1) physical impairment (as when an organ system fails to function and leads to increased morbidity, as in diabetes); (2) cognitive-behavioral impairment, as when a delay in intellectual or general cognitive ability becomes so delayed or deficient that it leads to deficient self-care and hence an increased risk for personal suffering, morbidity, or even mortality; and (3) psychosocial impairment, as when an individual's symptoms of a psychiatric disorder result in the loss of friendships, personal suffering, or increased morbidity (such as accidental injuries) or mortality (as in suicide). This manual concerns itself with the last or upper level of this hierarchy—the psychosocial arena of functional effectiveness. Its principal focus is on evaluating impairment in the context of psychiatric disorders or psychological problems, although the scales contained herein may also be of use in evaluating psychosocial impairment related to medical disorders. These major domains of human psychosocial life are likely to encompass the adaptive problems that some physical organs (the human brain) and most cognitive-behavioral adaptations evolved to address. It is likely to be at this level of adaptive problem solving that evolution (natural selection) has acted in the history of the species to create these lower-level cognitive-behavioral and even neurological adaptations.

This manual also adopts the criterion of the ADA that the normal, average, or typical human of that age is to serve as the standard for judging functional ineffectiveness and its harmful consequences. To make such a determination, there must be information on the normal or general population—the average person—with which the reports of the individual can be compared to assist with this judgment of impairment. One purpose of this manual is to provide normative information on the degree of functional ineffectiveness experienced by the general population of children and adolescents (ages 6–17) in their performance in a wide range of psychosocial domains of major life activities as reported by their parents.

Guidelines for Assessing Impairment or Disability

This manual is not intended to set forth detailed guidelines for the clinical evaluation of disorders and impairment. The American Academy of Child and Adolescent Psychiatry and the American Academy of Pediatrics, among others, have published detailed practice standards that should be consulted for such information, and many textbooks on assessment also contain such information (e.g., Mash & Barkley, 2003). Here I merely summarize the essential or basic structure of such an evaluation as might be recommended by several advisory or governing bodies or laws in the United States.

Guidelines of the American Medical Association

The American Medical Association (AMA; 2008) guidelines for evaluating impairment in adult mental disorders specify six areas of functional impairment for review in the evaluation of adults, many of which would apply to children and adolescents: (1) self-care and personal hygiene; (2) social and recreational activities; (3) the capacity for travel, including driving and using public transportation; (4) interpersonal relationships; (5) the capacity for concentration, persistence, and pace; and (6) employability. Five of these are psychosocial and one, interestingly, is cognitive-behavioral (concentration, persistence, and pace). In determining the presence of impairment in an adult, the evaluator is encouraged to review information from other reliable sources, such as records from inpatient hospitalizations, outpatient treatment, day treatment programs, occupational therapy, work evaluations, and disability assessments. The patient's self-report of symptoms, their impact on these six functional areas, and the information gathered from other sources, as well as the findings from the objective clinical examination, are to be analyzed by the examiner in making a judgment of impairment or disability. The existence of any widely disparate or incongruent findings between patient self-reports and the other sources of information, including the clinical evaluation, should be scrutinized to determine the reasons for this disparity. (For a more detailed discussion of the AMA guidelines, see Leclair, Leclair, & Brigham, 2009.) Obviously, these requirements cannot be extrapolated to children as written. Self-reports of impairment in children or even teens may not be especially reliable and should be amended with the reports of parents and others who know the child well, such as teachers. Also, school (and education generally) is among the major domains of life activities of a child or teenager and would be substituted in the preceding AMA guidelines for the occupational domain of adults. The domain of travel might also be omitted for a child, at least until he/she is of an age as an adolescent to be permitted to drive a motor vehicle or take public transportation unsupervised.

Also noteworthy is the fact that nowhere in the AMA guidelines is there any consideration given to comparing the patient's self-reports with those of a general population sample to determine the extent to which the patient's reports are normal, typical, or deviant (abnormal). This raises the question of just to what extent typical, average, or normal people consider themselves to be functioning effectively or ineffectively (impaired) in these psychosocial domains. This problem is only somewhat less difficult in the evaluation of impairment in children and teenagers, for which very few instruments are available for parent-reports with norms from a representative sample of the child or adolescent population. It is typically left to the clinician to make the determination of impairment based on his/her experience and training.

But on what is the clinician relying in doing so? Besides their training and experience, most clinicians likely rely on the reports of the parents and teachers and, to some degree, that of the child or teen patient. However, a few clinicians rely on more structured methods for evaluating impairment, such as the GAF Scale, for which there is no normative information on the general population. And fewer still rely on the very limited number of standardized methods commercially available that have normative information for determining psychosocial impairment.

Guidelines of the Social Security Administration

The Social Security Administration(SSA) guidelines (*www.ssa.gov/disability/professionals/bluebook/112.00-MentalDisorders-Childhood.htm*) that are provided for the determination of a disability in children closely follow the guidelines for adults, especially in requiring the establishment of the presence of a recognized medical or mental disorder. Those guidelines also stipulate that medical and psychological evidence of that disorder must be documented by the clinician and that evidence of impairment be documented for up to five functional domains (depending on age). These include "motor function; cognitive/communicative function; social function; personal function; and concentration, persistence, or pace. In most functional areas, there are two alternative methods suggested for documenting the required level of severity: (1) Use of standardized tests alone, where appropriate test instruments are available, and (2) use of other medical findings."

Consistent with other definitions of impairment and the "average" or "normal" person standard for its determination, impairment in the SSA guidelines is determined relative to the chronological age of the child in most cases. Degree of impairment is also specified as mild, moderate, marked, or extreme. The guidelines further state that

> a marked limitation may arise when several activities or functions are impaired, or even when only one is impaired, as long as the degree of limitation is such as to interfere seriously with the ability to function (based upon age-appropriate expectations) independently, appropriately, effectively, and on a sustained basis. When standardized tests are used as the measure of functional parameters, a valid score that is two standard deviations below the norm for the test will be considered a marked restriction.

Apart from the use of standardized tests for assessing the degree of motor and cognitive impairment in a child or teen, the judgment of impairment in the remaining domains (social, daily self-care) is largely determined by the clinician. Again, no emphasis is given to comparing the parent ratings of impairment with those provided by parents in a general population sample, something that would seem to be a necessary piece of the overall determination of impairment and disability.

This is not to say that some structured methods for evaluating psychosocial impairment in children have not been developed previously in the research literature on the subject. Several certainly have; however, just a few of them were given to a large sample of the U.S. population of parents for reports about their children or teenagers to determine the extent to which those parents reported various degrees of functional impairment in specific psychosocial domains. Furthermore, those methods cover a very limited number of domains of daily life activities. A few methods for evaluating impairment in children are considered here to illustrate their differences from the BFIS-CA.

Methods for Evaluating Psychosocial Impairment

Clinician Ratings

One of the most commonly used clinician ratings for determining the presence of psychosocial impairment in children is the CGAS (Shaffer et al., 1983). It is essentially the downward extension of the GAF Scale for adults as set forth in the current version of the DSM (as of this writing, DSM-IV-TR; American Psychiatric Association, 2000, p. 32). The GAF Scale is to be completed by a clinician using a single dimension on a single scale from 1 to 100 concerning the person's overall general functioning. For adults, the clinician is to "consider psychological, social, and occupational functioning on a hypothetical continuum of mental health–illness" but is not to include "impairment that is due to physical (or environmental) limitations." The CGAS specifies a somewhat different range of domains: psychological, social, and school functioning (home, school, and peer relations). The developers of the CGAS indicate that

> raters are expected to synthesize their knowledge about the child's social and symptomatic functioning and condense this information into a score. For example, a score of 61–70 indicates that the child has some difficulty in a single area but is generally functioning pretty well. Scores above 70 are considered to be in the normal range, whereas scores on the lower end of the continuum (below 60) indicate greater impairment. For instance, the lowest ratings refer to a need for constant supervision (1–10) or considerable supervision (11–20).

To illustrate this hypothetical continuum, consider the lowest rating of 1–10 for the CGAS: "Needs constant supervision (24-hour care) due to severely aggressive or self-destructive behavior or gross impairment in reality testing, communication, cognition, affect or personal hygiene." Now contrast this with the highest rating of 91–100: "Superior functioning in all areas (at home, at school and with peers); involved in a wide range of activities and has many interests (e.g., has hobbies or participates in extracurricular activities or belongs to an organized group such as Scouts, etc.); likeable, confident; 'everyday' worries never get out of hand; doing well in school; no symptoms."

Several problems exist with such a simple global judgment, especially as applied to children or teens. Interjudge (clinician) reliability of the scale is reported to range from .83 to .90 in research settings in which training on the rating system with clinical cases, videotaped vignettes, or test reports is likely to have been received (Bird, Canino, Rubio-Stipec, & Ribera, 1987). However, reliability is only moderate or lower in more routine clinical settings (.66 or less). The scale has been used widely in a number of research studies (at least 69 studies as of 2004; see Schorre & Vandvik, 2004) for various child psychiatric disorders. It thus has some evidence of validity for indicating degree of childhood competence or functional effectiveness, as well as in response to various interventions. Another disadvantage is that the scale does not distinguish among various major domains of psychosocial functioning. Instead, it involves simply a global summary rating that incorporates principally three domains (home, school, and peer relations) that are to be considered in the single summary judgment of the clinician. It is therefore unclear as to just what the specific nature of the impairment is or, more precisely, in what domains of life the impairment is occurring. Lower ratings appear to represent not just more severe but more pervasive impairment across multiple domains. Again, the nature of these domains is unclear. Just as important is the lack of any information on just how the general population of either adults or children would be rated on such a scale, information that would serve as a critical benchmark in determining what is normal or average for people in the United States. If the clinician has no information on how the general population would rate on such a scale, especially relative to a specific age group, then the reliability (and hence validity) of such judgments surely has to be limited. Finally, because clinicians are determining the ratings of impairment on this scale, this approach becomes costly and cumbersome, requiring a clinical evaluation by a professional. Such a measure could not be employed effectively as a screening tool for detecting impairment in various settings that did not involve a trained professional.

Two other clinician rating systems have been used with children in various research studies, including the GAF Scale without modification, as published in the DSM, and the Global Assessment of Psychosocial Disability in the 10th edition of the *International Classification of Diseases* (ICD-10; World Health Organization, 2001; Schorre & Vandvik, 2004). Both utilize the 1–100 single-dimensional rating method similar to the CGAS. They vary in their guidelines, their anchor-point descriptions for the numerical codes, and their psychometric properties. Both also suffer from many of the same problems discussed for the CGAS. Though employed in numerous research studies, these scales are rarely utilized in clinical practice. This is most likely owing to both lack of training and lack of normative information from which to draw valid conclusions about an individual's actual level of functioning relative to the population. An alternative to the CGAS used in some studies of children is the Child and Adolescent Functional Assessment Scale (Hodges & Kim, 2000; Hodges & Wong, 1996), which requires clinicians to rate a child for his/her impairment in eight domains (and to rate the caregiver in two domains). Although it provides a much broader range of domains of potential impairment, this scale suffers from the same limitations as the other clinician ratings. These include the requirement that a trained clinician provide the score and the absence of norms on a general population sample to assist with the interpretation and even validity of the ratings, among others.

Parent Ratings

Several parent-completed rating scales exist for the evaluation of psychosocial impairment. Two of these include normative information for the United States and other nations and provide scores reflecting impairment in several different domains. One such scale is the first page of the Child Behavior Checklist (CBCL; Achenbach, 2001) for parents. Parents are asked to rate their children's proficiency in seven areas (sports, hobbies, organizations and clubs, chores, number of friendships, quality of social relationships, and academic performance in various subjects). Each of these items is rated on a 3-point scale (below average, average, above average) of proficiency. The first two domains are also rated for both engaged time and proficiency. Three other questions also ask about school: receipt of special educational services at school, grade repetition, and academic or other problems in school. The item responses are then converted to a numerical score and scores summed to obtain a total domain score. Three domains of impairment are computed: activities, social engagement, and school. The CBCL has been employed in numerous research studies, is widely used in clinical practice, and has satisfactory evidence for its reliability and validity. Drawbacks to the impairment portion of this scale might include its limited range of scores for each item (3-point ratings) and the small range of domain scores (three domains). But clearly the CBCL covers a broader range of domains than do the CGAS or GAF Scale clinician ratings.

A similar rating scale to the CBCL that is well normed and contains some items reflecting impairment is the Behavior Assessment System for Children–2 (BASC-2; Reynolds & Kamphaus, 2004). Items on the scale that reflect impairment are combined to form ratings in two domains: activities of daily living and social skills. The psychometric properties (reliability, validity) of the scale are considered sound or satisfactory (Flanagan, 1995; Gladman & Lancaster, 2003; Reynolds & Kamphaus, 2004). Versions are available for ages 2–5, 6–11, and 12–21 years. Limitations of this scale are probably the same as those for the CBCL—a limited scoring range for the impairment items (4-point scale) and a limited range of domains of impairment (daily living, social engagement).

A more recently developed scale designed specifically to assess impairment in children and adolescents in several domains of major life activities is the Impairment Rating Scale (IRS; Fabiano et al., 2006). The parent version of the scale evaluates six domains: peer relationships, sibling relationships, relationships with parents, academic progress, self-esteem, and influence on family functioning. An overall impairment score is also calculated. The parent describes the nature of the impairments in each domain in his/her own words (not scored) and then places an "X" along a line approximately 7.25 inches in length to indicate the child's degree of impairment in this domain ranging from "*no problem/definitely does not need treatment or special services*" to "*extreme problem/definitely needs treatment or special services*" (Fabiano et al., 2006, p. 371, original emphasis). The mark is converted to a score by subdividing the line into seven equal segments (of 1 inch) and giving a numerical score of 0 ("no problem") to 6 ("extreme problem"), depending on which segment the "X" is placed on. This is a rather cumbersome scoring system made all the more problematic by the fact that there are no descriptors of any anchor points between the lowest and highest (beginning and end) endpoints of the line. The rating scale has some evidence for satisfactory reliability and validity from four separate studies reported by the authors (Fabiano et al., 2006). Besides the scoring system, another problem with this scale is the lack of nationally representative norms for children and teens to permit clinicians to use the scale to determine how the parent rates the child relative to a sample of children of the same age and sex. Although two of the studies reported by the authors used large samples, they were limited mainly to the western New York state area (mainly a single school district) in one study and to Halifax, Nova Scotia, schools in the other study. Such samples are not representative of all U.S. (or Canadian) children and so limit what normative information is available for clinical use. As of this writing, the IRS and the New York State normative information could be obtained for free from *www.wings.buffalo.edu/adhd.*

It is certainly the case that rating scales assessing quality of life (QOL) in children (see Riley et al., 2006, for an example) may overlap in their domain content with rating scales of impairment (such as in school, recreation, social relationships, family, and other domains). But the former scales are not evaluating the degree of functional ineffectiveness (impairment) being reported in these areas, which is the meaning of "impairment." Instead, QOL scales evaluate the extent of satisfaction, happiness, or sense of personal well-being of an individual within these domains of life. Degree of happiness or satisfaction in any domain may be low, but that does not mean the individual can be considered to be functioning ineffectively or to be impaired or disabled in them. For instance, factor analysis of the scale used in the Riley and colleagues (2006) study revealed five dimensions labeled as satisfaction (with health and self), comfort (physical, emotional, restricted activity), resilience, risk avoidance, and achievement (peer relations, academic performance). Except for the latter, most of the remaining dimensions would not be considered to reflect domains of impairment.

Some of the same problems that afflicted clinician ratings of psychosocial impairment also plague these and other parent rating scales. Although the range of major domains of life activities appears to be broader on many of these scales, especially the six-item IRS, even that scale appears to miss some important domains of children's lives, such as self-care, participation in community activities (clubs, sports, etc.), interactions with classmates, performing chores at home, and so forth; some of these were covered by the CBCL and BASC. These scales may also cluster some domains into global categories, such as social functioning, rather than distinguishing among relations with parents, with siblings, with friends, with classmates, and with strangers or acquaintances, for instance. The range of item ratings for many of these scales is also restricted, thus creating artificially low relationships with other measures of impairment in those domains.

For the CBCL and IRS, some evidence is available on just how valid the individual domain ratings are in capturing actual impairment in that domain as judged by other methods or sources for evaluating that domain. For instance, if a child is rated as impaired in school, other evidence exists for such impairment that correlates with this domain rating. More such evidence would be useful, however. Showing that ratings of impairment are distinct from ratings of symptoms of psychopathology is fine as one source of evidence for validity of impairment as a distinct construct from psychopathology, as many of these scales have done, but it is not sufficient evidence of construct, discriminative, or criterion validity. Furthermore, scales such as the IRS and the clinician rating methods lack normative information on a nationally representative sample of parents that would permit some determination of the position of these ratings within the larger distribution of parent-rated impairment in a general population sample of children and adolescents. For this reason, scales such as the IRS cannot be used in clinical practice or other settings for the evaluation of impairment in patients or others in which the issue of psychosocial impairment relative to the average person is exceptionally important.

Suggestions for Assessing Psychosocial Impairment

As evident in the foregoing discussions of AMA and SSA guidelines, the clinical assessment of psychosocial impairment in children should typically include:

- An initial interview to determine *both* the presence of disorder(s) and the nature of the impairments. The clinician seeks to establish the major life domains in which impairment may be occurring and their respective severities, as well as the symptoms and the disorders that may be giving rise to those impairments.
- A carefully taken history of the child's symptoms, other concerns, medically

relevant information, and prior evaluations of and treatments received for these same complaints.

- A determination of the developmental inappropriateness of the symptoms of the disorder(s) relative to others in the general population (using, e.g., behavior rating scales such as the CBCL or BASC-2).
- Establishing the age of onset and course of the relevant disorders and their impairments to date.
- A physical exam of the child or teen if functional impairment is thought to have arisen from a medical disorder.
- Psychological testing if general cognitive ability, academic achievement, or specific neuropsychological abilities are believed to be deficient and are contributing to impairment in psychosocial functioning.
- Ruling in or ruling out other treatable medical and psychiatric disorders that may be contributing to the child's or teen's clinical presentation, symptoms, and impairments.
- A review of the available archival records related to particular domains of psychosocial impairment that may be of key importance to the purpose of the evaluation, such as school-related records, official driving records (for teens), official juvenile criminal records, educational transcripts or report cards, prior medical records related to disability determinations, and prior medical, psychiatric, psychological, or educational evaluations and treatment records.
- *A determination of the degree of statistical deviance (abnormality) of the child's parent-reported impairment relative to the reports of parents in the general population for children of the same age and sex.*

This latter source of information is not included in most guidelines for the evaluation of impairment or disability, but it is essential to establishing the position of the individual relative to the normal, average, or typical child or teen (the average of the general population). After all, if impairment is to be judged relative to the average person, as recommended by the SSA and ADA and as implied or explicit in various definitions of the term, then some means of comparing the parents' complaints about children's psychosocial functioning with those given by the general population of parents is indispensable to the determination of child or adolescent impairment.

An essential method for assessing most of these issues remains the clinical interview. As noted, behavior rating scales of psychiatric symptoms are also highly useful both for the initial screening for risk for disorders and for establishing the degree of developmental deviance (age-inappropriateness) of the patient's symptoms where mental disorders are believed to be the source of the functional impairment. Psychological testing may be useful as well in establishing the extent of cognitive-behavioral deficits as a possible origin of the difficulties in psychosocial functioning. Moreover, as the AMA and SSA guidelines make plain, the physical examination is often essential to establishing the presence of medical disorders that also may be contributing to psychosocial impairment. Until now, only a few well-normed rating scales of functional impairment in major psychosocial domains for children were available to clinicians. But even those, such as the CBCL and BASC-2, cover a limited range of domains out of the many in which children participate. The BFIS-CA was invented to help correct this problem, as it provides individual ratings of impairment across 15 primary domains of psychosocial functioning. In addition, eight secondary impairment questions focus more specifically on friendships, community activities, sports participation, and academic performance and adjustment. The BFIS-CA is also exceptionally convenient for evaluating change in psychosocial impairment resulting from various interventions, such as medications or efforts at rehabilitation. It can also be used to evaluate possible changes in psychosocial impairment status pre- and postinjury.

The Seven Sources of Information

As emphasized in the various governmental and professional guidelines for evaluating impairment, no single source of information can serve as the sole or gold standard in making the final determination of the existence and degree of psychosocial impairment. Seven types or sources of information are frequently needed in making such a determination. These are:

1. Patient- and parent-reports of symptoms and impairments.
2. Patient- and parent-reported history of symptoms and impairments.
3. Psychological testing where necessary, including symptom validity tests for detecting malingering (discussed subsequently).
4. Physical (medical) examinations as appropriate.
5. Archival (official) records (the paper trail of impairment).
6. Population norms for comparison with the parent-reported symptoms and impairments.
7. Reports of significant others who know the patient well (i.e., teachers).

These last two sources and types of information are rarely, if ever, mentioned in guidelines for conducting evaluations of disability, yet they can provide valuable information with which the other sources can be compared and against which these additional sources can be judged by comparison. Indeed, the determination of the extent to which parent-reported impairment compares with reports provided by a general population sample would seem to be essential.

The Need for Triangulation among the Sources

As I have noted elsewhere (Barkley, 2011b), clinicians should then engage in a process of triangulation of these sources of information against each other and comparing them with the clinician's own training and experience in these matters to arrive at this final determination of impairment. A useful metaphor for the evaluation of these different sources of information in arriving at a determination of impairment is the global positioning system (GPS) method. This method triangulates the position of the individual against two or more other sources of information about his/her position to arrive at a reasonably accurate report of the individual's geographical location on the planet. Likewise, clinicians should arrive at the relative position of the patient within the general population concerning his/her degree of impairment by comparing multiple sources of information with each other and the child-, parent-, and teacher-reports about a patient. Truth is an assembled thing, and this holds for impairment determination in clinical practice. Each source of information can be judged against the information provided by two others to gauge the integrity or validity of the initial source. This process is repeated across all seven domains until all possible combinations of three-way comparisons have been achieved. This procedure is more likely to lead the clinician to arrive at the most valid and reasonable approximation of reality—in this case the degree of psychosocial impairment of the individual.

The Issue of Malingering

A major problem in determining disability or impairment is the possibility of malingering, defined in DSM-IV-TR as "the intentional production of false or grossly exaggerated physical or psychological symptoms, motivated by external incentives such as avoiding military duty, avoiding work, obtaining financial compensation, evading criminal prosecution, or obtaining drugs" (American Psychiatric Association, 2000, p. 683). This is typically thought of as a problem exclusively with adults. As a result, a substantial literature exists on this issue with adults (see Lovett, Gordon, & Lewandowski, 2009, for a more detailed discussion). Space precludes a detailed review of that literature here. Suffice it to say that even the AMA and SSA guidelines forewarn clinicians to evaluate the possibility that the individual is feigning the severity of his/her symptoms and impairments, usually for some personal gain.

The issue can also arise in the evaluation of disorders and impairment in children, for instance, as in neuropsychological assessments of children (Faust, Hart, & Guilmette, 1988) and adolescents (Faust, Hart, Guilmette, & Arkes, 1988). Children can be intentionally instructed by others, such as parents, to "fake bad" on the neuropsychological tests (Ku & Boone, 2002). In one study, such instructions given by an experimenter resulted in as many as 93% of typical children being diagnosed as abnormal by clinicians, and 87% of those cases were attributed to cortical dysfunction. Moreover, none of the clinicians in that study detected the malingering (Faust, Hart, & Guilmette, 1988). Subsequent studies confirmed that this can be a problem in neuropsychological assessments of children (McKinzey, Prieler, & Raven, 2003), though not on all tests or under all instructional conditions (Nagle, Everhart, Durham, McCammon, & Walker, 2006).

There is no foolproof means of detecting malingering. In the realm of psychological evaluations, one often sees "validity scales" being included in such assessment methods as personality tests. In neuropsychology, "effort tests" may be given to trick the patient into believing that the test being given is evaluating disability when in fact it is being used to detect feigning (Morgan & Sweet, 2008). For instance, the Test of Memory Malingering (Tombaugh, 2004) may be useful in detecting malingering in children (Constantinou & McCaffrey, 2003; Donders, 2005), as may several other symptom validity tests (Blaskewitz, Werten, & Kathmann, 2008). Whenever some obvious or external benefit would be an end result of the determination of impairment, clinicians should be alert to the possibility of malingering (Lovett et al., 2009; Morgan & Sweet, 2008; Walker, 2011). No single method of assessment can necessarily be free of the possibility of feigning or malingering, and so a combination of methods may be the most useful (Slick, Tan, Strauss, & Hultsch, 2004). Probably the best means of detecting the possibility of malingering is the method of triangulation of sources against each other, including symptom validity tests. Each source is compared against two others so that all possible combinations are considered and the clinician can gain a more thorough perspective on the issue of impairment and on the possibility of malingering. This method is effective because it is rarely, if ever, possible for an individual to coordinate the data from all of these sources so that they are consistent with and abet the scheme of misrepresentation.

Conclusion

This brief introduction to the nature and assessment of psychosocial impairment in children and adolescents has argued for a distinction among the terms "symptom," "disorder," and "impairment/disability" so as to avoid confusion in readers' thinking and in their evaluation of the literature on these topics. A symptom can be considered to be a physical, cognitive, or behavioral manifestation of a disorder. Symptoms often form a pattern or syndrome, as noted in the DSM-IV-TR. Disorders are dysfunctions in physical or psychological (mental) adaptations that result in reducing or diminishing the individual's functional effectiveness in meeting the demands of daily life. Such ineffectiveness leads to harm. Impairment represents both this functional ineffectiveness in major domains of daily life activities and the harm resulting from it. Impairment is diminished functioning relative to the normal, average, or typical child; it is *abnormal* in its degree and thus must be judged relative to the "normal person" standard. Various guidelines exist for the determination of impairment, and various structured assessment tools have been developed to assist with that determination (clinician ratings, parent ratings). But until now there has been little normative information available on the extent to which parents in the general population view their children as being impaired in the major domains of life activities. Yet comparing a child with this general population would seem to be an indispensable part of the larger process of assessing impairment. The BFIS-CA was developed to address that problem.

CHAPTER 2

Development of the BFIS-CA

This chapter describes the history and initial development of the BFIS-CA and the methods used to collect information on the scale from the normative sample of U.S. parents having children ages 6–17 years.

Developmental History of the BFIS-CA

The BFIS-CA was initially developed as the HSQ (Barkley, 1981). (For more information on the early history of the HSQ and research on it, see Barkley & Edelbrock, 1987, and Barkley & Murphy, 1998, 2006.) The HSQ was itself developed from a semi-structured parent interview created by the late Constance Hanf, PhD, at the Oregon Health Sciences Center, but never published. It was intended to evaluate the extent to which various disruptive behavior problems occurred in and interfered with various home and public situations. Parents reported on the nature and extent to which their children manifested significant noncompliance with or defiance of their parents in each situation. I had the privilege of training with Hanf in 1976–1977 and using this interview. From the situations listed in the interview, I developed a rating scale to be completed by parents; this was the HSQ. The scale was expanded from the initial interview to include 16 different situations around the home and in public places. Parents were asked to indicate whether or not they thought their children had behavior problems in each situation. If so, they were to rate the severity of the problem on a scale from 0 (*mild*) to 9 (*severe*). Those situations were the following: playing alone; playing with other children; at mealtimes; getting dressed; washing/

bathing; while the parent is on the telephone; watching television; when visitors are in the home; when the parent is visiting others; in supermarkets, stores, churches, restaurants, and other public places; when asked to do chores at home; at bedtime; in the car; with a babysitter; when father is home; when asked to do school homework. Two scores were computed from this scale: the number of problem settings (number of answers indicating that a setting was a problem) and the mean severity score (average rating across all domains indicated to be problems). Initial information on reliability and validity was satisfactory (Altepeter & Breen, 1992; Barkley & Edelbrock, 1987; DuPaul & Barkley, 1992). Not surprisingly, given the instruction to rate the degree of problem behavior in each situation, the scores were found to correlate significantly with ratings of aggression, hyperactivity, and delinquent conduct from the CBCL (*r*'s = .83, .73, and .48, respectively) in samples of children with attention-deficit/hyperactivity disorder (ADHD), as well as with the depressed and social withdrawal scales (*r*'s = .62 for each) (Breen & Barkley, 1988). Similar results were found for the HSQ in its relationship to subscales of the Personality Inventory for Children (Breen & Barkley, 1983). The HSQ was also significantly associated with degree of parenting stress (Breen & Barkley, 1988). As expected, the HSQ showed substantial differences between children with ADHD and various control groups of children and significant changes as a function of treatment of the children with ADHD with medication (Barkley & Edelbrock, 1987). The scale scores contributed unique information to predicting group membership between children with and without ADHD apart from that contributed by ADHD symptoms (Barry, Pinard, Barry, Garland, & Lyman, 2011). The scale has often been used as a parent rating of child impairment (Gathje, Lewandowski, & Gordon, 2008). Some normative data were collected on a sample of 995 children from central Wisconsin between ages 4 and 11 years (Altepeter & Breen, 1992) for the original scale and on a sample of 588 girls and 539 boys ages 6–12 in Massachusetts for a revised version of the scale that focuses on attention problems alone rather than on the broader domain of behavior problems (DuPaul & Barkley, 1992). An adolescent version of the scale has also been developed with sound psychometric properties (Adams, McCarthy, & Kelly, 1995). The scale was also sensitive to changes in problem behavior as a function of psychiatric medications (Abikoff et al., 2004; Aman et al., 2010; Barkley, Fischer, Newby, & Breen, 1988), the effects of parent training in child management (Aman et al., 2010; Danforth, Harvey, Ulaszek, & McKee, 2006; Lauth, Otte, & Heubeck, 2009), and of the effects of anger control training in adolescents (Sukhodolsky et al., 2009), among other interventions. The HSQ therefore has shown considerable promise as a measure of the situational pervasiveness and degree of impairment that children experienced in various home and public situations as a result of their disruptive behavior problems, such as defiance and noncompliance (Crowe, Beauchamp, Catroppa, & Anderson, 2011; Naglieri, Goldstein, & LeBuffe, 2010).

As a measure of general psychosocial impairment, however, the HSQ suffers from some significant limitations. One is that the instructions make it clear that degree of functional ineffectiveness in any given situation is to be based on the extent of externalizing types of behavioral problems. A more general and thus useful scale would not specify the types of symptoms that produced impairment in any situation but would simply ask parents to rate the degree of difficulties the child had in functioning effectively in those situations. This would help to assess impairment independent of some specific disorder. In this way the scale could be used to assess impairment in children who have many different disorders besides externalizing ones. A further problem with the scale was the lack of nationally representative norms for the U.S. childhood and adolescent population. The norms collected on the scale came from a limited region of the United States (two states) and from children ages 4–11 (Altepeter & Breen, 1992) and 6–12 (DuPaul & Barkley, 1992).

It was therefore decided to reconstruct the HSQ as the BFIS-CA. The instructions to the rater were altered to make it explicit that the child was being rated on his/her degree of problems in functioning effectively in each setting without regard to any specific types of symptoms or disorders that may be causing the problems in that situation. Some of the situations in the HSQ were removed from the scale, such as mealtimes, watching television, and others, and replaced with other domains of major life activities thought to be more important in evaluating psychosocial impairment, such as self-care, school performance, and so forth. The number of situations on the BFIS-CA was set at 15, as follows: (1) interactions with the mother, (2) interactions with the father, (3) school performance, (4) social interactions with brothers or sisters, (5) playing with other children in the neighborhood, (6) activities in the community (church, clubs, Scouts, social groups, organizations), (7) visiting other people's homes, (8) playing with other children at school, (9) managing any money they may earn or receive as an allowance, (10) daily self-care (dressing, bathing, hygiene), (11) completing chores or other assigned work at home, (12) doing school homework, (13) following rules, (14) interactions with other adults (visitors to the home, in other community settings) and (15) playing sports. The same range of item responses from the HSQ, 0–9, was retained, but more explicit descriptions of points across the scale were used to indicate the child's degree of impairment (0 = *not at all*, 1–2 = *somewhat*, 3–4 = *mild*, 5–7 = *moderate*, and 8–9 = *severe*). Parents were also given the response option of circling the number 99, for *does not apply*.

As noted in Chapter 1, an important issue here is just how the term "psychosocial impairment" is to be defined and explained to parents in the instructions for the scale. For the BFIS-CA, the following explicit instructions were given to respondents in the normative sample to guide them in making a judgment of how impaired they viewed their children as being in each domain:

> How much difficulty does your child have functioning effectively in each of these major life activities <u>compared to other children of the same age</u>? That is, to what degree is he/she impaired in each of these life domains? Please circle the number next to each item that best describes his/her degree of difficulty in functioning in that domain **DURING THE PAST 6 MONTHS.** If that situation does not apply to him/her (for instance, he/she has no siblings) please circle the 99 in the last column (under "Does not apply"). If your child is currently taking medication for any psychiatric or psychological disorder, please rate his/her functioning based on how he/she functions while **OFF** of his/her medication.

Unlike the older HSQ, here it is evident that "impairment" means the degree of difficulty a parent believes his/her child or teen experiences in functioning effectively in each of the 15 psychosocial domains listed on the scale. Hence, *degree of impairment refers to degree of difficulty in functional effectiveness in a particular domain of major life activity.* How much difficulty does a parent have to report for his/her child to be considered impaired on this scale relative to the average child in the U.S. population (the "average person" standard used in the ADA)? That question is addressed in Chapter 3, after an examination of the extent to which the normative sample responded with each of the possible 0–9 ratings for each of the 15 domains on the BFIS-CA.

Normative information is *not* available for the interview form of the BFIS-CA. Instead, that form is used to obtain more detailed information on the nature of each impairment rated as being clinically significant so as to further validate the parent's rating.

The BFIS-CA scale items focus on rating the degree of functional impairment that parents believe their children are experiencing in each psychosocial domain, rather than on positive or normative functioning. The scale was intended for clinical purposes—to be used to evaluate the range of functional impairment in clinic-referred or high-risk children or adolescents. In that situation, the examiner is faced with the question of the extent to which the complaints about a clinical patient concerning his/her problems are indicative of impairment in psychosocial functioning from medical or mental disorders. The question here is how *typical or atypical* the complaints of the parents about their children are, rather than where a child falls within the distribution of normal variation in normal functioning in these various major life domains in the general population. In other words, the BFIS-CA approaches the issue of impairment from the standpoint of deficit measurement.

Deficit measurement is typical in the development of clinical assessment devices such as those used to assess child behavioral problems, for example, the CBCL and BASC-2, as discussed in the previous chapter. The distribution of such scores is quite different from the more typical bell-shaped curve of the distribution of normal variation in a typical psychological ability, such as intelligence or academic achievement. The score distribution of a deficit measurement tool can be expected to have a highly skewed distribution toward the zero point or low-score end on the scale with a steep dropoff in the percentage of the general population that manifests an increasing degree of impairment. Deficit assessment evaluates the likelihood that the complaints of a parent are sufficiently severe or numerous as to place their child or teen significantly outside the distribution of typical complaints for the general population. The BFIS-CA is a deficit measurement method, not a test of normal variation in a human ability. Hence its instructions direct respondents to report the degree of functional difficulties their children experience rather than trying to assess the range of normal abilities in each of these 15 domains.

It is very important to note here that the BFIS-CA contains instructions to parents to rate the degree of functional impairment *without reference to any specific mental or medical disorder.* In this manner, degree of impairment can be established separately from the existence of a specific disorder. This type of instruction permits the BFIS-CA to be used as part of the evaluation of *any* medical or mental disorder that could lead to difficulties in psychosocial functioning in these 15 domains. Determining the cause(s) of the psychosocial impairment is a separate issue involving a follow-up interview and differential diagnosis. If a disorder or set of symptoms were specified in the instructions of the rating scale, as was done in the original HSQ, then the scale would be applicable only to patients known to have that disorder. Thus the applicability and value of such a scale would be limited, as the parent might rate only the degree of impairment related to that disorder or set of symptoms, not the overall degree of his/her child's impairment in general.

Methods of Collecting the Normative Sample

The 15-domain BFIS-CA was then given to a nationally representative sample of 1,922 parents in the United States who had children between the ages of 6 and 17. The survey company contracted to obtain this national sample was instructed to ensure that males and females were equally represented in each of 12 age groups for each of nine regions representing the United States. The company chosen for this task was Knowledge Networks of Menlo Park, California (see *www.knowledgenetworks.com* for more information on the company). Knowledge Networks conducted the survey using the Web-enabled Knowledge Panel®, a probability-based panel designed to be representative of the U.S. population. Initially, participants were chosen scientifically through a random selection of telephone numbers and residential addresses. Persons in selected households were then invited by telephone or by mail to participate in the Knowledge Panel. For those who agreed to participate but did not already have Internet access, Knowledge Networks provided a laptop and Internet service provider connection at no cost. This was very important, as surveying only people who already had computers and Internet connections would immediately have biased the sample away from one that was representative of the U.S. population. People who already had computers and Internet service were permitted to participate using their own equipment. Panelists then received unique log-in information about accessing surveys online and were sent emails throughout each month inviting them to participate in research. Panelists were paid for their completion of the survey. More technical information is available at *www.knowledgenetworks.com/ganp/reviewer-info.html.*

The parent-report version of the BFIS-CA was provided to Knowledge Networks as a rating scale on which respondents were to answer each item using a 10-point Likert scale (0–9) with anchor points for rating degree of impairment in their children or teens, as described before. The scale was uploaded to an Internet site, and members of the Knowledge Panel were invited to complete them. The interview version was not used in this study. The survey was conducted in August 2011 and was completed within 3 weeks of the initial invitation. The company was contracted to obtain parent-completed scales for at least 1,800 children broken down into 12 age groups (one for each age from 6 to 17) having at least 75 males and 75 females in each age group. A final sample of 1,922 children was obtained.

Knowledge Networks requires that participants be given the option of choosing not to answer a question. In rare cases a participant did refuse to rate every domain, with percentages ranging from 1.5 to 3.1% and averaging 1.9%, or 36 respondents out of 1,922. In these cases, the missing answers were replaced with the response of

"Does not apply" so that the remaining data for these participants could be used in the project. These responses, along with the reported responses of "Does not apply," were then all coded as missing data for purposes of analyzing each domain.

It is important to note here that this sample was not subsequently filtered to remove individuals with a prior history of special education, who took psychiatric medication, who had any psychiatric diagnosis, or who may have had any learning, developmental, neurological, or medical disorders. This filtering technique has been used in the collection of normative information for other scales. Performing such filtering, however, creates a supernormal comparison group, not a general population sample, and can result in impairments being found to occur at far lower levels of deviance on the ratings than would be the case had a general population sample been used without such filtering. The BFIS-CA is based on just such an unfiltered general population sample, so that individual impairment scores on it can be compared with the "average person" standard so important in the definition of the term "impairment" (see Chapter 1).

Demographic Characteristics of the National Sample

Knowledge Networks was originally contracted to obtain completed scales on at least 1,800 children, broken down into 12 age groups (years 6–17), with at least 75 boys and 75 girls in each age group. The company was able to obtain ratings from 1,922 parents with at least 80 boys and 80 girls in each of these age groups. Initial analyses of the demographic profile showed that male respondents (fathers) were slightly overrepresented in the sample (53% vs. 47% female). Ethnically White individuals were also somewhat overrepresented (74%) compared with the 2000 U.S. Census (69.1%). College-educated (bachelor's degree or higher, 42%) people were also overrepresented compared to the U.S. Census (25%). Consequently, the original sample was reduced by 6% ($N = 122$) by removing White males having bachelor's degree or higher. Those chosen for removal were proportionately weighted across bachelor's ($N = 62$), master's ($N = 40$), and doctoral degrees ($N = 20$) and equally distributed between male ($N = 61$) and female ($N = 61$) children so as to retain an equal representation of boys and girls at each of the original age levels. The selection of an individual for removal from among those meeting these characteristics was done at random. The final sample used to create the norms reported here therefore consisted of 1,800 parents (and their children). This slightly reduced sample is referred to henceforth as the *normative sample.* All further analyses reported in the remainder of this chapter are based on this normative sample.

Age, Sex, and Biological Relationship

The ages of the parents in the normative sample who completed the rating scale ranged from 18 to 68 years, with a mean age of 42.3 years ($SD = 7.9$). The parent respondents reported that 95.3% of the children in this survey had another parent known to them ($N = 1,715$). Those other parents ranged in age from 21 to 76 years, with a mean age of 42.5 ($SD = 7.5$). The mean age of the children in the sample was 11.8 years (*SD* = 3.7). The parent respondents were equally represented by sex: 50% fathers (*N* = 900) and 50% mothers (*N* = 900). Biological parents represented 91% of the sample. The specific breakdown of the status of the parents' biological relationships to the children follows: biological mothers, 46.4%; stepmothers, 1.5%; adoptive mothers, 1.3%; foster mothers, 0.1%; biological fathers, 44.8%; stepfathers, 3.1%; adoptive fathers, 1.7%; and foster fathers, 1.1%.

Education

The breakdown in educational categories for the parent respondents in comparison with the 2000 U.S. Census (*www.census.gov*) is shown in the following:

Education category	Normative sample	U.S. Census
Less than high school	4.1%	19.1%
High school (diploma or equivalency)	28.1%	28.6%
Some college, no degree	20.6%	21.0%
Associate's degree	9.2%	6.3%
Bachelor's degree	22.6%	15.5%
Graduate degree	15.4%	8.9%

The present sample is generally comparable to the U.S. population in the percentage having high school diplomas or equivalency, some college, or Associate's degrees but has a slight overrepresentation of individuals with bachelor's or graduate degrees. The sample also contains a lower percentage of those having less than a high school education than appear in the U.S. Census. The breakdown of educational levels of the nonrespondent parents follows: less than high school, 6.6%; high school, 20.6%; some college, no degree, 20.6%; associate's degree, 10.2%; bachelor's degree, 22.8%; graduate degree, 14.8%. These percentages are very similar to those for the respondent parents. The mean educational level for the children in the sample was 7.4 years (*SD* = 3.5, range = kindergarten [1] to 12th grade [13]), or roughly a mid-sixth-grade education.

Geographic Region

The geographic distribution of the participants was as follows in comparison with the 2000 U.S. Census:

U.S. geographic region	Normative sample	U.S. Census
Northeast	18%	19%
Midwest	28%	23%
South	31%	36%
West	23%	22%

The normative sample thus represents all regions of the United States and appears to approximate the geographic distribution of the U.S. adult population.

Ethnicity

The racial/ethnic breakdown of the normative sample is as follows relative to the 2000 U.S. Census:

Ethnic group	Normative sample	U.S. Census
White, alone	73.0%	75.1%
Black	7.7%	12.3%
Other (Asian, Native U.S.)	4.3%	6.6%
Hispanic	12.4%	12.5%
Multiracial	2.7%	2.4%

The sample contains members of all major ethnic groups in the United States and appears to approximate the racial/ethnic distribution of the United States except for a somewhat lower representation of Blacks in the normative sample relative to the U.S. Census.

Household Income

The breakdown of the normative sample by income categories follows, again relative to the 2000 U.S. Census:

Income category	Normative sample	U.S. Census
Less than $10,000	5.4%	9.5%
$10,000–$14,999	2.9%	6.3%
$15,000–$24,999	5.5%	12.8%
$25,000–$34,999	7.7%	12.8%
$35,000–$49,999	11.4%	16.5%
$50,000–$74,999	20.4%	19.5%
$75,000–$99,999	18.8%	10.2%
$100,000–$149,999	18.7%	7.7%
$150,000+	9.3%	4.6%

The mean income ranged from $50,000 to $59,999, whereas both the median and mode fell in the range of $60,000–$74,999. The median household income of the United States is $41,994 as of the 2000 U.S. Census. The results suggest that this sample of parents had a somewhat higher average household income than that of the entire U.S. population. However, once again these figures are not directly comparable given that the U.S. Census does not break down household income into categories such as parents with children in the age ranges used here. It is possible that parents have a somewhat higher mean household income than do individuals who are not parents in the population.

Marital Status of Parents

The marital status of the parents in the normative sample relative to parents reported in the 2000 U.S. Census follows:

Marital status	Normative sample	U.S. Census
Married	81.3%	69.0%
Separated, divorced, widowed	8.3%	19.0%
Never married	4.3%	11.9%

As this table shows, the normative sample has a slightly higher representation of married parents than is the case in the U.S. population.

Employment Status of Parents

The employment status of the normative sample was as follows: working as paid employees, 64.8%; self-employed, 8.7%; not working, on temporary layoff, 1.2%; not working, looking for work, 6.8%; retired, 1.1%; disabled, not working, 4.5%; and not working for other reasons (wife or husband working as a homemaker, for instance), 12.9%. Approximately 74% of the sample was working. Comparable figures could not be located from the U.S. Census for the age range of parents and children in the normative sample. However, overall employment in the U.S. 2000 Census was 64% for individuals 18 years of age and older. The employment figure for the normative sample is similar to this figure from the 2000 U.S. Census.

To summarize the demographic characteristics, it appears that the normative sample recruited here reasonably approximates that of the U.S. adult population as based on the U.S. Census from the year 2000 concerning regional distribution, sex, race/ethnic group, and employment status. It is unclear how this sample compares with the U.S. population in household income, as such figures are not readily available from the U.S. Census for parents within this age range having children within this age range of the normative sample. The normative sample has a somewhat higher representation of parents who are married and who are college graduates.

Developmental and Psychiatric Diagnoses of Children

Parents were asked whether or not their children had ever received any of the following diagnoses from a professional. Alongside each diagnosis is the percentage of the normative sample that had received such a diagnosis:

Diagnosis	Sample
Physical disability (unable to talk or use arms unassisted)	0.3%
Language delay	5.0%
Motor skill or coordination delay	3.3%
Reading disorder or disability	4.2%
Math disorder or disability	2.4%
Spelling disorder or disability	2.4%
Writing disorder or disability	2.3%
Other academic learning disorder	1.7%
General developmental delay or mental retardation	1.2%
Tic disorder or Tourette syndrome	0.6%
Deafness or hearing disability	0.4%
Blindness or visual impairment	0.6%
Seizure disorder or epilepsy	0.8%
Attention-deficit disorder (ADD) or ADHD	9.2%
Oppositional defiant disorder	1.6%
Conduct disorder	0.3%
Any anxiety disorder	3.0%
Any depression disorder	1.8%
Bipolar disorder or manic–depression	0.8%
Autism or autistic spectrum disorder or Asperger syndrome	1.8%
Childhood schizophrenia or psychosis	0.1%
No diagnosis of any of the above	77.1%

The rates for various disorders are well within the ranges found in various epidemiological studies of the U.S. population of children (American Psychiatric Association, 2000; Mash & Barkley, 2003; see also Chapter 7) except that children diagnosed with oppositional defiant disorder and conduct disorder appear to be underrepresented. Approximately 23% of the sample had one or more disorders. The results are reasonably consistent with research showing that on average 12–13.5% of children ages 6–12 and 16.5% of children ages 13–18 have at least one psychiatric disorder (Costello, Egger, & Angold, 2005; Roberts, Attkinsson, & Rosenblatt, 1998), typically ranging between 14 and 20%, depending on methods used for diagnosis (Brandenburg, Friedman, & Silver, 1990). Some recent studies found an overall prevalence for psychiatric disorders for a 3-month period of 13.5% and lifetime prevalence throughout a 3-year follow-up during childhood of 36.7% (Costello, Mustillo, Erkanli, Keeler, & Angold, 2003). Add to the average prevalence of 13–16% the percentage having intellectual, learning, language, and motor disorders that account for another 10–12% of the population exclusive of psychiatric disorders (Boyle, Decoufle, & Yeargin-Allsop, 1994; Mash & Barkley, 2003), and one finds that on average 23–29% of the U.S. population of children have at least one developmental, learning, or psychiatric disorder. The overall prevalence of 23% in the present normative sample is therefore a close approximation of the prevalence of these disorders in the U.S. population of children.

Treatment Status of the Children

Parents were also asked to indicate whether their children had ever received any of the following types of treatment:

Treatment type	Sample
Any medication for a psychiatric or psychological disorder	8.1%
Formal tutoring outside of school for school performance	4.1%
Special education services of any type	9.4%
Speech and language therapy	11.4%
Occupational therapy	4.3%
Physical therapy	3.0%
Individual psychological counseling	9.4%
Family psychological counseling	3.9%
Group psychological therapy	0.9%
Placement in an inpatient psychiatric unit	0.7%
Attendance at a residential treatment school for children with psychological or psychiatric disorders	0.3%
None of the treatments listed above	71.6%

It is not possible to find comparable figures for the United States for all of these therapies, but a comparison with those for which figures are available suggests that these rates are reasonably similar to those found in other studies. For instance, one study using data from the National Ambulatory Medical Care Survey found a rate of psychotropic drug use of 8.3% for adolescents in 2000–2001 (Thomas, Conrad, Casler, & Goodman, 2006), a figure that had more than doubled since 1996 and one very close to that found for such drug use in our normative sample. Likewise, several studies found rates of 3.9–6.3% for children in the United States in 1996 (Olfson, Marcus, Weissman, & Jensen, 2002; Zito et al., 2003), a rate that also had more than doubled since 1987 (see Olfson et al., 2002). Given the results for the Thomas and colleagues (2006) study of teenagers over the subsequent term to 2001, this rate for children likely doubled again by the early 2000s (to at least 7–12%). Again, the expected rate is very similar to that found here.

The results for the factor analyses of the scale and construction of the individual subscales based on this normative sample are discussed in the next chapter.

CHAPTER 3

Factor Analysis, Scale Construction, and Item Frequencies

This chapter first reports the results of the factor analyses intended to uncover the underlying dimensions of impairment on the BFIS-CA. Then the frequencies with which the domains were endorsed by the normative sample are presented and discussed.

Factor Analysis

On average, participants in the entire initial sample (N = 1,922) answered that 13 of the 15 domains were applicable to their children (M = 13.7, SD = 3.2). The median and mode were both 15 out of 15. Just 5% of the normative sample endorsed only 8 or fewer domains as applicable to their children, whereas 90% answered that 13 or more of the domains applied to their children and so chose to rate them. Analysis of variance (ANOVA) was used to evaluate the effect of child age (12 age groups) and sex on the number of domains rated by parents, and both were not significant (age: F = 1.08, df = 11/1,921, p = NS; sex: F = 0.42, df = 1/1,921, p = NS). In short, most participants gave answers to the majority of the 15 domains of the BFIS-CA regardless of the age or sex of the participant's child. This suggests that the domains listed on the scale are widely applicable across the childhood and adolescent population.

The ratings of the 15 domains on the BFIS-CA were submitted to a principal-components factor analysis (PCFA) using the entire initial sample of 1,922 parents described in Chapter 2. Missing data (for those who marked a domain as "does not apply") were replaced with the mean. The initial results revealed two factors that had eigenvalues greater than 1. The first accounted for most of the variance (65.7%). All of the 15 domains loaded highly on this dimension, thus indicating that impairment in children can be conceptualized as a single construct, just as was found recently for an adult impairment rating scale (Barkley, 2011b). The second dimension was considerably smaller and explained an additional 7% of the variance. It was composed primarily of community domains. The results were then submitted to a varimax rotation, designed to maximize as many values in each column of the factor-loading coefficient table as close to zero as possible. This approach is typically used in an attempt to reduce the degree of correlation among the items (variables). But the ratings were also submitted to a promax rotation as it is frequently used when variables are known to be correlated, as are the BFIS-CA domains. That rotation allows items to be correlated with more than one factor. Both approaches yielded the same eventual factor structure. The results of the PCFA with rotations are shown in Table 3.1.

The first factor (eigenvalue = 9.85) accounted for 38% of the variance after rotation and contained nine domains that were entirely related to home and school activities. The factor was therefore labeled as the Home–School factor and had its highest loadings on the domains related to doing chores and tasks at home, doing school homework, performance in school, and following rules. It is largely a dimension of work or handling responsibilities and rules. The second factor (eigenvalue = 1.05) accounted for 34% of the variance after rotation and contained the six remaining domains, which dealt with community and leisure activities. Its highest loadings came from the following domains: visiting others' homes; playing with other children at school; community activities, such as church, Scouts, and clubs; and playing with other children in the neighborhood. It is largely a leisure activities dimension. It was therefore labeled as the Community–Leisure factor. The relationship of the two factors was moderate to high, $r = .68$, indicating approximately 46% of shared variance between the two dimensions.

Frequency of Domain Responses

It is clinically and scientifically informative to examine the percentage of respondents in the normative sample who endorsed each of the item answers. This gives an indication of how common or uncommon the different answer levels of impairment are for each domain (item). This information can also be used to determine what severity rating for each item can be used to indicate that this item at that rating can be judged to be functionally impaired—that is to say, that such an answer or rating in that domain would be very atypical of the general population. For instance, if the vast majority of parents respond to a domain with answers ranging from *not at all* to *somewhat* to *mild* (0–4 on the BFIS-CA), then responses more severe than this (*moderate, severe*) could be considered to be indicative of a likely domain of impairment relative to the average child. Of course, whether or not that domain is actually functionally impaired in reality is a question of validity. The clinician must evaluate that issue against other forms of information that would corroborate such a parent rating of a child, as discussed in Chapter 1. But it can still be of great clinical value to

TABLE 3.1. Factor Loadings for BFIS-CA Domains Based on PCFA with Varimax and Promax Rotations

	Factors	
BFIS-CA domain	1	2
1. Interactions with his/her mother	**.737** (**.820**)	.360 (.633)
2. Interactions with his/her father	**.703** (**.775**)	.326 (.587)
3. School performance	**.782** (**.875**)	.394 (.682)
4. Interactions with brothers and sisters	**.650** (**.784**)	.466 (.693)
5. Playing with other children in the neighborhood	.412 (.700)	**.793** (**.892**)
6. Activities in the community (church, Scouts, clubs, etc.)	.372 (.669)	**.808** (**.889**)
7. Visiting other people's homes	.395 (.694)	**.817** (**.907**)
8. Playing with other children at school	.424 (.718)	**.810** (**.913**)
9. Managing any money he/she may earn or be given as an allowance	**.640** (**.756**)	.421 (.647)
10. Caring for him/herself (dressing, bathing, and hygiene)	**.553** (**.723**)	.533 (.714)
11. Getting chores or other assigned tasks completed at home	**.838** (**.896**)	.321 (.638)
12. Doing school homework	**.833** (**.890**)	.319 (.634)
13. Ability to follow rules	**.773** (**.885**)	.439 (.719)
14. Interactions with other adults (visitors to the home, when visiting others, in community settings, etc.)	.486 (.744)	**.734** (**.896**)
15. Playing sports	.264 (.548)	**.752** (**.794**)

Note. Numbers in **boldface** type indicate the dimension receiving the highest loading for that domain. Promax rotation factor loadings are in parentheses.

know just how often children are rated as having difficulty in functioning effectively in each of the 15 domains evaluated in the BFIS-CA. To gain some idea about how often parents in a general population sample endorsed each possible answer for each domain, the percentage of parents in the normative sample ($N = 1{,}800$) who endorsed each of the possible answers to each domain was computed. The results appear in Table 3.2. This is important information for medical and mental health professionals and others who may have an interest in knowing the proportion of the population of parents that endorses particular levels of functional difficulties

TABLE 3.2. Percentage of the Normative Sample Endorsing "Does Not Apply" and Percentage of Normative Sample to Whom the Domain Did Apply, and Who Endorsed Each Level of Impairment for Each Domain on the BFIS-CA

		Degree of rated impairment (functional difficulties)[b]									
	Does not	None	Somewhat		Mild		Moderate			Severe	
BFIS-CA domain	apply[a]	0	1	2	3	4	5	6	7	8	9
1. In his/her interactions with his/her mother	6.7	67.4	10.1	4.5	4.0	3.5	2.6	3.6	1.9	1.5	0.9
2. In his/her interactions with his/her father	9.3	63.0	12.3	5.0	5.2	3.7	3.1	2.8	1.9	1.8	1.2
3. In his/her school performance	5.7	59.6	12.3	5.2	4.4	4.6	3.0	3.6	2.9	2.5	1.9
4. In his/her interactions with brothers and sisters	15.6	57.8	14.3	5.6	5.7	4.9	3.0	2.6	2.6	1.6	1.8
5. When playing with other children in the neighborhood	10.7	66.4	11.9	5.5	4.0	3.5	3.0	2.0	1.7	1.1	0.9
6. In his/her activities in the community (church, Scouts, clubs, etc.)	12.8	70.7	10.8	3.9	4.1	3.5	1.5	2.9	1.3	0.6	0.7
7. When he/she is visiting other people's homes	6.1	69.0	12.3	5.0	4.1	3.1	2.3	2.1	1.1	0.5	0.5
8. When playing with other children at school	8.4	68.0	10.8	5.0	4.6	3.3	2.5	2.4	1.3	1.1	0.8
9. Managing any money he/she may earn or be given as an allowance	9.9	63.2	12.8	5.9	5.2	3.4	2.3	2.9	1.8	1.1	1.4
10. In caring for him/herself (dressing, bathing, and hygiene)	6.6	69.7	12.0	5.0	3.5	2.6	2.0	1.8	1.3	1.0	1.0
11. Getting chores or other assigned tasks completed at home	5.2	44.1	22.5	8.1	6.8	4.4	3.2	4.2	2.3	1.9	2.5
12. Doing school homework	5.6	50.6	18.7	6.2	6.2	3.6	3.2	3.5	2.8	2.8	2.4
13. In his/her ability to follow rules	5.6	60.4	15.9	5.1	4.2	3.4	2.8	2.1	2.3	2.1	1.6
14. In his/her interactions with other adults (visitors to the home, when visiting others, in community settings, etc.)	5.4	70.9	11.4	3.6	3.7	3.4	2.2	1.7	1.5	0.8	0.8
15. Playing sports	16.7	68.1	12.8	4.2	4.1	3.5	2.1	2.0	1.3	0.9	0.9

[a]Percentages in this column reflect the percentage of the normative sample ($N = 1{,}800$) specifying that this domain did not apply to their child.
[b]Percentages in the remaining columns (marked 0–9) are the percentages of parents who did believe this domain applied and so chose to rate their child's degree of impairment.

(impairment) in their children in these 15 domains of major life activities. Six of these domains are graphically depicted in Figure 3.1.

Table 3.2 and Figure 3.1 clearly show the extent of the non-normality of the distributions for these domains. The distributions of the answers are highly skewed to the left (toward low ratings), as expected for a scale that focuses on impairment in a general population. Such a result has been observed with other rating scales of impairment or of children's psychiatric symptoms (see Achenbach, 2001; Reynolds & Kamphaus, 2004). This explains why raw scores were not converted to *T*-scores to smooth out and partially normalize these distributions in creating the scoring sheets for the BFIS-CA. Such a practice would artificially warp the percentiles that would be determined from such a conversion, so they would not be those actually obtained in the normative sample. Instead, the score sheets reported in the Appendix indicate the actual percentile in the normative sample associated with each score.

Table 3.2 and Figure 3.1 also clearly show that, for the vast majority of domains, a great majority of a general population sample of parents endorses most items at a severity of impairment of *not at all, somewhat,* or *mild*. Answers reflecting moderate or severe impairment (6–7 and 8–9, respectively) are statistically unusual and even rare in the case of scores of 8 or 9. The latter ratings were endorsed by less than 3% of the population in most domains and by less than 5% of the population in the remainder. Less than 7% in most cases gave answers of 6 or 7. How much dif-

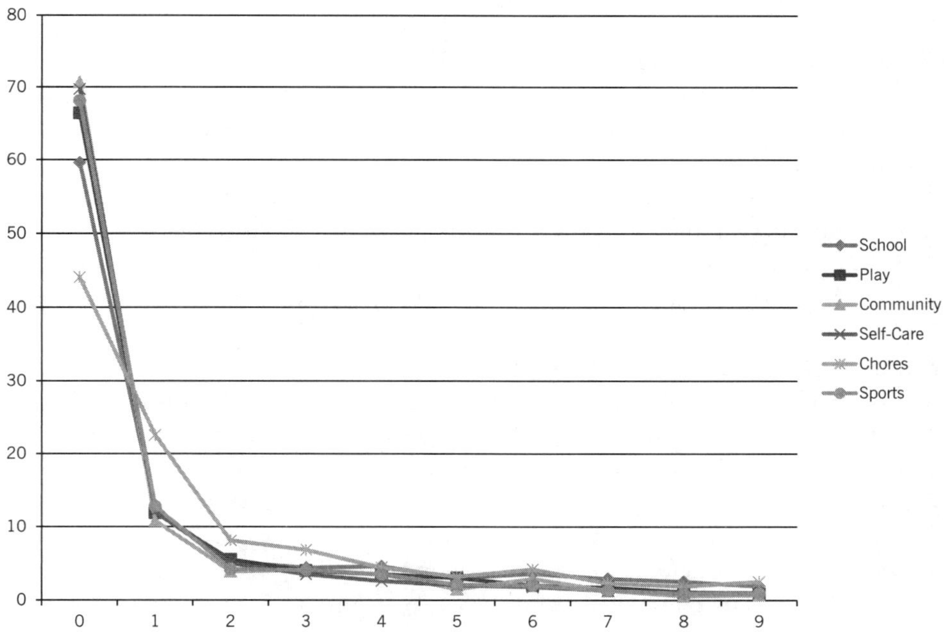

FIGURE 3.1. The percentage of the sample (to whom this setting applied) reporting each degree of impairment for each of six domains from the BFIS-CA. School, school performance; Play, play with other children in the neighborhood; Community, participation in community activities; Self-Care, caring for him- or herself (e.g., dressing, bathing, and hygiene); Chores, getting chores or other assigned tasks completed at home; and Sports, playing sports.

ficulty (how high a rating) must a child have to be considered statistically unusual or abnormal? Most rating scales consider the 93rd to 95th percentiles as probably indicative of being statistically deviant in a population (this translates to between 1 in 14 and 1 in 20 people, respectively). So if one wanted to identify a domain as being impaired to a degree that is statistically rare (say, the top 7%), then each domain can be examined for the score that signifies this threshold (93rd percentile or higher). Here are the thresholds used to signify abnormality for the various domains when based on the entire normative sample:

- A score of 5 or higher would reach this threshold for these five domains: (1) activities in the community; (2) visiting other people's homes; (3) caring for themselves; (4) interactions with other adults; and (5) playing sports.
- A score of 6 or higher would reach this threshold for these five domains: (1) interactions with mother; (2) interactions with father; (3) playing with other children in the neighborhood; (4) playing with other children at school; and (5) managing money.
- A rating of 7 or higher surpasses this threshold for the remaining five domains: (1) school performance; (2) interactions with brothers and sisters; (3) getting chores or other assigned tasks completed at home; (4) doing school homework; (5) ability to follow rules.

These thresholds are indicated on the scoring sheets in the Appendix in **boldface** type in order to signify them (and higher scores) as the threshold used to determine functional impairment in that domain relative to the average child in the population. From this information a clinician can compute a score for the number of domains in which the individual placed in the impaired range, or a number of impaired domains score.

Besides the score (rating) given on each of the 15 domains, a separate mean impairment score can be computed for the two major dimensions of the scale: Home–School and Community–Leisure. To do so, the scores for the domains in which a child was rated (as opposed to *does not apply*) were summed. This sum was then divided by the number of domains that were rated as applying to the children (the number of domains that contributed a score to the summation). To summarize, the BFIS-CA can be used to obtain 18 scores: 15 individual domain ratings, a Home–School mean impairment score, a Community–Leisure mean impairment score, and a number of impaired domains score. These are considered to be the primary scores for the scale. There are also eight secondary impairment questions on the scale, as noted previously, that deal with friends, community organizations, sports, and academic performance and adjustment. The answers that parents provide to these questions can be compared as well against the responses provided by the normative sample should the clinician be interested in them.

In the next chapter, the manner in which these scores are related to various demographic features of the children and parents will be examined in order to determine how best to present the norms (percentiles) on score sheets.

CHAPTER 4

Relationship of BFIS-CA Scores to Demographic Factors in the Normative Sample

This chapter reports the relationships of various demographic factors to the BFIS-CA scores for the entire normative sample of 1,800 parents. This was done to determine the best means of presenting the normative data (percentiles) on the Impairment Profiles (score sheets) in the Appendix. Yet it also sheds light on the relationship of these demographic factors (age, sex, ethnicity, geographic region) to parent-reported levels of impairment in a general population sample of children ages 6–17 years.

Age

Age was found to correlate to a low but significant and negative degree with 6 of the 15 domain scores, with significant Pearson correlations ranging from .05 (managing money) to .12 (interactions with father; all *p*'s $< .05$). All six significant correlations were within the Home–School (work) domains, whereas none of the correlations for domains within the Community–Leisure dimension were significant. These are small positive correlations indicating that age accounts for minimal variance within this sample. The results suggest that impairment scores may increase slightly as a function of age. As a consequence, both the Home–School mean impairment score ($r = .08$, $N = 1{,}715$, $p < .001$) and number of domains impaired score ($r = .05$, $N =$

1,232, $p = .037$) were significant as well. In general, specific ratings of impairment in the domains on the BFIS-CA share less than 1.5% of their variance with age.

Such correlation analyses can disguise nonlinear effects, particularly when there is good reason to believe that a nonlinear relationship might exist between impairment ratings and age. For instance, impairment could be elevated in very young children, may decline with age to late childhood, but then increase again in adolescence as a consequence of growing independence and individuation from parents. The relationship of age to the impairment scores was therefore also analyzed using the 12 age groups (6–17 years) in the normative sample in a one-way (age group) ANOVA. The effect of age was significant (all p's $< .05$) for just 3 of the 15 BFIS-CA domains: interactions with father ($F = 2.54$, $p = .003$); doing chores ($F = 2.01$, $p = .024$); and doing school homework ($F = 2.25$, $p = .01$). There was also a marginally significant effect on the domain of interactions with mother ($F = 1.76$, $p = .056$). Therefore, age was not a significant factor in most domains. It was also not significant in analyses of the summary scores (Home–School mean impairment score, Community–Leisure mean impairment score, number of impaired domains score). The results for the Home–School and Community–Leisure mean impairment scores are shown graphically in Figure 4.1. Despite the apparent rise in severity scores for the Home–School domains, age was not a statistically significant factor. But in the three specific domains in which it was significant, pairwise comparisons of each age group against the others showed that it was the 6- to 9-year-olds who were likely to differ from the 16- to 17-year-olds, with no other age

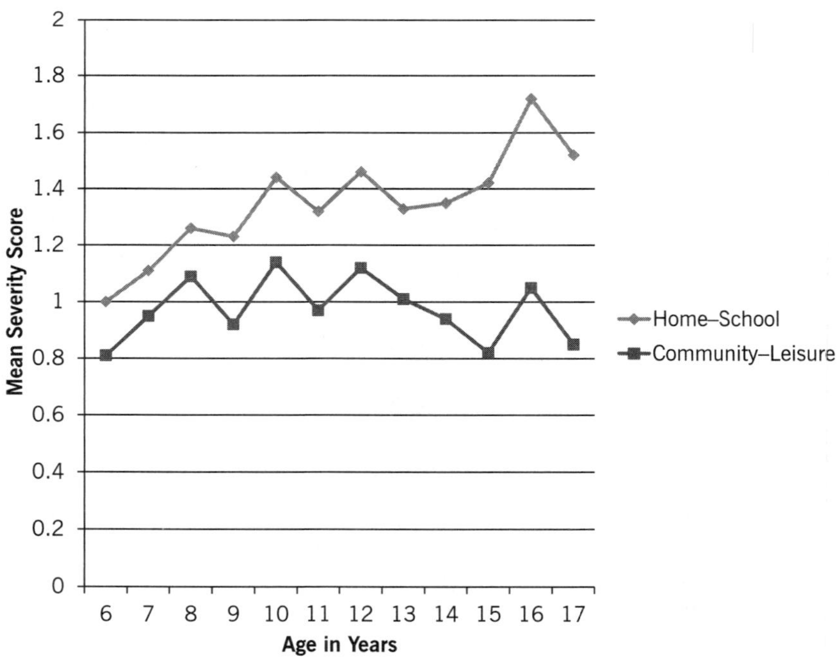

FIGURE 4.1. BFIS-CA mean impairment severity scores for each of 12 age groups in the normative sample ($N = 1{,}800$).

comparisons being significant. Therefore, age could pose a significant problem for scoring these specific domains, and even for the Home–School mean impairment score based on them, if all ages were to be collapsed together for portrayal of the norms on the scoring sheets. For this reason, it appeared to be advisable to cluster the age groups into two broad age ranges for displaying the norms (percentages) in the scoring sheets in the Appendix. Those age ranges are 6–11 ($N = 902$) and 12–17 ($N = 898$), thus dividing the sample into nearly equal sample sizes for these two age groups.

Also evident in Figure 4.1 is the finding that mean impairment ratings across the Home–School (work-related) domains are significantly higher than the mean impairment ratings across the Community–Leisure domains. This makes perfect sense given the greater demands for compliance, responsibility, work, and even self-reliance in the former settings compared with the latter.

The two larger age groups were then compared on all of the 15 domain scores and three summary scores using ANOVAs. Results showed that five of the domain scores were now significant: interactions with mother ($F = 7.79$, $p = .005$), interactions with father ($F = 17.54$, $p < .001$), school performance ($F = 5.97$, $p = .015$), doing chores ($F = 12.03$, $p = .001$), and doing school homework ($F = 10.92$, $p = .001$). In all five domains, impairment ratings were higher in the older than in the younger age groups. As a result, given that all of these domains are contained within it, the Home–School mean impairment score was also significant ($F = 6.53$, $p = .011$). Such findings underscore the decision to present the normative information using these two age groups on the Impairment Profiles in the Appendix.

Sex

A comparison of the 901 males with the 899 females from the normative sample was conducted using ANOVAs on all domain and summary scores. The results indicated significant main effects of sex on 11 of the 15 domain scores; the exceptions were interactions with mother, interactions with father, interactions with brothers and sisters, and playing with other children in the neighborhood. These results are shown in Figure 4.2. In all instances in which significant differences were found, males had significantly higher impairment ratings than females. But the mean differences are rather small in magnitude, and so it is most likely that the large sample sizes being compared here have driven these small effects to statistical significance. As a result of so many significant sex effects, there was also a significant effect on all three summary scores that is depicted in Figure 4.3. All of these main effects are shown in Table 4.1. These analyses were repeated, this time examining the interaction of sex with age grouping. Of interest here would be any significant interactions of sex with age grouping. There were none for any domain specific or summary scores. Those results are also shown in Table 4.1. What all of this makes clear is that norms need to be presented on the scoring sheets in the Appendix for each sex separately, as has been done.

(text resumes on page 42)

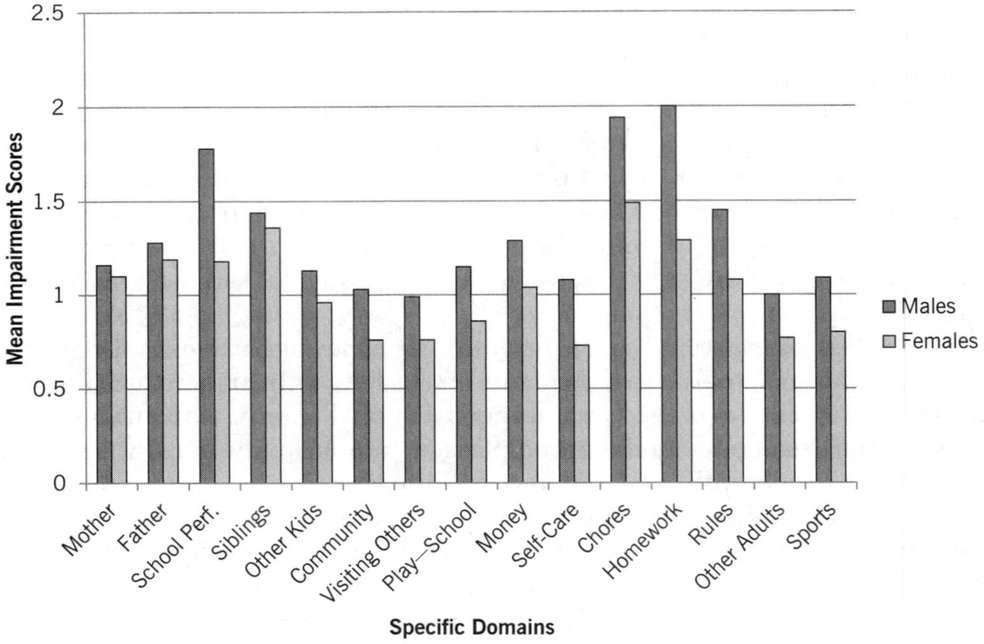

FIGURE 4.2. Mean impairment ratings for each specific domain on the BFIS-CA for each sex. All comparisons were statistically significant except for interactions with mother, interactions with father, interactions with brothers and sisters, and playing with other children (kids) in the neighborhood.

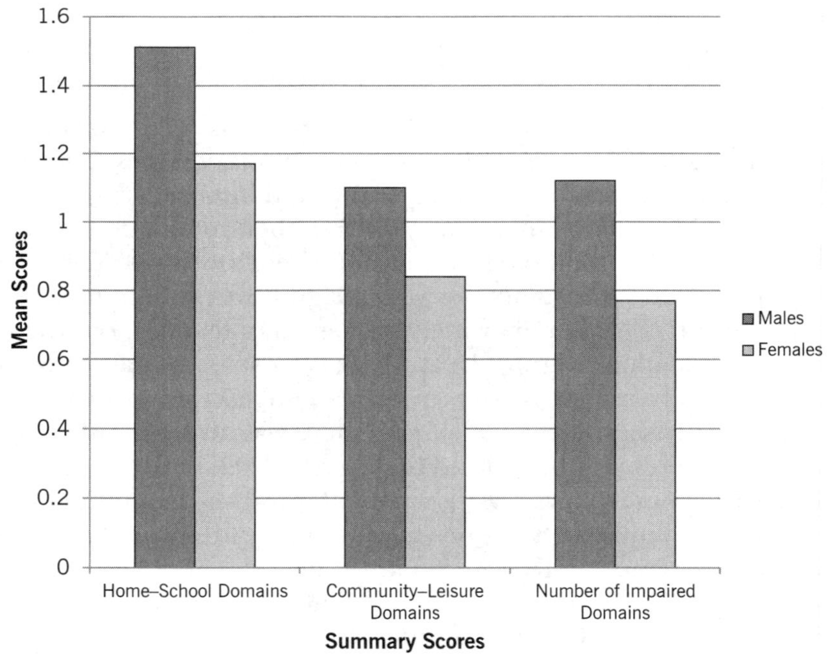

FIGURE 4.3. Mean impairment ratings for the Home–School domains, the Community–Leisure domains, and the number of impaired domains summary scores from the BFIS-CA for males and females. All comparisons were statistically significant.

TABLE 4.1. BFIS-CA Results for Each Sex within Each of the Two Age Groups Used to Create the Impairment Profiles in the Appendix

	Age groups × sex									
	Males				Females					
	6–11 years		12–17 years		6–11 years		12–17 years			
Subscale	Mean	*SD*	Mean	*SD*	Mean	*SD*	Mean	*SD*	*F*	*p*
With mother	1.00	2.00	0.97	1.94	1.32	2.29	1.23	2.21	S = 0.37	NS
									A = 7.78	<.001
									A × S = 0.07	NS
With father	1.08	1.98	1.50	2.40	0.95	1.93	1.42	2.29	S = 0.88	NS
									A = 17.63	<.001
									A × S = 0.05	NS
School performance	1.58	2.39	1.98	2.82	1.09	2.15	1.27	2.18	S = 26.43	<.001
									A = 6.15	0.03
									A × S = 0.95	NS
With siblings	1.45	2.30	1.43	2.25	1.31	2.25	1.42	2.30	S = 0.44	NS
									A = 0.16	NS
									A × S = 0.31	NS
Playing in neighborhood	1.16	2.00	1.09	2.08	0.96	1.91	0.96	1.87	S = 2.98	NS
									A = 0.13	NS
									A × S = 0.16	NS
Community activities	0.95	1.81	1.12	2.10	0.71	1.65	0.82	1.75	S = 8.81	.003
									A = 2.28	NS
									A × S = 0.10	NS
Visiting others	1.01	1.84	0.97	1.88	0.79	1.71	0.74	1.55	S = 7.25	.007
									A = 0.32	NS
									A × S = 0.01	NS
Playing at school	1.17	2.08	1.13	2.12	0.88	1.85	0.84	1.67	S = 9.11	.003
									A = 0.16	NS
									A × S = 0.01	NS
Managing money	1.25	2.13	1.33	2.24	0.95	1.88	1.12	2.06	S = 5.89	.015
									A = 1.52	NS
									A × S = 0.17	NS
Self-care	1.04	1.96	1.12	2.08	0.79	1.73	0.66	1.67	S = 14.74	<.001
									A = 0.09	NS
									A × S = 1.27	NS
Doing chores	1.75	2.35	2.14	2.65	1.28	2.02	1.69	2.32	S = 16.10	<.001
									A = 12.37	<.001
									A × S = 0.01	NS
School homework	1.73	2.40	2.27	2.88	1.17	2.09	1.42	2.25	S = 36.34	<.001
									A = 11.33	.001
									A × S = 1.58	NS

(cont.)

TABLE 4.1. *(cont.)*

	Age groups × sex									
	Males				Females					
	6–11 years		12–17 years		6–11 years		12–17 years			
Subscale	Mean	*SD*	Mean	*SD*	Mean	*SD*	Mean	*SD*	*F*	*p*
Following rules	1.38	2.22	1.53	2.47	0.98	2.05	1.17	2.09	S = 12.51 A = 2.31 A × S = 0.04	<.001 NS NS
With other adults	1.02	1.95	0.97	1.96	0.77	1.81	0.77	1.61	S = 6.51 A = 0.12 A × S = 0.05	.011 NS NS
Playing sports	1.13	2.01	1.06	2.11	0.76	1.55	0.85	1.80	S = 9.04 A = 0.01 A × S = 0.66	.003 NS NS
Home–School mean impairment	1.38	1.87	1.65	2.12	1.07	1.76	1.28	1.77	S = 13.98 A = 6.69 A × S = 0.09	<.001 .010 NS
Community–Leisure mean impairment	1.12	1.85	1.09	1.89	0.84	1.64	0.84	1.54	S = 9.92 A = 0.03 A × S = 0.05	.002 NS NS
Number of impaired domains	0.99	2.52	1.25	2.79	0.72	2.37	0.82	2.17	S = 9.13 A = 2.33 A × S = 0.44	.003 NS NS

Note. F, results for the *F*-test from the analysis of variance; A, main effect for age group; S, main effect for sex; A × S, interaction of age group × sex; *p*, probability value for each of the *F*-tests if ≤ .05; NS, not significant.

Ethnic Group

The next issue to address was whether there existed any significant relationship of ethnic group to the BFIS-CA scores. One-way ANOVAs were done comparing the ethnic groups on each of the specific domain ratings. There were significant main effects for ethnic group on 7 of the 15 BFIS-CA domain ratings on the omnibus ANOVAs. However, when pairwise comparisons between the groups were conducted, 6 of these 7 domains were found not to be statistically significant. This suggests that any differences among the ethnic groups were quite small. The significant omnibus tests likely arose from evaluating such large sample sizes, which can drive even small effects to be significant. The one domain in which pairwise comparisons were significant was managing money. Here the only contrast that was significant was between children whose parents were classified as belonging to two or more ethnic groups and those classified as Other, Non-Hispanic (largely Asian). The former reported less impairment than the latter. No other pairwise comparisons on this domain were significant. Also no effect was found for ethnicity on the three summary scores: Home–School and Community–Leisure mean impairment scores and the number of domains impaired score. Given the fact that the vast majority of domains involved no significant ethnic differences between any of the groups and the one comparison that was significant was trivial, the norms do not need to be portrayed for each ethnic group on the Impairment Profiles in the Appendix.

Geographic Region

The next analyses concentrated on determining whether any differences on the BFIS-CA scores were associated with the geographic regions in which the parents lived. One-way ANOVAs were again used to compare the four major regions. No significant differences were found for any of the 15 specific domain ratings for the Home–School or Community–Leisure mean impairment scores and for the number of domains impaired score. These results indicate that the norms do not need to be portrayed for each geographic region and so they can be collapsed together to create the Impairment Profiles in the Appendix.

Secondary Impairment Questions

Eight additional questions related to impairment were collected on the normative sample and are provided in the second section of the BFIS-CA Parent Rating Scale in the Appendix. They have to do with specific issues of some significance in the typical daily lives of children and adolescents related to friendships, community activities, sports participation, and school performance and adjustment. Parents either gave a specific answer (e.g., "How many friends does your child have?") or checked one of several possible answers (e.g., "During the most recent grading period at school, what was your child's average grade across all his/her subjects on his/her report card?"). These questions were:

- How many friends does your child have?
- In the past year, in how many clubs or community organizations did your child participate (Scouts, church groups, hobby groups, etc.)?
- In the past year, in how many *organized* sports did your child participate at school and in your community?
- During the most recent grading period at school, what was your child's average grade across all his/her subjects on his/her report card?
- During the past school year, did any of your child's teachers tell you that your child was having problems with his/her behavior or with doing his/her schoolwork?
- Has your child ever been retained in a grade or held back a grade after he/she started school?
- Has your child ever been suspended or expelled from school?
- Has your child ever received special education services?

The answers to such questions are important in gathering a more comprehensive picture of any child's potential impairments in the domains of peer relations, community activities, sports, and especially academic performance and school adjustment. Although they cannot be captured so easily using the 0–9 Likert scale ratings used for each of the 15 BFIS-CA primary domains, they can still provide some corroborative evidence for those ratings that pertain to these domains of child life activities. A separate score sheet for these secondary impairment questions is provided for each of the BFIS-CA Impairment Profiles in the Appendix in case the clinician is interested in how the parent's answers for a specific child or adolescent compare with the information available from the normative sample for that child's age group and sex.

The above analyses pertaining to age, sex, ethnic group, and geographic region were also conducted on these eight questions. The results were as follows.

Number of Current Friends

Parents in the normative sample who chose to answer this question (N = 1,779) reported a mean number of 7.47 (SD = 7.30) friends, but the distribution was highly skewed, with a few parents reporting as many as 85 friends for their child. Both the median and the modal number of friends was 5. Children with 20 or more friends would place at the 93rd percentile or above in this sample, and those with 1 or none would be in the bottom 5.6%. In other words, 94.4% of the sample had at least 2 or more friends. The younger age group (6–11) had slightly but significantly fewer friends (M = 7.08, SD = 6.85) than did the 12–17 age group (M = 7.85, SD = 7.73; F = 4.96, p = .026). There was no significant difference between boys (M = 7.18, SD = 6.87) and girls (M = 7.76, SD = 7.71) in number of friends (F = 2.83, p = NS). There were also no significant differences among the ethnic groups (F = 0.83, p = NS) and no regional differences on this measure (F = 1.19, p = NS).

Number of Organized Community Activities in Previous Year

A total of 1,776 parents in the normative sample reported on this question. Results indicated a mean number of community activities of 2.19 (SD = 2.35), but again the distribution was highly skewed, with parents reporting a range of 0–50 such organized activities in which their children had participated in the previous year. The median and mode were both 2. Children participating in 5 or more such activities would place at the 95th percentile or higher, whereas those having no such activities would be in the lowest 21.2%. Overall, 79.8% of the children participated in 1 or more community activities. The younger (6–11) age group (M = 2.12, SD = 1.76) did not differ significantly from the older one (12–17; M = 2.26, SD = 2.82) in this respect (F = 1.53, p = NS). But girls (M = 2.36, SD = 2.27) participated in slightly but significantly more such activities than did boys (M = 2.02, SD = 2.41; F = 9.01, p = .003). The ethnic groups did not differ significantly (F = 0.62, p = NS). There was a small but significant difference across the four major regions of the United States on this question (F = 6.30, p < .001), with pairwise comparisons showing that children in the northeast region (M = 2.65, SD = 3.60) participated in slightly but significantly more activities than did children in the south (M = 2.06, SD = 1.79), midwest (M = 2.23, SD = 1.94), or west (M = 1.95, SD = 2.19) regions, who did not differ among each other.

Number of Sports in Previous Year

Reports on this question were provided by 1,776 parents. The range of responses was 0–25, with just 7 parents reporting that their children were in 7 or more sports. The distribution was therefore highly skewed such that the mean number of organized sports in which a child had participated in the preceding year (other than school physical education classes) was 1.19 (SD = 1.43), with a median of 1 and a modal response of 0. Parents reported that 38.9% of children had not participated in any sports in the prior year. Children participating in 3 or more sports would place at or above the 86th percentile, and children in 4 or more would be at or above the 94th percentile. Eliminating the single parent who reported 25 would result in a mean of 1.18 (SD = 1.32), with children participating in 3 or more sports being at or above the 86th percentile; just 5.6% of parents reported that their children were in 4 or more sports. The 6- to 11-year-olds participated in slightly but significantly more sports (M = 1.26, SD = 1.32) than did the 12- to 17-year-olds (M = 1.09, SD = 1.30; F = 7.36, p = .007). Boys (M = 1.28, SD = 1.36) also participated in slightly but significantly more sports than did girls (M = 1.08, SD = 1.26; F = 10.19, p = .001). The ethnic groups differed slightly but significantly (F = 3.12, p = .014) on this measure, with Hispanic children participating in significantly fewer sports (M = 0.93, SD = 1.18) than children in the Other, Non-Hispanic (M = 1.43, SD = 1.40) and multiethnic (two or more ethnicities; M = 1.42, SD = 1.58) groups, who did not differ from each other nor from those in the Black (M = 1.18, SD = 1.49) or White, Non-Hispanic (M = 1.20, SD = 1.30) groups. Regional differences were found in sports participation (F = 7.55, p < .001). Children living in the south (M = 1.05, SD = 1.14) and west (M = 1.05, SD = 1.27) participated in slightly but significantly fewer sports than did those in the northeast (M = 1.39, SD = 1.42) or midwest (M = 1.30, SD = 1.43). The former two regions did not differ from each other, nor did the latter two regions.

School Performance and Adjustment

Grade Point Average

Of a total of 1,743 parents who reported on their children's grade point average (GPA) from the children's last report card: 53.6% reported that their children had an A average (or 90–100%), whereas 32.3% reported a B average (80–89%), 11.6% a C average (70–79%), 1.8% a D average (60–69%), and just 0.7% reported an average of E or F or failing (50–50%). In other words, 86% of this sample had a B average or better on their last report cards. However, the two age groups differed significantly in these categories (χ^2 = 55.93, df = 4, p < .001) with the 6- to 11-year-olds having a higher percentage in the A category than the 12- to 17-year-olds (62 vs. 46%, respectively), whereas somewhat more of the older group than the younger group placed in the B (36 vs. 28.4%) and C (14.5 vs. 8.6%) categories. Girls also differed significantly from boys on this categorical measure (χ^2 = 18.43, df = 4, p = .001). Girls were slightly more likely to be in the A-average category than boys (57.2 vs. 50%) but less likely to be in the remaining categories: B average (31.4 vs. 33.3%), C average (10.1 vs. 13%), D average (0.9 vs. 2.7%), and E/F/failing (0.3 vs. 1%). There was a significant difference among the ethnic groups in the percentages placing in each of these categories (χ^2 = 27.25, df = 16, p = .039). The same results were reanalyzed treating this measure as dimensional, with 1 = A, 2 = B, 3 = C, 4 = D, and 5 = E/F averages. This permitted a simpler means of examining such ethnic comparisons. Again, the omnibus ANOVA was significant ($F = 5.16$, $p < .001$), with pairwise comparisons showing that Blacks, Non-Hispanic had a significantly lower GPA (1.84) than did the Other, Non-Hispanic category (mostly Asian; $M = 1.48$) and the multiethnic category ($M = 1.48$), who did not differ from each other. The White, Non-Hispanic ($M = 1.61$) and Hispanic ($M = 1.76$) groups did not differ from each other or any of the other ethnic groups. Potential regional differences were also examined in this same manner, with the omnibus ANOVA indicating no significant differences in GPA ($F = 1.40$, p = NS).

Teacher-Reported Behavior or Schoolwork Problems

Parents were asked whether their child's teacher had told them that their child was having problems with behavior or doing schoolwork during the preceding school year. A total of 1,789 parents answered this question. Overall, 26.1% of children had received such reports. There were no differences between the age groups in the percentage of children having such teacher reports (6–11 = 26.9% vs. 12–17 = 25.7%; $\chi^2 = 0.57$, $df = 1$, p = NS). But boys were significantly more likely than girls (32.5 vs. 20%) to have received such reports ($\chi^2 = 35.69$, $df = 1$, $p < .001$). There were also ethnic differences on this question, with parents of White (24.3%) or Other, Non-Hispanic (22.1%) children being less likely to have received such reports than Black (38%), Hispanic (30.6%), and multiethnic (33.3%) groups. There were no significant differences among the four geographical regions in these reports (24.8 to 27.2%; $\chi^2 = 0.80$, $df = 3$, p = NS).

Grade Retention

A total of 1,792 parents reported on whether or not their children had ever been retained in a grade (held back a grade) at least once. In general, just 5.4% of children had been retained. As might be expected from the inherent differences in opportunity for this event, the older age group of 12- to 17-year-olds had a low but significantly greater percentage of such cases than did the younger age group of 6- to 11-year-olds (7.3 vs. 3.7%, respectively; $\chi^2 = 11.20$, $df = 1$, $p = .001$). The sexes did not differ in this respect (boys = 6.2% vs. girls = 4.7%; $\chi^2 = 2.05$, $df = 1$, p = NS). But the differences among the ethnic groups were significant ($\chi^2 = 21.08$, $df = 4$, $p < .001$). Blacks (13%) were most likely to have been retained than the other ethnic groups, who varied in this measure as follows: Hispanic = 7.2%, multiethnic = 6.3%, White = 4.6%, and Other, Non-Hispanic (1.3%). Surprisingly, there were also significant regional differences in the percentage of children having been retained in a grade ($\chi^2 = 9.83$, $df = 3$, $p = .02$), with the south (7.9%) having the highest percentage, followed by the northeast (5.3%), west (4.4%), and midwest (3.8%).

Suspension/Expulsion

There were reports from 1,790 parents on the question of whether or not their children had ever been suspended or expelled from school. Across the entire sample, just 6.9% of children had experienced this event. Again, because of greater time in school and hence more opportunity for this outcome, the older age group (12–17) was significantly more likely than the younger one to have had this outcome (10.3 vs. 3.6%; $\chi^2 = 31.48$, $df = 1$, $p < .001$). Boys were also significantly more likely to have experienced this outcome than girls (9.9 vs. 3.9%; $\chi^2 = 25.14$, $df = 1$, $p < .001$). And as with grade retention, there were significant ethnic group differences, with Blacks (15.2%) being most likely to have had this outcome, followed by multiethnic (10.4%), Hispanic (9.4%), White (5.7%), and lastly Other, Non-Hispanic (2.6%) groups ($\chi^2 = 22.75$, $df = 4$, $p < .001$). Differences among the geographic regions, however, were not significant (range = 5.9%–7.3%; $\chi^2 = 0.70$, $df = 3$, p = NS).

Special Education Services

Within the entire sample, 9.2% of children ($N = 176$) had received special education services, according to parent reports. Here again, because of greater time in school and hence opportunity for this outcome, the older age group (12–17) was more likely than the younger one to have had this outcome (10.0 vs. 8.3%), but not significantly so ($\chi^2 = 1.56$, $df = 1$, p = NS). Once more, boys were also significantly more likely to have experienced this outcome than girls (13.0% vs.5.39%; $\chi^2 = 34.08$, $df = 1$, $p < .001$). The ethnic groups did not differ significantly in this outcome: Blacks (10.9%), multiethnic children (10.4%), Hispanic (6.7%), White (9.7%), and lastly Other, Non-Hispanic (2.6%) groups ($\chi^2 = 6.62$, $df = 4$, p = NS). Differences among the geographic regions also were not significant ($\chi^2 = 4.07$, $df = 3$, p = NS).

Creation of Impairment Profiles

In view of the preceding findings, the norms are presented on the Impairment Profiles in the Appendix separately for each sex and, within sex, for each of two age groups, 6–11 years and 12–17 years, thus creating four profiles. The means and standard deviations for each domain for each of these two age groupings for each sex are shown in Table 4.1 and were discussed earlier. These are the distributions that were used to create the Impairment Profiles that appear in the Appendix. The percentile scores for each age group and sex are shown in their respective tables on the Profiles. Raw score ranges for each domain score are presented starting with the 1st–50th percentile, the 50th–75th, and the 76th–84th because scores in these ranges are normal and not of clinical interest other than to signify that the rating was in the normal range. Percentile equivalents for each individual score from the 85th percentile onward are provided separately up to the 99th percentile. This was done because it is only as one nears the extreme upper end of the distributions that the percentiles become the most useful for clinical purposes—that is, in identifying individuals who are age-inappropriate in their impairment ratings. *T*-scores were not created due to the substantial skewing of these distributions and the fact that such conversions tend to try to normalize what is an abnormal distribution. This can result in percentiles based on *T*-scores for a given raw score that are not in fact the percentiles associated with that raw score in the sample. Instead, the actual percentiles are provided for the raw scores directly. The reliability information available on the scale is discussed in the next chapter.

CHAPTER 5

Reliability

This chapter presents information concerning the various forms of reliability for the BFIS-CA. Of course, additional research on these and other psychometric characteristics of the scale is welcome. What information is available indicates that the reliability of the scale is quite satisfactory for use of the scale in clinical, research, and school or other organizational settings in which the assessment of psychosocial impairment in children and teens is of interest.

Internal Consistency

The internal consistency of the BFIS-CA domain ratings (Cronbach's alpha) was found to be quite satisfactory (alpha = .970, $F = 33.28$, $p < .001$). This is to be expected given the relatively high factor loadings of each of the 15 domains onto the two initial factors found in the PCFA prior to rotation reported in Chapter 3. All of this suggests that higher impairment ratings in any one domain are also related to a strong tendency for higher ratings to be found in other domains. The internal consistency of the 9 domains forming the Home–School factor was .948 ($F = 19.24$, $p < .001$), and that for the 6 domains composing the Community–Leisure factor was .960 ($F = 25.30$, $p < .001$).

Test–Retest Reliability

Test–retest reliability reflects the temporal consistency of a measure. It was assessed by having a subset of the original sample complete the scale on a second occasion 3–5 weeks after initial completion. A total of 86 parents completed the scale a second time, with at least 5 children for each age level from 6–17 years. There were 45 boys and 41 girls in this sample. The breakdown for the sex of the parents was 36 males and 50 females. These parents were randomly chosen by Knowledge Networks within each child age group and sex and invited to return to the website to complete the scale for a second time. They were, of course, paid for their participation, just as were all participants on the first occasion of assessment. No parents refused to answer the questions for the 15 domains.

The Pearson product–moment correlations between the first and second administrations follow: interactions with mother, .81; interactions with father, .73; school performance, .82; interactions with siblings, .66; playing with other children, .75; community activities, .69; visiting others' homes, .56; playing with other children at school, .89; managing money, .63; self-care, .77; doing chores/tasks, .69; doing school homework, .74; following rules, .79; interactions with other adults, .82; and playing sports, .85 (all ps < .001). The test–retest reliability for the Home–School mean impairment score was .86; for the Community–Leisure mean impairment score, .83; and for the number of impaired domains score, .87 ($p < .001$). These results show high reliability across this time period for most domains and especially for the three summary scores, but with only moderate reliability for a few others, such as visiting others' homes, managing money, and interactions with siblings.

Test–retest stability of the BFIS-CA domain scores can also be examined by comparing the actual scores from the initial testing with those from the retesting. This was done using a paired-samples t-test. The results are shown in Table 5.1. Those findings indicate that the second administration did not yield results significantly different from the first administration on any specific domain scores or on the three summary scores. These results suggest that there is satisfactory stability of the BFIS-CA scores over this time period.

The eight additional secondary questions mentioned in the previous chapter that form the second section of the BFIS-CA were also examined for their test–retest reliability. For number of friends, the correlation between first and second assessment was .66 ($p < .001$); for number of community organizations, it was .67 ($p < .001$); for number of sports, .83 ($p < .001$); and for GPA on previous report card, .70 ($p < .001$). Comparisons of these three scores between the first and second assessment was done using paired-samples t-tests. The results indicated no significant change in the answers over this time period (friends: t = 0.88; organizations: t = 1.22; sports: t = 0.17; all p's = NS).

The remaining four questions were categorical and so were analyzed using chi-square. For the question of whether or not teachers had reported to parents that their children had a problem with behavior or school performance, results indicated that 85% of those who had said "yes" gave the same report on the retesting 3–5 weeks later, and 90% of those parents who had said "no" on the first assessment said so again on the retesting (kappa = 0.73, approximate T = 6.73, $p < .001$). Concerning the question about grade retention, 100% of the parents stating "yes" on the first assessment said the same on the second assessment, whereas 97.5% of those who said "no" the first time also gave that same answer the second time (kappa = 0.84, approximate T = 7.93, $p < .001$). On the question about suspension/expulsion from school, 89% of those who said "yes" on initial assessment said so again at the retest point, whereas 99% of those who had said "no" initially gave this same answer at retesting (kappa = 0.88, approximate $T = 8.12$, $p < .001$). In conclusion, there is moderate to high agreement from the initial survey to retesting on these secondary questions related to social, community, and school impairment.

The next chapter addresses the various types of evidence available for the validity of the BFIS-CA.

TABLE 5.1. Comparison of Initial and Retesting Sample Results on BFIS-CA Domain Ratings, Mean Impairment, and Percent Domains Impaired Scores (N = 86)

	Initial		Retesting				
Domain	Mean	SD	Mean	SD	Mean Diff.	*t*	*p*
1. Interactions with his/her mother	0.96	1.95	1.01	2.02	.05	0.37	NS
2. Interactions with his/her father	1.25	2.56	1.38	2.38	.13	0.67	NS
3. School performance	1.30	2.08	1.41	2.31	.11	0.74	NS
4. Interactions with brothers and sisters	1.11	1.91	1.31	2.27	.20	0.95	NS
5. Playing with other children in the neighborhood	1.23	1.99	1.35	2.12	.12	0.74	NS
6. Activities in the community (church, Scouts, clubs, etc.)	0.80	1.74	1.14	2.20	.34	1.82	NS
7. Visiting other people's homes	0.80	1.58	0.91	1.71	.11	0.65	NS
8. Playing with other children at school	0.95	1.88	0.96	1.79	.01	0.14	NS
9. Managing any money he/she may earn or be given as an allowance	1.14	2.02	0.88	1.61	–.26	1.42	NS
10. Caring for him/herself (dressing, bathing, and hygiene)	0.74	1.76	0.83	1.76	.09	0.66	NS
11. Getting chores or other assigned tasks completed at home	1.63	2.22	1.83	2.44	.20	0.96	NS
12. Doing school homework	1.59	2.37	1.95	2.82	.36	1.63	NS
13. Ability to follow rules	1.31	2.26	1.51	2.48	.20	1.14	NS
14. Interactions with other adults (visitors to the home, when visiting others, in community settings, etc.)	0.72	1.66	0.94	1.89	.22	1.75	NS
15. Playing sports	0.85	1.76	1.02	2.02	.17	1.28	NS
Home–School mean impairment	1.26	1.79	1.36	1.86	.10	0.96	NS
Community–Leisure mean impairment	0.94	1.61	1.14	1.81	.20	1.75	NS
Number of impaired domains	0.77	2.32	0.98	2.52	.22	1.57	NS

Note. Mean diff., differences in the initial and retesting means; *t*, results for the paired samples *t*-test; *p*, probability value for the *t*-test if ≤ .05; NS, not significant.

CHAPTER 6

Validity

In general, "validity" means the accuracy, correctness, or truth value of an assertion or conclusion (Bryant, 2000). Often it is judged against the empirical evidence available in support of or contradicting the statement, as well as any criticism of the logical basis for it. It answers the question of the degree to which any truth claim agrees with the evidence from reality. In scale development, the term means the extent to which the measure does what it claims to do; here it refers specifically to the degree to which the BFIS-CA evaluates psychosocial impairment.

Construct Validity

Face Validity

Establishing construct validity starts with a clear and explicit definition of the construct the scale is intended to assess (Bryant, 2000; Cook & Campbell, 1979). Without such a definition, it is not possible to evaluate a rating scale to determine whether its items are correctly sampling from and hence evaluating the conceptual domain of that construct. The construct measured by the BFIS-CA is "psychosocial impairment." "Impairment" has been defined earlier in this manual as the extent of difficulty a child or adolescent experiences in functioning effectively in a major domain of life activity relative to others of the same age (and often, sex). It is considered a dimensional construct in that children are believed to vary in their degrees of functional ineffectiveness in performing major life activities. This form of construct validity is usually called face validity; it refers to the degree to which the scale appears to sample the construct (its semantic content or meaning) it claims to assess. The BFIS-CA must be viewed as having high face validity because (1) the instructions direct the respondent to evaluate his/her child's performance in 15 major domains of psychosocial functioning and (2) the respondent is directed to rate the child as to his/her degree of difficulty functioning effectively in those domains, that is, the degree to which he/she experiences impairment. The instructions incorporate the very definition of the term "impairment" as it is used here and thus should have high face validity.

Factor Analysis

Some evidence for the construct validity of the BFIS-CA does come from the results of the factor analysis described in Chapter 3. There it was evident that the 15 domains on the BFIS-CA comprised one large factor in the initial PCFA before rotation, with one much smaller factor that reflected community and leisure activities. After rotation, the scale appears to assess two semidistinct yet interrelated dimensions of impairment: Home–School (mainly work-related) and Community–Leisure (mainly nonwork or low responsibility) domains. This makes sense given that the level of demands for effective functioning in work-related contexts as represented in the Home–School dimension may differ markedly from the demands made in play or leisure situations, or in far less demanding community activities, such as Scouts, sports, hobbies, and so forth. Yet the moderate correlation between the two dimensional scores ($r = .82$, $p < .001$) makes it evident that the degree to which children or adolescents may be having difficulties with functioning effectively in any particular domain is highly related to the degree of difficulties they may be having functioning in the other domains assessed on the BFIS-CA. The two dimensions of impairment, therefore, share over 67% of their variance. This makes it apparent that a general factor of impairment or functional ineffectiveness underlies all of these domains of major human life activities, much like the general factor, *g*, that has been found to exist across all specific intelligence scale subtests.

Relationship to Other Measures of Impairment

Evidence is not yet available on the relationship of the BFIS-CA scores to other ratings of impairment, such as those on the CBCL (Achenbach, 2001) or BASC-2 (Reynolds & Kamphaus, 2004). But, as indicated in Chapter 4, several additional secondary questions related to impairment were collected on the entire sample besides the 15 domain dimensional ratings. These dealt with number of friends, number of community activities, number of sports, and educational performance and school adjustment. Some of these same questions appear on the CBCL or BASC-2. Answers to these questions can serve as one means of validating the 15 specific primary domain ratings—particularly those dealing with the same domain, such as school, sports, and peer relationships—as well as the three summary scores.

Unpopularity

One means of examining the validity of impairment ratings in social functioning is to compare children in the entire sample ($N = 1{,}922$) who were unpopular (had one or no friends) to those who had a more typical number of friends (two or more) on the relevant social domains within the 15 primary domain ratings and on the three summary scores. As indicated in Chapter 4, very few children had just one or no friends. Just 5.6% of the sample fell into this unpopular category. The results are shown in Figure 6.1. Unpopular children had ratings more than three times higher in the domain of playing with other children in the neighborhood ($M = 3.26$, $SD = 2.99$) compared to children having two or more friends ($M = 0.92$, $SD = 1.81$; $F = 133.50$, $p < .001$). The same was true for playing with other children at school: unpopular children had far higher scores ($M = 3.18$, $SD = 2.99$) than children with at least two friends ($M = 0.87$, $SD = 1.76$; $F = 144.87$, $p < .001$). The unpopular children also had significantly higher scores on all three of the BFIS-CA summary scores, as shown in this figure (all p's $< .001$). Alternatively, children could be sorted into two groups: those who placed at or above the 93rd percentile (score of 6 or higher) on each of the domains concerning play and those who placed lower. The former group would be considered to be impaired in those domains. These two groups could then be compared on the number of friends they had, as reported by parents. When these comparisons were done on the sample, children impaired in playing with others in their neighborhoods had significantly fewer friends ($M = 5.2$; $SD = 10.7$, $N = 96$) than did those not rated as impaired ($M = 7.8$, $SD = 8.2$, $N = 1{,}809$; $F = 8.78$, $p = .003$). The same comparison was done for children rated as impaired in playing with other children at school (score of 6+) and those not so impaired in the

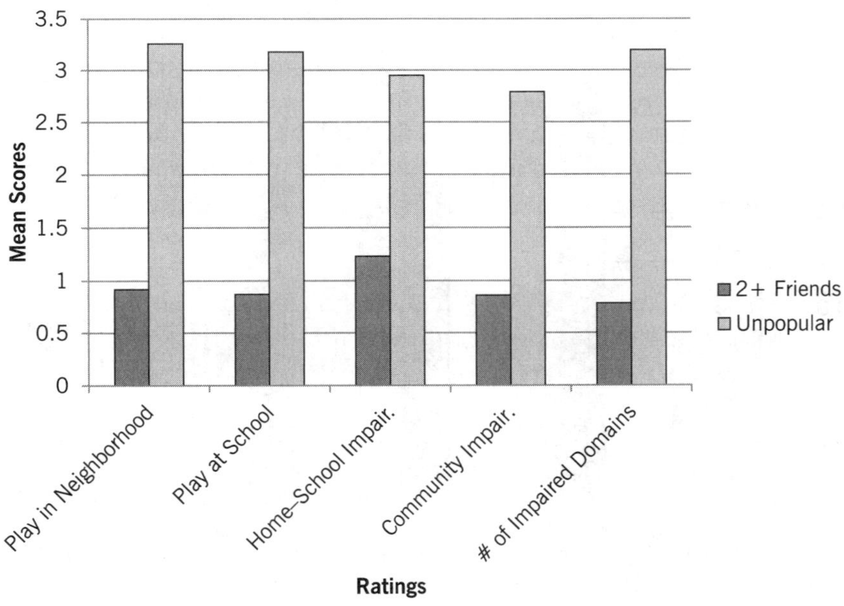

FIGURE 6.1. Comparison of children having two or more friends to those having one or none (Unpopular) on the specific domain scores of playing with children in the neighborhood and playing with children at school from the BFIS-CA, as well as the three summary scores of Home–School mean impairment, Community–Leisure mean impairment, and Number (#) of Impaired Domains scores. Impair., mean impairment score. All comparisons are significant (p's $< .001$).

number of friends reported by parents. Again, children rated as impaired in play at school had significantly fewer friends (M = 5.68, SD = 11.1, N = 98) than did those not placing in the impaired range (M = 7.8, SD = 8.2, N = 1,807; F = 5.84, p = .016).

Community Involvement

Seemingly, ratings of impairment in community activities might be expected to be related, albeit imperfectly, to the reports of number of organized community activities that children participated in during the previous year. To examine this issue, children from the entire sample were classified into two groups; those involved in two or more community activities and those involved in one or none during the preceding year. The former group composed 60% of the sample. The results are shown in Figure 6.2; all comparisons were significant at $p < .001$. Children less involved in community activities had significantly higher impairment ratings (M = 1.24, SD = 2.13) on the specific domain of activities in the community on the BFIS-CA than did children involved in two or more such activities (M = 0.71, SD = 1.59). The less involved children also had higher ratings on all three of the BFIS-CA summary scores, as shown in Figure 6.2. This suggests some evidence of validity for this specific domain rating on the scale, as well as for the three summary scores. As before, this relationship can be examined in the inverse direction by comparing children who placed at or above the 93rd percentile (score of 5+) in the specific rating of

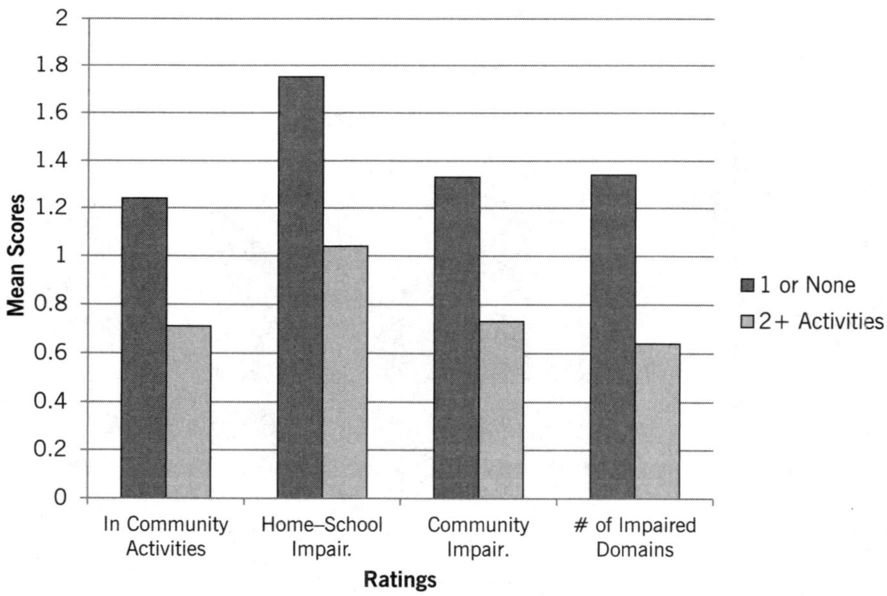

FIGURE 6.2. Comparison of children less involved in their community activities (1 or none) to those more involved (2+ activities) as reported by parents on the specific domain score of activities in the community from the BFIS-CA, as well as on the three summary scores of Home–School mean impairment, Community–Leisure mean impairment, and the Number (#) of Impaired Domains scores. Impair., mean impairment score. All comparisons are significant (p's < .001).

activities in the community on the number of community organizations in which they participated the previous year, as reported by parents. The results showed that impaired children (M = 1.8, SD = 2.1, N = 114) participated in significantly fewer community organizations than did those not rated as impaired in this domain (M = 2.4, SD = 2.3, N = 1,555; F = 6.96, p = .003).

Sports Participation

One of the domains being rated on the BFIS-CA is the degree to which a child may be impaired in playing sports. This domain can be partially validated with parent reports of the frequency of sports participation in the prior year. But in examining the relationship of that rating to actual organized sports participation as reported by parents, a problem arises in that 39% of the children were reported to have not been involved in any organized sports during the previous year. With this in mind, this relationship was examined by comparing children who were not involved in sports in the previous year with those who were involved on the specific domain rating of playing sports, as well as on the three BFIS-CA summary scores. The results are shown in Figure 6.3. All comparisons were significant ($p < .001$). Children not involved in sports (M = 1.36, SD = 2.22) had nearly double the magnitude of impairment ratings in this domain than children who were involved (M = 0.76, SD = 1.66; F = 35.06, $p < .001$). They were also significantly more impaired on the three BFIS-CA summary scores. Again, the inverse relationship can also serve as evidence of validity for this scale. Children placing in the impaired range (93rd percentile or

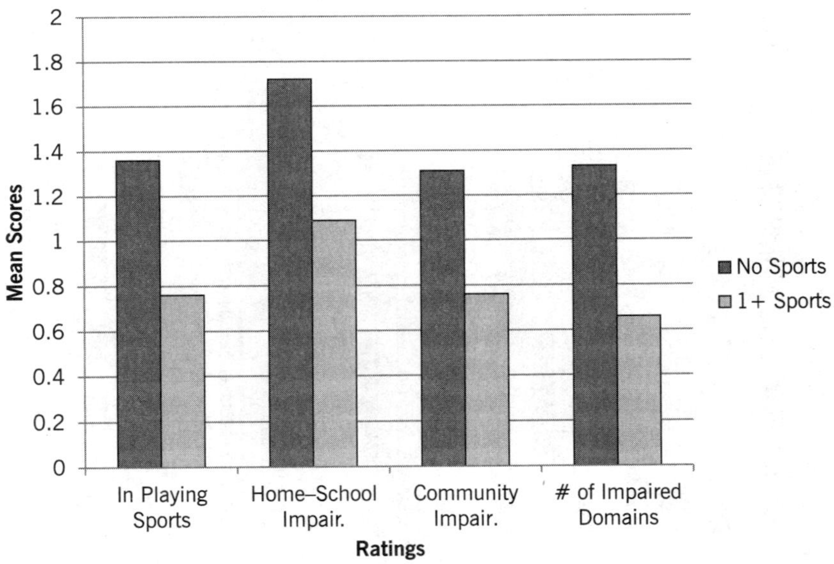

FIGURE 6.3. Comparison of children not involved in organized sports in prior year with those involved (1+ activities) on the specific domain score of playing sports from the BFIS-CA, as well as on the three summary scores of Home–School mean impairment, Community–Leisure mean impairment, and the Number (#) of Impaired Domains scores. Impair., mean impairment score. All comparisons are significant (p's < .001).

higher) in the specific domain rating of playing in sports (score of 5 or higher) can be compared with those not so impaired in parent-reports of organized sports participation in the previous year. When that is done, children impaired in this domain participated in significantly fewer sports ($M = 1.0$, $SD = 1.3$, $N = 114$) than children not placing in the impaired range ($M = 1.4$, $SD = 1.5$, $N = 1{,}481$; $F = 6.79$, $p = .009$). This provides evidence of validity for the specific domain rating concerning playing sports on the BFIS-CA.

School Performance and Adjustment

As noted in Chapter 4, parents were asked several questions about school (GPA, teacher-reported problems, retention in grade, suspensions/expulsions) besides being asked to rate their children specifically in the domains of school performance and school homework. The first analysis involved comparing children in the five different GPA classifications on their specific domain ratings of school performance, playing with other children at school, and homework performance, as well as the three summary scores from the BFIS-CA. These results are shown in Figure 6.4.

The findings clearly provide evidence for the validity of these specific domain ratings. In the specific ratings of impairment in school performance, children with differing GPAs differed significantly from each other ($F = 173.85$, $p < .001$). Pairwise comparisons on this domain rating in fact showed significant differences across all GPA levels with the pattern of significant differences being A < B < C < D < E/F. On the specific domain rating of playing with other children at school, again the children in the five GPA levels differed significantly from each other ($F = 39.11$,

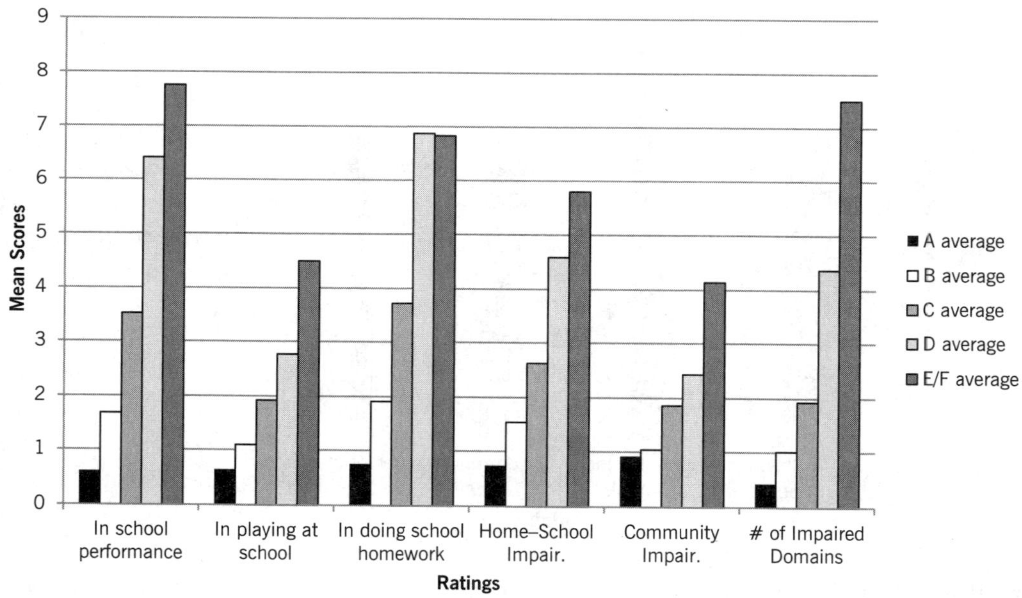

FIGURE 6.4. Comparison of children grouped based on GPA on previous year's report cards in specific domain ratings related to school and on the three summary scores from the BFIS-CA. Impair., mean impairment score. All comparisons are significant (p's < .001).

$p < .001$). This time, pairwise comparisons showed the following: A, B < C < D < E/F, such that the children in the highest two GPA categories (A and B) did not differ from each other but had lower impairment ratings than the other three GPA categories. The results for the specific domain rating of doing school homework also showed that these GPA categories differed significantly among themselves in this impairment rating ($F = 165.84$, $p < .001$). Pairwise comparisons in this instance showed the following differences: A < B < C < D, E/F, such that children in the lowest two GPA categories (D and E/F) did not differ from each other but were rated as more impaired than those in the other three categories.

Similar results were evident on the three BFIS-CA summary scores when comparing the five different GPA categories. For the Home–School mean impairment score, all five GPA categories differed among themselves ($F = 115.85$, $p < .001$), with pairwise contrasts showing that A < B < C < D < E/F. Differences in categories on the Community–Leisure mean impairment score were not quite as distinctive, but then this would be expected given that the domains contained in this score are not those related to school adjustment. Still, there were significant differences across the GPA categories ($F = 43.97$, $p < .001$). This time, pairwise comparisons showed that students with A and B averages scored lower than those with C and D averages, who scored lower than those with E or F averages. The A- and B-average students did not differ from each other. Neither did the C- and D-average students. On the number of impaired domains score, differences among the GPA categories were again significant ($F = 66.43$, $p < .001$). In this case, students with A averages had significantly fewer impaired domains than those with C averages, with neither of them differing from those with B averages, who fell between the A- and C-group ratings. But those with D and E/F averages not only differed from each other but also from the other GPA categories. The pattern was A < C < D < E/F.

The inverse relationships also demonstrated validity for the BFIS-CA specific domain scores concerning school performance and doing homework. Children who fell in the impaired range on the domain rating of school performance (93rd percentile and higher; scores of 7+) had lower GPAs ($M = 2.72$, $SD = 1.15$, $N = 119$) than did those not classified as impaired in this domain rating ($M = 1.54$, $SD = 0.71$, $N = 1,643$; $F = 279.65$, $p < .001$). [Note: GPA ratings ranged from 1 = A to 5 = E/F or failing.] The same held true for children placing in the impaired range (93rd percentile and higher) on the specific domain rating of doing school homework. Children rated as impaired (scores of 7+) had lower GPAs ($M = 2.65$, $SD = 1.13$, $N = 132$) than did those classified as not impaired ($M = 1.54$, $SD = 0.70$, $N = 1,633$; $F = 272.61$, $p < .001$).

Parents also reported whether or not they had received a report from their children's teachers during the prior school year about their children having a problem with behavior or with school performance. When children who had received such a report ($N = 488$) were compared with those who had not ($N = 1,338$), the groups differed significantly in the three specific BFIS-CA domain ratings of school performance, playing with children at school, and doing school homework, as well as in the three BFIS-CA summary scores (F's range 332.32–829.38; all p's < .001). The findings for all six measures are portrayed in Figure 6.5. The ratings are dramatically different between these two groups of children, lending further evidence to the validity of the BFIS-CA scores.

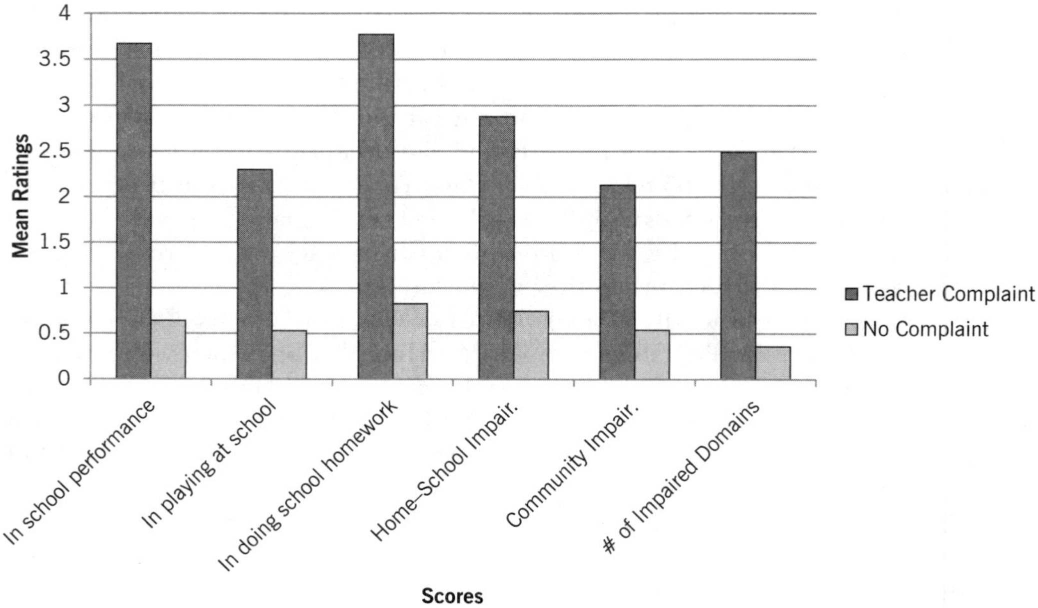

FIGURE 6.5. Comparison of children whose parents received teacher complaints of school behavior or school performance problems with those not receiving such teacher complaints on the three specific domain ratings related to school and on the three summary scores from the BFIS-CA. Impair., mean impairment score. All comparisons are significant (p's < .001).

Likewise, parents in the entire sample had stated whether or not their child had ever been retained in a grade. Those so retained ($N = 97$) were compared with those not retained ($N = 1{,}733$) on the same six scores from the BFIS-CA. All results were significant (F's range 25.86–72.31, all p's < .001). These results are graphically depicted in Figure 6.6. As with the results for teacher-reported school problems, these results also show marked differences in the BFIS-CA scores between those retained and not retained, providing further evidence of validity.

Parents in the entire sample also provided information on whether or not their children had ever been suspended or expelled from school. The children in each of these groups were compared on the three specific domain ratings related to school and on the three summary scores from the BFIS-CA. These comparisons are shown in Figure 6.7. All comparisons were significant (F's ranging from 128.32 to 196.63, all p's < .001). Children who had been suspended or expelled ($N = 124$) had significantly and substantially higher ratings on these six BFIS-CA scores than did those who had not been suspended or expelled ($N = 1{,}704$). To summarize, the BFIS-CA is clearly able to distinguish between children having various school performance and adjustment problems and those not having such problems, and thus it has some evidence of validity as an indicator of school-related impairment.

Once more, examining these relationships in the opposite direction can also give evidence of validity to the BFIS-CA scores. In this case, 81.3% of the children who scored in the impaired range (93rd percentile or higher; score of 7+) on the

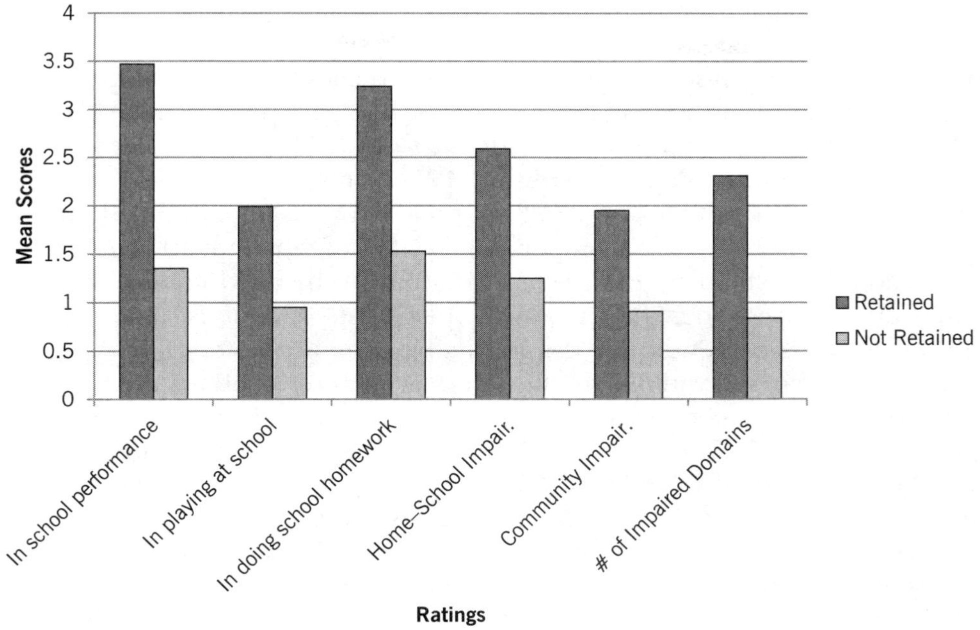

FIGURE 6.6. Comparison of children who had ever been retained in grade in school (held back a year) with those not retained on the three specific domain ratings related to school and on the three summary scores from the BFIS-CA. Impair., mean impairment score. All comparisons are significant (p's < .001).

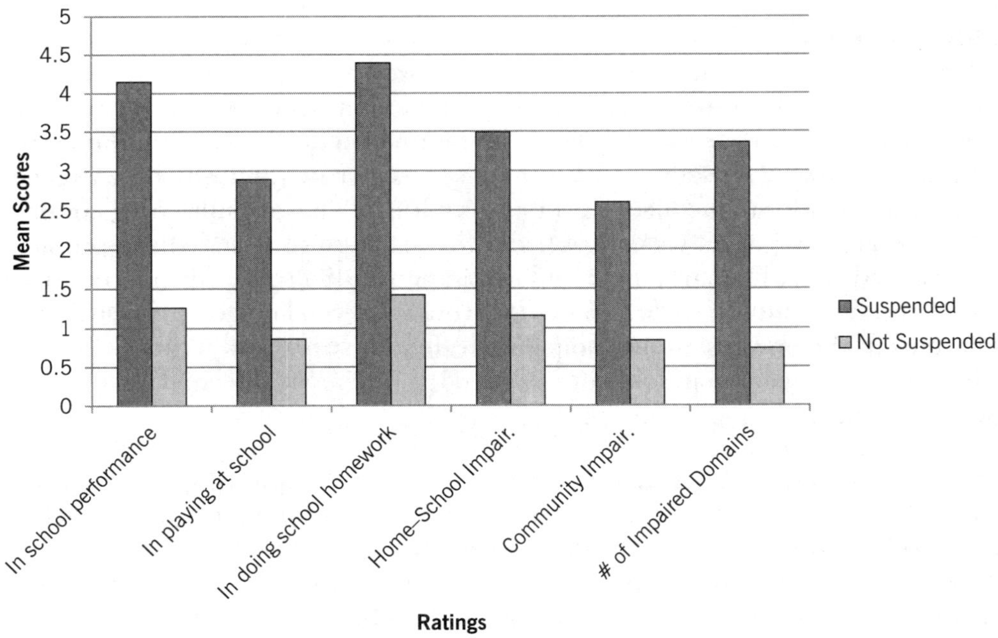

FIGURE 6.7. Comparison of children who had ever been suspended or expelled from school with those not suspended or expelled on the three specific domain ratings related to school and on the three summary scores from the BFIS-CA. Impair., mean impairment score. All comparisons are significant (p's < .001).

specific domain rating of school performance had received teacher complaints during the prior year concerning behavior at school or school performance compared with 22.3% of those not impaired ($\chi^2 = 206.31$, $p < .001$); 20.3% had been retained in a grade at least once compared with just 4% of the group not impaired in this domain ($\chi^2 = 64.00$, $p < .001$); and 28.9% of those rated as impaired had been suspended or expelled at least once compared with 5.2% of those not rated as impaired in their school performance ($\chi^2 = 104.91$, $p < .001$). Of the children who were rated as being impaired in doing their school homework (scores of 7+) and thus placing above the 93rd percentile for the normative sample, the rates of these same outcomes in comparison with those not so impaired were as follows: 81.3 vs. 22.3% had received a teacher complaint of school behavior or performance problems in the past year ($\chi^2 = 227.03$, $p < .001$); 15.1 vs. 4.5% had been retained in a grade ($\chi^2 = 28.30$, $p < .001$); and 30.2% vs. 4.9% had been suspended or expelled at least once in their school careers ($\chi^2 = 128.90$, $p < .001$). Thus being impaired on either school domain rating (performance or homework) is significantly associated with adverse outcomes in the school history of those children in comparison with those not placing in the impaired range on these BFIS-CA domain ratings. The results for the eighth secondary impairment question, dealing with receipt of special education services, are discussed in Chapter 8, along with the evidence related to other treatments that the children in the normative sample had received.

Criterion Validity

Validity can also be evaluated by the degree to which a measure is associated with or otherwise predicts an individual's status on a well-accepted measure (criterion) believed to be related in some way to that construct. As Bryant (2000) explained, if a measure is valid at assessing a construct-like impairment, then it should be shown to be related to past, present, and future measures or outcomes believed to have some association with that construct. The preceding evidence concerning construct validity in regard to parent-reports of friendships, community activities, sports participation, and school performance and adjustment can also be considered to support the criterion validity of the BFIS-CA scores. Additional evidence for such validity was available on other ratings collected on the entire sample.

Association with Ratings of Executive Functioning

Further evidence of BFIS-CA validity can be found in its relationship to measures of executive functioning (EF). EF often refers to self-regulation across time to achieve goals (Barkley, 2011a, 2012) and to those processes needed to sustain problem solving toward goals (Welsh & Pennington, 1988). It is likely to be involved in nearly all domains of major life activities; although it is more likely to be demanded in work-related than in leisure situations, as the former call for more self-restraint, time management, self-organization, problem solving, self-motivation, and emotional self-regulation than do the latter situations in most cases. Ratings were collected on the Barkley Deficits in Executive Functioning Scale—Children and Adolescents (BDEFS-CA; Barkley, 2012) for the entire sample studied here. The specific domain and summary scores from the BFIS-CA were correlated with the five scores from the BDEFS-CA, as well as with the Total EF Summary Score from that scale. The results are shown in Table 6.1. As is evident, all impairment ratings were significantly and moderately related to the EF scores. And, as hypothesized, correlations were higher for those domains related to work (Home–School mean impairment score) than to those related to leisure (Community–Leisure mean impairment score). As is evident in the relationships among the summary scores from both scales, impairment ratings share from 36 to 55% of their variance with the EF measures. Yet although there is substantial overlap in these measures of these distinct constructs, it is also clear that the measures each contain substantial unique variance that would indicate that impairment and EF are not the same construct. Children having greater deficits in EF are more likely to have higher impairment ratings than are children with fewer EF deficits, as one would expect knowing the nature of these constructs.

TABLE 6.1. Correlations of the BFIS-CA Domain and Summary Scores with Ratings from the BDEFS-CA

	BDEFS-CA subscale					
BFIS-CA subscale	TM	SO	SR	SM	SRE	EF
With mother	.47	.40	.54	.50	.53	.56
With father	.46	.41	.49	.48	.50	.53
School performance	.61	.58	.59	.67	.53	.67
With siblings	.49	.49	.59	.54	.60	.62
Playing in neighborhood	.42	.51	.53	.50	.55	.57
Community activities	.44	.51	.50	.49	.50	.55
Visiting others	.43	.51	.49	.47	.47	.53
Playing at school	.47	.54	.54	.52	.54	.59
Managing money	.50	.50	.56	.55	.49	.58
Self-care	.46	.48	.46	.51	.42	.53
Doing chores	.67	.53	.61	.71	.55	.69
School homework	.67	.56	.60	.72	.52	.69
Following rules	.61	.55	.67	.68	.61	.70
With other adults	.44	.52	.51	.50	.51	.56
Playing sports	.41	.49	.47	.49	.49	.53
Home–School mean impairment score	.65	.60	.68	.71	.63	.74
Community–Leisure mean impairment score	.48	.56	.56	.55	.56	.61
Number of impaired domains	.51	.50	.55	.56	.53	.60

Note. Analyses: Pearson product–moment correlations. All correlations are significant at $p < .001$. Sample sizes for correlations range from 1,607 to 1,824. TM, Self-Management to Time; SO, Self-Organization/Problem Solving; SR, Self-Restraint; SM, Self-Motivation; SRE, Self-Regulation of Emotion; EF, EF Summary Score.

For instance, children who placed in the impaired range on the BDEFS-CA (above the 93rd percentile for age and sex; *N*'s = 168–173) were compared with those not so impaired (*N*'s = 1,665–1,749) in the three BFIS-CA summary scores. The results are shown in Figure 6.8. All comparisons were significant (*p*'s < .001). It is abundantly evident that children deficient in EF are substantially impaired on the BFIS-CA.

Additional data on 22 children ages 6–17 years were collected by asking parents to complete both the BRIEF scale (Gioia, Isquith, Guy, & Kenworthy, 2000) and the BFIS-CA. This was a sample of convenience that included nondisordered children, those with learning disorders, and several with ADHD. The correlations between the BRIEF main factor scores and BFIS-CA three summary scores were:

	BRIEF scores		
BFIS-CA Summary Scores (*N* = 22)	Behavior Regulation	Metacognition	Total EF Score
Home–School mean impairment score	.70	.89	.89
Community–Leisure mean impairment score	.60	.78	.78

As with the BDEFS-CA results, these results indicate that ratings of impairment on the BFIS-CA are highly related to deficits in EF on this scale. The two constructs (EF and impairment) share between 36 and 79% of their variance. EF appears to play a substantial role in contributing to children's difficulties with functional effectiveness in a wide variety of domains of daily life activities, being somewhat more

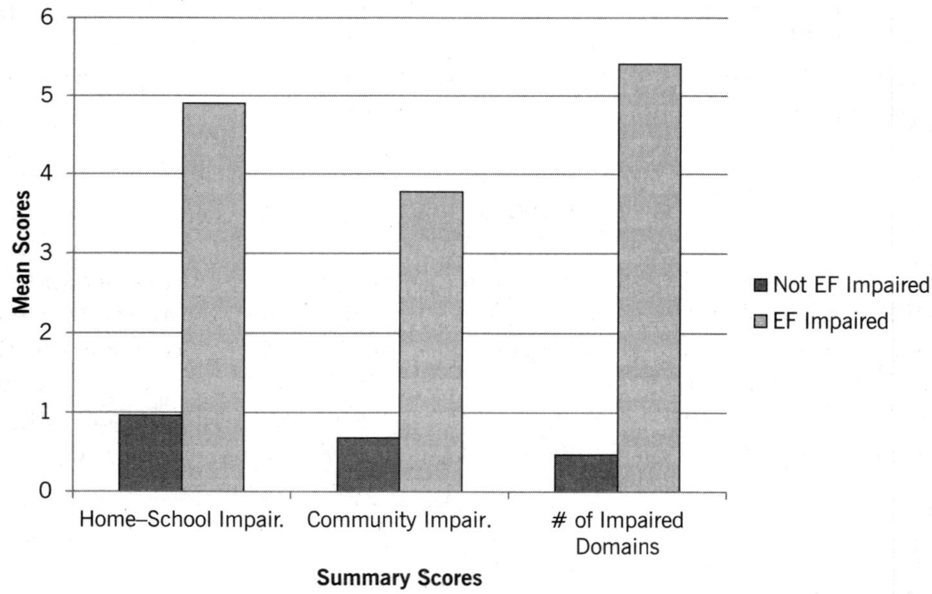

FIGURE 6.8. Comparison of children who were classified as impaired on the BDEFS-CA (at or above the 93rd percentile) on Total EF Summary Score with those not so impaired on the three summary scores from the BFIS-CA. Impair., mean impairment score. All comparisons are significant (*p*'s < .001).

highly related to work domains than to leisure ones, but clearly related to both dimensions of impairment.

Association with ADHD Symptom Ratings

One disorder known to produce rather pervasive difficulties in functioning across nearly all of the domains being examined on the BFIS-CA is ADHD (see Barkley, 2006). In the present project, ratings were collected on the 18 DSM-IV symptoms of ADHD using a 4-point Likert scale (0–3) as on the ADHD Rating Scale—IV (DuPaul, Power, Anastopoulos, & Reid, 1998) on the entire sample. Scores were computed separately for the nine inattention and nine hyperactive–impulsive symptom lists besides computing the total ADHD symptom score. These scores were found to be significantly correlated with the three summary scores from the BFIS-CA, as follows:

	ADHD ratings		
BFIS-CA Summary Scores (N = 1,833)	Inattention	Hyperactive–Impulsive	Total ADHD score
Home–School mean impairment score	.71	.63	.73
Community–Leisure mean impairment score	.56	.60	.63
Number of impaired domains	.58	.58	.63

It is obvious from this table that higher levels of ADHD are associated with higher levels of impairment to a substantial degree. The ratings of each construct share from 31 to 53% of their variance with each other. The highest relationships occur, as might be expected, between ADHD and the work-related impairment ratings summarized in the Home–School mean impairment score.

Conclusion

This chapter has reviewed some of the evidence concerning the construct and criterion validity of the BFIS-CA scores. What was provided clearly supports the validity of the scale scores and their utility in evaluations of children with regard to their degree of functional impairment in major life activities. In the next chapter, more evidence of validity is provided as derived from comparisons of children with various psychiatric, developmental, and learning disorders with those with disorders on the BFIS-CA scores.

CHAPTER 7

Relationship of BFIS-CA Scores to Disorders

As noted in the previous chapter, if a measure is valid at assessing a construct such as impairment, then it should be shown to be related to past, present, and future measures or outcomes believed to have some association with that construct (Bryant, 2000). This is especially so for psychiatric disorders in which functional impairment is a requirement for making the diagnosis, according to DSM-IV-TR (American Psychiatric Association, 2000). We had information for the entire normative sample about the percentages that had received professional diagnoses of various developmental, learning, psychiatric, and even a few neurological disorders as reported by patients. We also collected the percentage that had received various forms of psychiatric, psychological, and educational interventions. The BFIS-CA scores of groups receiving these various diagnoses or treatments were compared with scores of those who had not received them as further evidence for their validity.

Neurodevelopmental Disorders

Attention-Deficit/Hyperactivity Disorder

Another way of examining the relationship of ADHD to impairment ratings is to identify those children in the sample who might qualify for a research diagnosis of ADHD. They are the ones who place above the 93rd percentile on the ADHD rating scale and are rated as impaired in at least one domain on that scale (not using the BFIS-CA). Children so identified were compared with the rest of the sample on the BFIS-CA summary scores. All comparisons were significant (F's ranging from 722.32 to 1,093.91, all p's < .001). The results are shown in Figure 7.1. Here it can be seen that children empirically diagnosed as having ADHD (N = 125) have substantially higher impairment ratings than do those not so diagnosed (N = 1,797). As would be expected from the nature of ADHD, impairment ratings are greater in those domains related to work, which place greater demands on self-regulation than those domains related to community or leisure situations. Yet even the latter are more impaired in children with ADHD than in the control group.

Information was also collected from the parents on whether or not children had received various professional diagnoses, including ADHD or attention-deficit disorder (ADD). Children receiving such a diagnosis were compared with the rest of the sample on all of the BFIS-CA scores using one-way ANOVAs. Those results appear in Table 7.1. Children with ADHD/ADD received ratings of impairment in most domains that were three to four times higher than those found in children without ADHD, clearly supporting the view that ADHD is a highly and pervasively impairing disorder. Such results also support the validity of the BFIS-CA and its utility in the evaluation of such children. Given this fact, as well as findings that ADHD is often a comorbid condition with many other psychiatric, developmental, and learning disorders, those children having research (empirical) diagnosis of ADHD are removed from all of the comparisons that follow. This is done so as to get a clearer picture of the association of each disorder with impairment ratings on the BFIS-CA, controlling for any contribution that ADHD may have been making to those ratings.

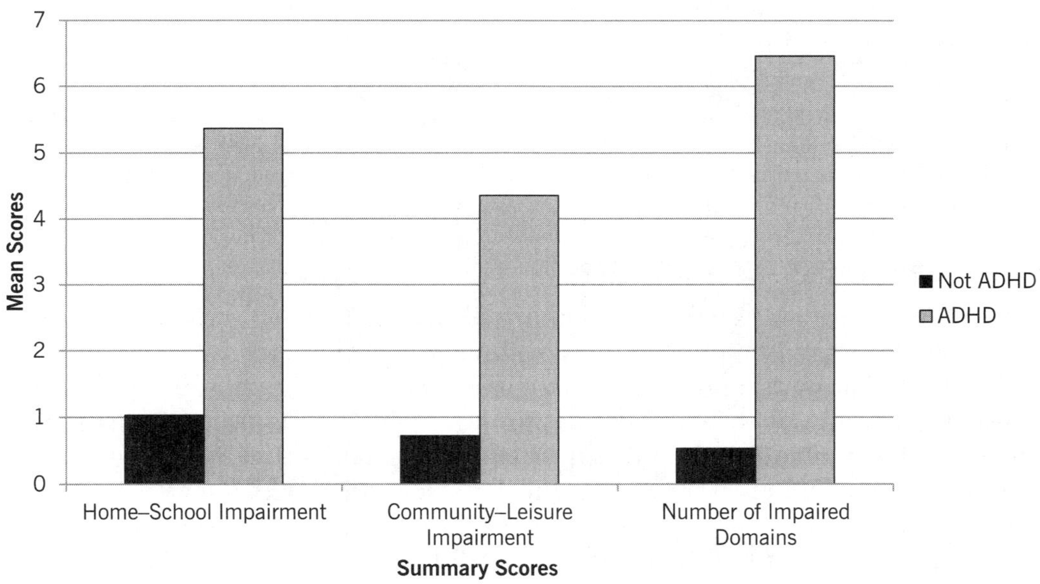

FIGURE 7.1. Comparison of children who were classified as having a research (empirical) diagnosis of ADHD (≥ 93rd percentile and one or more impairments) with those who did not on the three summary scores from the BFIS-CA. All comparisons are significant (p's < .001).

TABLE 7.1. BFIS-CA Scores for Children in the Entire Sample Having Parent-Reports of a Professional Diagnosis of ADHD/ADD and the Sample Remainder

	No ADHD/ADD (N = 1,749)		ADHD/ADD (N = 173)[a]			
Subscale	Mean	*SD*	Mean	*SD*	*F*	*p*
With mother	0.90	1.86	3.33	2.88	227.48	<.001
With father	1.02	1.95	3.16	2.85	153.73	<.001
School performance	1.10	2.04	4.92	2.80	503.17	<.001
With siblings	1.14	2.01	3.92	2.93	223.63	<.001
Playing in neighborhood	0.83	1.71	3.15	2.79	231.70	<.001
Community activities	0.67	1.54	3.07	2.70	288.07	<.001
Visiting others	0.66	1.48	2.82	2.55	273.32	<.001
Playing at school	0.76	1.62	3.35	2.90	311.57	<.001
Managing money	0.91	1.79	3.51	3.01	258.01	<.001
Self-care	0.69	1.57	2.83	2.94	226.69	<.001
Doing chores	1.37	2.02	4.78	2.95	394.67	<.001
School homework	1.25	2.04	5.18	2.92	520.99	<.001
Following rules	0.94	1.83	4.10	3.09	390.38	<.001
With other adults	0.68	1.58	2.75	2.62	227.97	<.001
Playing sports	0.80	1.70	2.67	2.68	127.74	<.001
Home–School mean impairment score	1.05	1.59	4.00	2.26	488.68	<.001
Community–Leisure mean impairment score	0.75	1.47	3.02	2.43	318.14	<.001
Number of impaired domains	0.60	1.92	4.09	4.18	391.29	<.001

Note. F, results for the *F*-test; *p*, probability value for the *F*-test if ≤ .05; NS, not significant.
[a]The *N*'s shown here are the maximum sample sizes, which can vary across these comparisons due to some parents reporting a specific domain as not being applicable to their children (or in rare cases due to parents refusing to rate this domain).

Speech and Language Disorders

Parents in the original sample indicated whether or not their children had been previously diagnosed by professionals as having a speech and language disorder (SLD). Using indirect reports from parents is not the most rigorous approach to identifying children with particular diagnoses, such as SLD, but until more rigorous research can be done, such diagnoses can still serve as a useful proxy for identifying children who are at least likely to have such disorders. Obviously, further research on children who are better screened and diagnosed directly by researchers would be the next logical step in such validation of the BFIS-CA, but for the time being, this proxy method can provide some initial indication of validity. This problem of the limits of parent-reported diagnoses of their children occurs for each of the diagnoses discussed in this chapter, so it is not discussed again under each diagnosis.

Children with both speech–sound disorders and specific language impairments may have significantly greater likelihood of having ADHD, ranging from 16 to 66%

(McGrath et al., 2008). This is especially true of the inattentive type of ADHD given a greater association of such SLD with DSM-IV inattentive symptoms (McGrath et al., 2008). Therefore, any group differences in impairment ratings between children with SLD and other children might be a result of this comorbidity with ADHD. To control for this possibility, the group comparisons were done between the SLD group (*N* = 72) and nonimpaired children (*N* = 1,725), this time removing any children who met the research criteria above for ADHD from both groups. The results are shown in Table 7.2.

Evident in these results is that SLD is nowhere near as impairing a disorder, either in severity or in pervasiveness, as is ADHD. Indeed, several domain ratings were not significantly different between the groups: interactions with mothers, interactions with fathers, interactions with siblings, managing money, and following rules. The remaining differences were quite small despite being statistically significant. The statistical significance of such comparisons, when small in magnitude,

TABLE 7.2. BFIS-CA Scores for Children in the Entire Sample Having Parent-Reports of a Professional Diagnosis of SLD and the Sample Remainder, with ADHD Cases Removed

	No SLD (or ADHD) (*N* = 1,725)		SLD (not ADHD) (*N* = 72)[a]			
Subscale	Mean	*SD*	Mean	*SD*	*F*	*p*
With mother	0.88	1.82	0.76	1.71	0.31	NS
With father	0.99	1.88	0.99	1.90	0.01	NS
School performance	1.08	1.97	2.00	2.65	14.36	< .001
With siblings	1.09	1.91	1.48	2.30	2.28	NS
Playing in neighborhood	0.77	1.58	1.31	2.33	6.86	.009
Community activities	0.66	1.48	1.09	2.00	5.11	.024
Visiting others	0.62	1.37	1.28	2.05	14.91	< .001
Playing at school	0.70	1.48	1.29	2.26	9.76	.002
Managing money	0.88	1.70	1.28	2.00	3.42	NS
Self-care	0.62	1.40	1.23	2.06	12.24	< .001
Doing chores	1.33	1.93	2.04	2.19	9.11	.003
School homework	1.25	2.01	2.04	2.39	10.37	.001
Following rules	0.89	1.72	1.13	1.67	1.34	NS
With other adults	0.61	1.42	1.11	2.02	8.22	.004
Playing sports	0.73	1.57	1.44	2.45	11.23	.001
Home–School mean impairment score	1.01	1.48	1.46	1.70	6.17	.013
Community–Leisure mean impairment score	0.70	1.33	1.29	2.04	12.89	< .001
Number of impaired domains	0.50	1.61	1.08	2.53	8.42	.004

Note. F, results for the *F*-test; *p*, probability value for the *F*-test if ≤ .05; NS, not significant.

[a]The *N*'s shown here are the maximum sample sizes, which can vary across these comparisons due to some parents reporting a specific domain as not being applicable to their children (or in rare cases due to parents refusing to rate this domain).

most likely has to do with the large sample sizes being used here. This small degree of impairment in association with SLD is also apparent in the score for number of impaired domains, on which children with SLD averaged ratings of impairment in just a single domain (≥ 93rd percentile) only slightly higher than the control group. The most impairing domains for children with SLD were in school performance and school homework, as might be expected from the nature of SLD and the need for normal language functioning in those domains.

This dataset also offers the opportunity to study parent ratings of impairment in children with SLD who do and do not have comorbid ADHD. Thus we can see whether any unique patterns are associated with one disorder relative to the other, as well as the relative magnitude of impairment associated with each disorder alone and their comorbidity. In the next comparison, children with only SLD ($N = 72$) were compared with children having only ADHD (by the research criteria noted earlier; $N = 101$) and with those having both disorders (SLD + ADHD; $N = 24$). All three groups were compared with the remainder of the sample ($N = 1,725$). These comparisons were done for the three BFIS-CA summary scores. The results appear in Figure 7.2. The omnibus ANOVAs were all significant (all p's $< .001$). Pairwise comparisons indicated that children with SLD + ADHD scored significantly worse than all other groups on all three BFIS-CA summary scores. Pairwise comparisons, however, indicated that for the Home–School mean impairment score, the SLD-only and control groups did not differ. But both groups differed from the two

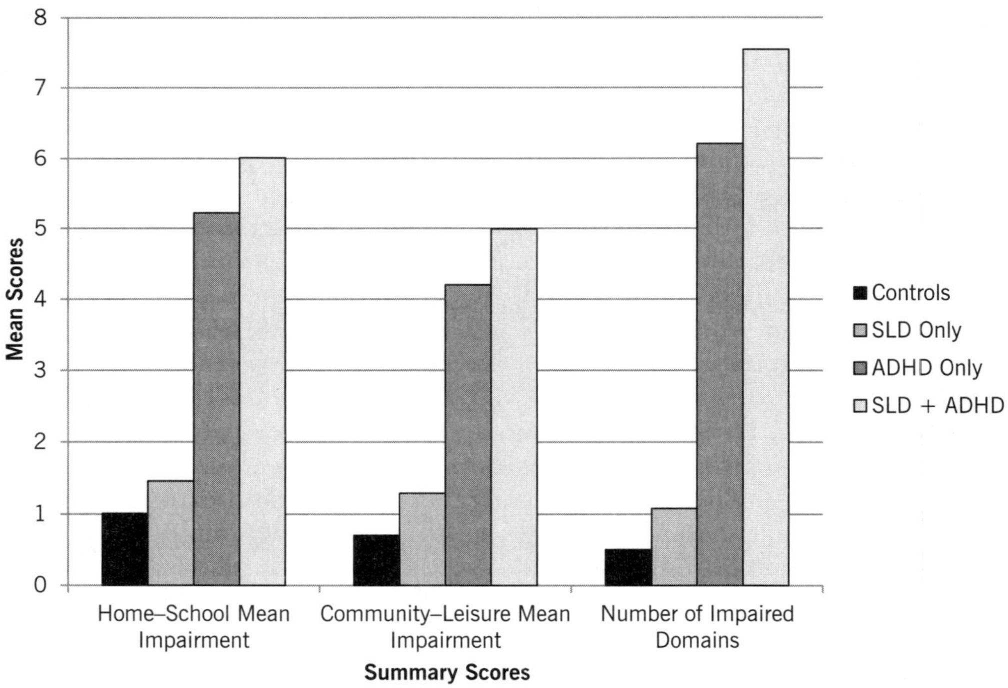

FIGURE 7.2. Comparison of children with SLD only, ADHD only, and SLD + ADHD with control children on the three summary scores from the BFIS-CA. See text for details concerning pairwise comparisons. ADHD diagnosed by research criteria (see text).

ADHD groups, with the pattern of significant comparisons being: SLD + ADHD > ADHD only > SLD only, controls. For the Community–Leisure score, the pattern was as follows: SLD + ADHD > ADHD only > SLD only > controls. Here, the two disorders appear to have unique impairments that are additive, whereas in the earlier comparison ADHD seemed chiefly to drive impairment, though the combination of the disorders makes matters significantly worse. This was also true for the score on number of impaired domains, on which the pattern was similar to that for the Home–School score: SLD + ADHD > ADHD only > SLD only, controls, with the latter two groups not differing from each other.

This is precisely the sort of evidence that provides substantial support for the criterion validity of the BFIS-CA. It is relatively easy to show differences between groups of children with disorders and typical samples on such a measure given that many disorders can lead to higher impairment ratings. It is a more difficult test of a measure to show that it can detect relatively unique patterns of associated impairment when comparisons are made among different disorders. The BFIS-CA can do so.

Delayed Motor Development or Coordination

Children with delayed motor development and coordination, also known as developmental coordination disorder (DCD), might be expected to be impaired in certain domains of daily life activities in childhood, such as sports participation, that unusually tax such abilities. Children with professional diagnoses of DCD or delayed motor development more generally ($N = 59$) were initially compared with those without such a diagnosis ($N = 1,859$) on all BFIS-CA scores. All comparisons were significant (all p's $< .001$).

However, comparisons of children with and without DCD are complicated by the high comorbidity of DCD with ADHD, which can range from 13 to 50% or more of such cases (Barkley, 2006; Kaplan, Crawford, Cantell, Kooistra, & Dewey, 2006; Piek, Dyck, Francis, & Conwell, 2007). The presence of ADHD in such comparisons can make DCD appear to be a far more impairing disorder than it might otherwise be if not for the comorbidity with ADHD. To address that problem, once again children with ADHD were removed from the groups both with and without DCD so that comparisons could be made between these two groups without being confounded with cases of ADHD that are likely to have substantial impairment in all domains tapped by the BFIS-CA. All comparisons remained significant (all p's $< .003$) and are shown in Table 7.3. As this table shows, a few domains were not significantly different in these comparisons: interactions with mother and interactions with father. However, on all other comparisons, children with DCD were significantly more impaired than children in the control group. Yet those differences were of a very small magnitude and, again, likely resulted from the use of large samples here, especially for the control group. The average ratings for the children with DCD were about twice the levels of those of the control children but still quite low on the 0–9 rating system. The greatest impairment ratings occurred in domains one might expect to be associated with this sort of disorder—sports, school and homework performance, and, to a lesser extent, playing with other children. And even then the number of impaired domains averaged just over one for the DCD group, which

TABLE 7.3. BFIS-CA Scores for Children in the Entire Sample Having Parent-Reports of a Professional Diagnosis of DCD and the Sample Remainder, with ADHD Cases Removed

	No DCD (or ADHD) (N = 1,757)		DCD (no ADHD) (N = 40)[a]			
Subscale	Mean	*SD*	Mean	*SD*	*F*	*p*
With mother	0.88	1.82	0.63	1.19	0.66	NS
With father	0.98	1.88	1.35	2.01	1.29	NS
School performance	1.08	1.97	2.89	3.03	28.97	< .001
With siblings	1.09	1.90	2.20	2.56	9.90	.002
Playing in neighborhood	0.76	1.59	2.06	2.59	21.40	< .001
Community activities	0.66	1.49	1.52	1.96	9.75	.002
Visiting others	0.63	1.40	1.42	1.87	10.87	.001
Playing at school	0.70	1.49	2.00	2.46	23.62	< .001
Managing money	0.87	1.66	2.21	3.05	20.25	< .001
Self-care	0.62	1.39	1.86	2.62	25.89	< .001
Doing chores	1.34	1.94	2.34	2.18	9.12	.003
School homework	1.24	2.00	3.03	2.90	26.09	< .001
Following rules	0.88	1.71	1.53	2.12	4.98	.026
With other adults	0.62	1.45	1.19	1.77	5.57	.018
Playing sports	0.73	1.58	2.31	2.72	30.43	< .001
Home–School mean impairment score	1.01	1.48	2.03	1.76	16.63	< .001
Community–Leisure mean impairment score	0.70	1.35	1.76	1.99	21.41	< .001
Number of impaired domains	0.51	1.64	1.35	2.22	10.63	.002

Note. F, results for the *F*-test; *p*, probability value for the *F*-test if ≤ .05; NS, not significant.
[a]The *N*'s shown here are the maximum sample sizes, which can vary across these comparisons due to some parents reporting a specific domain as not being applicable to their children (or in rare cases due to parents refusing to rate this domain).

is quite low when contrasted against the more than six impaired domains seen in the children with a research diagnosis of ADHD (and more than four for those with a history of a professional diagnosis of ADHD/ADD).

Again, of greater interest and importance to scale validity is the presence of any distinct patterns between different disorders that may sometimes be comorbid. To examine this possibility, children with DCD only ($N = 40$) were compared with those with ADHD only ($N = 102$) and with those with both disorders (DCD + ADHD; $N = 23$) on the three BFIS-CA summary scores. All were compared with the remaining control children. The results are shown in Figure 7.3. The omnibus ANOVAs were all significant (all p's < .001). The pairwise contrasts were quite interesting, showing that the DCD + ADHD and ADHD-only groups were significantly more impaired in the Home–School mean impairment score than the other two groups but did not differ from each other. Yet the DCD-only group was also more impaired than the

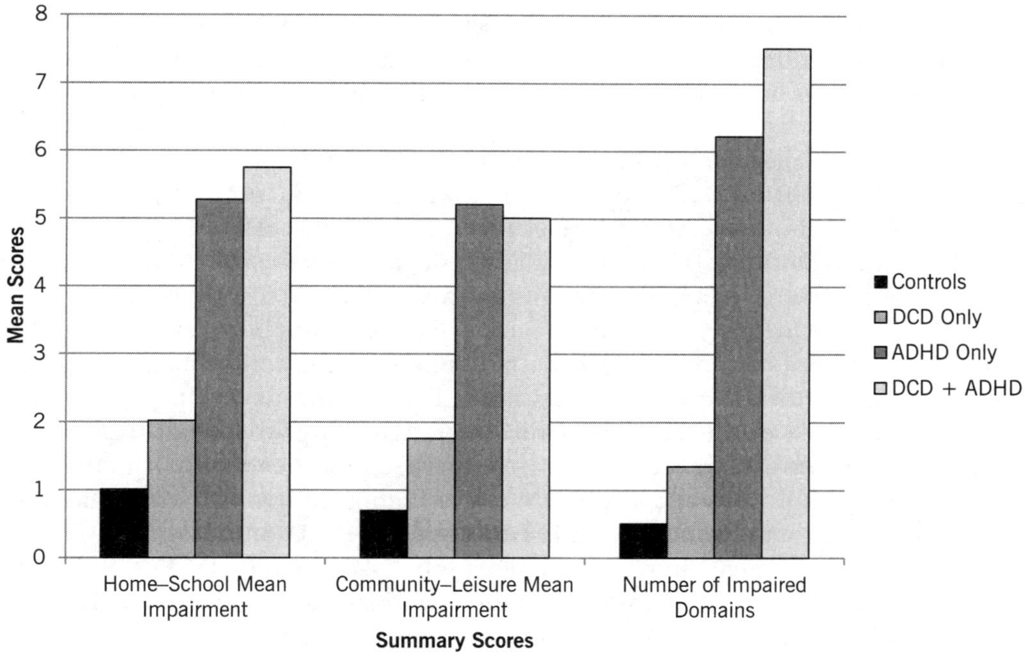

FIGURE 7.3. Comparison of children with DCD only, ADHD only, and DCD + ADHD with control children on the three summary scores from the BFIS-CA. See text for details concerning pairwise comparisons. ADHD diagnosed by research criteria (see text).

control group. The pattern was therefore: DCD + ADHD, ADHD only > DCD only > controls. For the Community–Leisure mean impairment score, all groups differentiated themselves from each other, with a pattern of DCD + ADHD > ADHD only > DCD only > controls. Such a pattern suggests that each disorder may have some unique effects on this domain of impairment that become additive when the disorders coexist. This was the same pattern found for the number of impaired domains score. Notice, however, that despite such distinctiveness among all groups, the two ADHD groups are markedly more impaired than the two groups without ADHD in the absolute magnitude of their scores. The BFIS-CA scores therefore differentiate not only the presence of disorders from their absence but also disorders from each other; this is yet more evidence for the validity of these scores.

Further evidence for the validity of the BFIS-CA in detecting differential patterns of impairments in daily life would come from comparing children with DCD only to those with SLD and those having both disorders. Each may arise from different neurodevelopmental mechanisms in the brain. One could anticipate that these disorders would have different patterns of impact on domains of daily life for children, even though they should be far less severe than those deficits associated with ADHD. In fact, given the overlap of both disorders with ADHD, its presence would contaminate or confound the results of such comparisons, especially if ADHD were more differentially associated with one disorder than the other. Consequently, ADHD cases were removed from the following comparisons. Doing so, however, results in small samples for the disordered groups and thus reduces the power to detect differences in these comparisons—a limitation that should be kept in mind for all subsequent comparisons of disorders discussed throughout the rest of this chapter.

There were 61 children in the sample who had been diagnosed as having SLD only (not ADHD or DCD), 29 who had been diagnosed with DCD only (not ADHD or SLD), and 11 who had comorbid DCD + SLD (but not ADHD). The omnibus ANOVAs comparing these groups were all significant (all *p*'s $< .001$). The results are shown in Figure 7.4 and clearly show a milder impact of these disorders than was the case for ADHD. Yet a differential pattern can still be detected between the disorders through the pairwise contrasts. In all comparisons, only the comorbid group differs from either the control group or those with SLD only, who never differ from each other on these three summary scores. And the DCD-only group never differs from the latter two groups. In the case of the Home–School mean impairment score, the DCD-only group does not differ from the comorbid group, falling between it and the other groups. The pattern is DCD + SLD > SLD only, controls. For the Community–Leisure mean impairment score, the pattern was: DCD + SLD > all other groups. The same is true for the number of impaired domains score. In short, no disorder alone is associated with significantly more impairment ratings than the

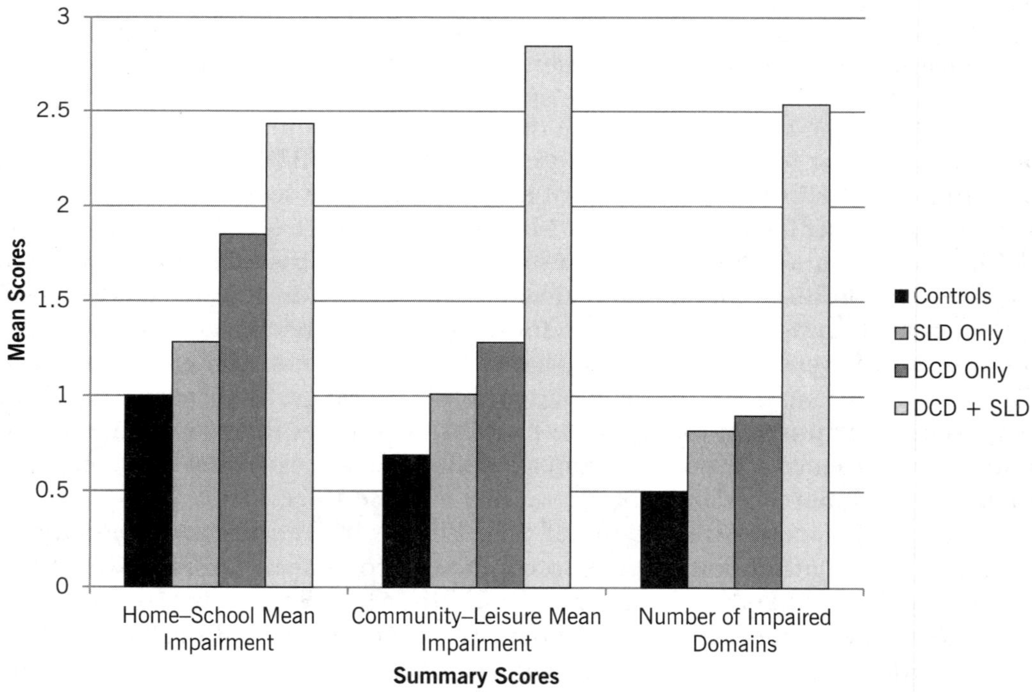

FIGURE 7.4. Comparison of children with DCD only, SLD only, and DCD + SLD with control children on the three summary scores from the BFIS-CA with all ADHD cases removed. See text for details concerning pairwise comparisons. ADHD diagnosed by research criteria (see text).

controls, but the comorbid DCD + SLD group does become more impaired, even if far less so than was seen in conjunction with ADHD.

Developmental Delay/Mental Retardation

Parents of 22 children in the original sample reported that the children had been diagnosed by a professional as having developmental delay/mental retardation (DD/MR). Impairments would be expected in various domains sampled by the BFIS-CA, such as in school performance and doing school homework, in individuals having such a generalized delay in development. To explore this possibility, the 22 children carrying a professional diagnosis of DD/MR according to parent-report were compared with the remainder of the sample (1,900). All comparisons were significant (all p's $< .001$). But 13 of these children also met the research criteria for ADHD, which is not an uncommon rate of comorbid ADHD within samples of children with DD/MR. Again, any differences in the impairment ratings here could be driven entirely by this comorbid ADHD. With these cases removed, some of the initial differences are no longer significant. This is the case for the domains of interactions with mothers, interactions with fathers, and following rules. But other differences stayed significant between those with DD/MR (without ADHD; $N = 9$) and the controls ($N = 1{,}788$; all p's $\leq .05$). These differences were significant despite the very low power of the comparison due to the very small DD/MR sample. These results are shown in Table 7.4. Where comparisons were significant, the average impairment ratings for the DD/MD-only group were two to four times larger than those ratings found in the control group, suggesting that this disorder may be more impairing than the more specific delays of SLD or DCD, yet nowhere near as impairing as ADHD. Mean impairment ratings were typically higher for Community–Leisure domains than for Home–School domains, with the exception of school performance specifically. Such a pattern suggests that children with DD/MD are somewhat more impaired in functioning outside the home than in functioning in it and especially when under parental supervision. On average, children with DD/MR were impaired in at least two domains on the number of impaired domains score relative to the 0.5 score for the controls, yet well below the scores of 4 to 6+ associated with ADHD.

As has been done for the other disorders discussed, additional comparisons were made with the children with DD/MR only, those with ADHD only, and those with both disorders (DD/MR + ADHD), as well as against the control group, on the three BFIS-CA summary scores. All omnibus ANOVAs were significant at $p < .001$. These results are graphically illustrated in Figure 7.5. In all comparisons, the ADHD-only and DD/MR + ADHD groups are the most severely impaired and do not differ from each other, though both differ from the DD/MR-only and control groups. Yet the DD/MR-only group is more impaired than the controls, even if considerably less so than the two ADHD groups. This makes it plain that DD/MR is a more impairing disorder than SLD or DCD but is far less so than is ADHD. There is no evidence here of additivity when the two disorders coexist, although the small sample sizes may have precluded adequate power to detect small to moderate effect size differences between those two ADHD groups.

TABLE 7.4. BFIS-CA Scores for Children in the Entire Sample Having Parent-Reports of a Professional Diagnosis of DD/MR and the Sample Remainder, with ADHD Cases Removed

	No DD/MR (or ADHD) (N = 1,788)		DD/MR (no ADHD) (N = 9)[a]			
Subscale	Mean	*SD*	Mean	*SD*	*F*	*p*
With mother	0.88	1.82	0.44	0.53	0.51	NS
With father	0.99	1.88	1.22	1.20	0.14	NS
School performance	1.10	2.00	3.78	2.68	15.95	< .001
With siblings	1.10	1.92	2.71	2.29	4.91	.027
Playing in neighborhood	0.78	1.60	3.75	3.06	27.09	< .001
Community activities	0.67	1.49	3.29	3.25	21.25	< .001
Visiting others	0.64	1.40	3.00	2.50	25.37	< .001
Playing at school	0.71	1.51	3.44	2.45	29.05	<.001
Managing money	0.88	1.70	2.88	3.31	10.84	<.001
Self-care	0.64	1.44	1.63	1.41	3.76	.053
Doing chores	1.35	1.94	3.38	2.72	8.62	.003
School homework	1.27	2.02	3.50	3.29	9.64	.002
Following rules	0.89	1.72	1.67	1.58	1.82	NS
With other adults	0.62	1.44	2.78	2.49	19.96	< .001
Playing sports	0.75	1.61	4.00	3.39	20.22	< .001
Home–School mean impairment score	1.02	1.49	2.29	1.50	6.47	.011
Community–Leisure mean impairment score	0.70	1.35	3.29	2.30	32.27	< .001
Number of impaired domains	0.52	1.65	2.22	2.72	9.44	.002

Note. F, results for the *F*-test; *p*, probability value for the *F*-test if $\leq .05$; NS, not significant.
[a]The *N*'s shown here are the maximum sample sizes, which can vary across these comparisons due to some parents reporting a specific domain as not being applicable to their children (or in rare cases due to parents refusing to rate this domain).

Seizure Disorders or Epilepsy

In the original sample, parents of 14 children reported that their children had seizure disorders or epilepsy by professional diagnosis. Those 14 children with diagnoses of seizure disorders were compared with the remainder of the sample (N = 1,908) on all BFIS-CA scores, and all were significant (all p's $< .05$) except for interactions with mother. Again, ADHD can coexist with seizure disorders in about 20% of all cases (Kaufmann, Goldberg-Stern, & Shuper, 2009), with each having at least a 2.5 times greater likelihood of occurring with the other disorder over base rates in the population (Hesdorffer et al., 2004). Just two of the children in the seizure-disorder group had a diagnosis of ADHD, and so they were removed from this group, along with those having ADHD in the control group. The groups were compared again, and the results are shown in Table 7.5. The results indicate that impairments are not significantly higher for children with seizure disorder on all scores; there are

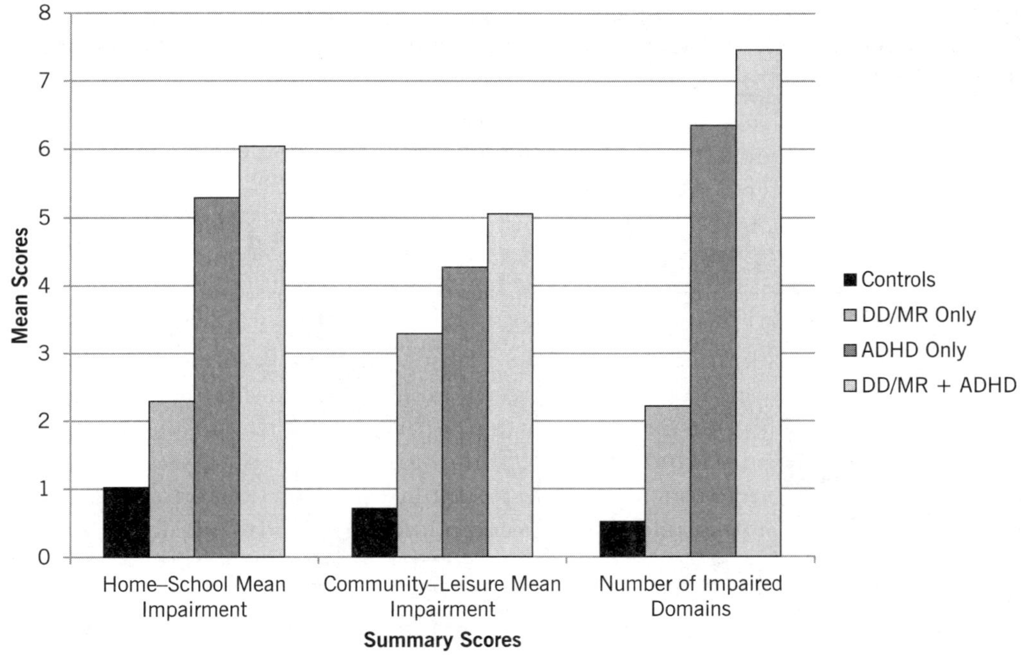

FIGURE 7.5. Comparison of children with DD/MR only, ADHD only, and DD/MR + ADHD with control children on the three summary scores from the BFIS-CA. See text for details concerning pairwise comparisons. ADHD diagnosed by research criteria (see text).

some exceptions. No group differences were evident in the domains of interactions with mother, interactions with siblings, following rules, and interactions with other adults. And the difference for the domain of managing money was only marginally significant ($p = .052$). Bear in mind that the samples here are small, and so the power to detect small or moderate effect sizes is quite limited. But what findings do emerge from such comparisons as being significant can be considered reasonably robust. The findings suggest that impairment in school performance and doing school homework are most problematic for children with seizure disorders, perhaps because of the learning and memory disorders often associated with seizure disorders. Although other differences in most other domains are significant, the levels are far below those degrees of impairment associated with ADHD and seem similar to those of children with DD/MR. They appear to be higher, however, than what was seen in children with SLD or DCD. Because of the small sample of children with seizure disorders, however, it was not possible to study these comparisons directly.

Tic Disorders or Tourette Syndrome

Studies suggest that simple or transient tics are a common occurrence in children, being found in 7–21% of general population samples of children (Khalifa & Knorring, 2007; Kurlan et al., 2002). Nearly 7% of children have experienced some form of tic in the preceding year (Khalifa & Knorring, 2007). Most such simple tics tend to remit within 4 years of onset (Leckman, 2004; Spencer et al., 1999). Such occur-

TABLE 7.5. BFIS-CA Scores for Children in the Entire Sample Having Parent-Reports of a Professional Diagnosis of Seizure Disorders or Epilepsy and the Sample Remainder, with ADHD Cases Removed

	No seizure disorders/ epilepsy (or ADHD) (*N*= 1,788)		Seizure disorders/ epilepsy (no ADHD) (*N*= 10)[a]			
Subscale	Mean	*SD*	Mean	*SD*	*F*	*p*
With mother	0.87	1.81	0.90	1.37	0.01	NS
With father	0.98	1.87	2.40	2.80	5.66	.017
School performance	1.10	1.99	4.00	3.65	20.89	< .001
With siblings	1.10	1.92	2.25	2.31	2.83	NS
Playing in neighborhood	0.78	1.61	2.40	2.87	9.92	.002
Community activities	0.67	1.50	2.50	2.51	11.76	.001
Visiting others	0.64	1.41	1.90	2.08	7.89	.005
Playing at school	0.72	1.53	1.78	1.79	4.27	.039
Managing money	0.89	1.70	2.00	2.78	3.79	.052
Self-care	0.63	1.42	2.10	3.21	10.40	.001
Doing chores	1.35	1.94	3.20	2.66	9.00	.003
School homework	1.26	2.01	4.10	3.66	19.57	< .001
Following rules	0.89	1.71	1.80	2.04	2.79	NS
With other adults	0.63	1.45	1.10	1.59	1.05	NS
Playing sports	0.75	1.62	2.11	1.96	6.28	.012
Home–School mean impairment score	1.02	1.49	2.56	1.83	10.64	.001
Community–Leisure mean impairment score	0.71	1.37	1.88	1.55	7.24	.007
Number of impaired domains	0.52	1.66	1.58	2.11	4.88	.027

Note. F, results for the *F*-test; *p* = probability value for the *F*-test if ≤ .05; NS, not significant.
[a]The *N*'s shown here are the maximum sample sizes, which can vary across these comparisons due to some parents reporting a specific domain as not being applicable to their children (or in rare cases due to parents refusing to rate this domain).

rences rarely result in a professional diagnosis of a disorder. Far less common are children with multiple tics that often do lead to a diagnosis of a chronic or multiple tic disorder (TD) or Tourette syndrome (TS). TS occurs in approximately 0.1–6 individuals per 1,000 population, or 0.01–0.60% (Khalifa & Knorring, 2007; Singer & Walkup, 1991). In the present sample, parents reported a professional diagnosis of TD/TS in 11 children, or 0.5% of our sample, consistent with that found in other studies using more rigorous ascertainment of the disorder.

The children in the present sample having TD/TS were compared with those without tics on all scores from the BFIS-CA. Most of the differences were significant (all *p*'s < .05) except for the specific domains of interactions with mother, interactions with father, interactions with siblings, and managing money. But there is a considerably higher incidence of ADHD (and obsessive–compulsive disorder) in children with TD/TS (typically 30–50% or more) (Banaschewski, Neale, Rothenberger, & Roessner, 2007; Kurlan et al., 2002; Leckman, 2004) than the base rates for either disorder would predict. Again, the coexistence of ADHD with TD or TS could be the basis for these differences in impairment ratings. TD/TS are also overrepresented in ADHD, being present in up to 20%, perhaps more, of those cases (Banaschewski et al., 2007; Barkley, 2006; Spencer et al., 1999). In this sample, 3 of the 11 children who had been professionally diagnosed with TD/TS also met criteria for a diagnosis of ADHD (27%). They were therefore removed from the sample, and the scores were reanalyzed. Those results are shown in Table 7.6.

All of the scores became nonsignificant except for the domain of playing sports. Again, the small sample size substantially limited the power to detect effects for these TD/TS cases. Even so, the absolute levels of rated impairment for this group are also very small relative to both the controls and the other disorders, such as ADHD or DD/MR. And the three summary scores show that children with TD/

TABLE 7.6. BFIS-CA Scores for Children in the Entire Sample Having Parent-Reports of a Professional Diagnosis of TD/TS and the Sample Remainder, with ADHD Cases Removed

	No TD/TS (or ADHD) (*N* = 1,789)		TD/TS (no ADHD) (*N* = 8)[a]			
Subscale	Mean	*SD*	Mean	*SD*	*F*	*p*
With mother	0.88	1.81	0.86	1.21	0.01	NS
With father	0.99	1.88	1.13	1.26	0.04	NS
School performance	1.12	2.01	1.38	2.13	0.13	NS
With siblings	1.11	1.93	1.75	1.28	0.89	NS
Playing in neighborhood	0.79	1.63	1.25	1.03	0.64	NS
Community activities	0.68	1.51	1.50	1.31	2.37	NS
Visiting others	0.65	1.41	1.38	1.19	2.11	NS
Playing at school	0.72	1.53	1.75	1.28	3.59	NS
Managing money	0.89	1.71	1.38	1.77	0.64	NS
Self-care	0.64	1.44	1.25	1.83	1.44	NS
Doing chores	1.35	1.95	2.50	1.77	2.75	NS
School homework	1.27	2.03	2.50	1.60	2.90	NS
Following rules	0.89	1.72	1.63	1.85	1.45	NS
With other adults	0.63	1.46	1.00	1.19	0.52	NS
Playing sports	0.75	1.61	2.71	2.36	10.24	.001
Home–School mean impairment score	1.03	1.49	1.60	1.42	1.19	NS
Community–Leisure mean impairment score	0.72	1.37	1.55	1.13	2.93	NS
Number of impaired domains	0.53	1.66	0.37	0.52	0.07	NS

Note. F, results for the *F*-test; *p*, probability value for the *F*-test if $\leq .05$; NS, not significant.

[a]The *N*'s shown here are the maximum sample sizes, which can vary across these comparisons due to some parents reporting a specific domain as not being applicable to their children (or in rare cases due to parents refusing to rate this domain).

TS are not more impaired nor impaired in more domains than control children so long as comorbid ADHD cases are removed from both. The results do suggest that it may be comorbid ADHD that results in much of the impairment associated with TD/TS.

This is not unexpected. When cases of TD/TS are separated on the basis of comorbidity with ADHD, deficits on tests of EF, for instance, are diminished considerably; they may be found only on tests of attention or motor control or are, more often, exclusively associated only with those children having ADHD (Groot, Yeates, Baker, & Bornstein, 1997; Harris et al., 1995; Roessner, Becker, Banaschewski, & Rothenberger, 2007). This appears to be the case with parent ratings of EF deficits as well; EF deficits on the BRIEF scale are evident only in individuals with ADHD or ADHD comorbid with TS but not in cases with TS alone (Mahone et al., 2002). Given the small sample size of TD/TS cases alone and those with ADHD, it was not possible to compare those with and without ADHD to directly evaluate this observation.

Autism Spectrum Disorders

Studies suggest that autism spectrum disorders (ASD) occur in approximately 0.6–1.0% of the child and adolescent population (Simonoff et al., 2008). In the present sample, parents of 36 children (1.8%) reported that their children had received professional diagnoses of autism, ASD, or Asperger syndrome. These children made up the ASD group and were compared with the remainder of the sample ($N = 1{,}886$) on all BFIS-CA scores. All comparisons were significant (all p's $< .001$). Differences between these groups were substantial, rivaling those magnitudes seen in the preceding comparisons involving children with ADHD and implying that substantial and pervasive impairment exists in all domains in daily life in children with ASD.

One must bear in mind, however, that ADHD is the second most common comorbid disorder associated with ASD after social anxiety disorder (Simonoff et al., 2008). Studies suggest that 28–53% of children with ASD may have ADHD (Simonoff et al., 2008; Sinzig, Walter, & Doepfner, 2009). The rate of comorbidity between ADHD and ASD in the present ASD sample was 47% (17 of 36), consistent with prior studies. Likewise, children with ADHD often have significant elevations in ASD symptoms even if they do not qualify for a diagnosis of ASD (Mulligan et al., 2009; Reiersen, Constantino, Volk, & Todd, 2007). Interestingly, behavioral genetic studies of twins show that these two symptom dimensions have a high degree of shared familial genetic contribution between them (Mulligan et al., 2009). That contribution is also shared with a degree of conduct disorder, oppositional defiant disorder, and motor disorders. Thus, removing children with ADHD from such studies of impairment ratings in children with ASD may remove some of the variance that is actually due to ASD (the independent variable of interest) or at least that is the result of this shared underlying familial trait. Even so, for the sake of showing what impairment may be unique to ASD, the ADHD cases were removed from the ASD sample, and the analyses were recomputed. These results are shown in Table 7.7. Some analyses became nonsignificant, though many of these could be considered marginally significant in view of the small sample size of ASD cases.

TABLE 7.7. BFIS-CA Scores for Children in the Entire Sample Having Parent-Reports of a Professional Diagnosis of ASD and the Sample Remainder, with ADHD Cases Removed

	No ASD (no ADHD) (N = 1,778)		ASD (no ADHD) (N = 19)[a]			
Subscale	Mean	*SD*	Mean	*SD*	*F*	*p*
With mother	0.87	1.81	1.26	2.23	0.88	NS
With father	0.98	1.87	1.74	2.60	3.03	NS
School performance	1.10	2.00	2.61	2.61	10.08	.002
With siblings	1.08	1.89	3.22	3.13	22.30	< .001
Playing in neighborhood	0.77	1.59	3.06	2.77	34.15	< .001
Community activities	0.66	1.48	2.76	2.84	33.44	< .001
Visiting others	0.64	1.40	2.00	1.85	16.74	< .001
Playing at school	0.71	1.50	3.06	2.57	38.53	< .001
Managing money	0.88	1.70	2.05	2.46	8.87	.003
Self-care	0.64	1.44	1.26	1.48	3.59	NS
Doing chores	1.35	1.94	2.16	2.43	3.22	NS
School homework	1.26	2.02	2.47	2.57	6.66	.010
Following rules	0.89	1.72	1.37	1.71	1.45	NS
With other adults	0.62	1.45	1.26	1.56	3.66	NS
Playing sports	0.74	1.58	3.33	3.13	38.99	< .001
Home–School mean impairment score	1.02	1.49	2.00	1.64	8.15	.004
Community–Leisure mean impairment score	0.70	1.35	2.49	1.94	32.54	< .001
Number of impaired domains	0.51	1.64	1.95	2.50	14.11	< .001

Note. *F*, results for the *F*-test; *p*, probability value for the *F*-test if ≤ .05; NS, not significant.

[a]The *N*'s shown here are the maximum sample sizes, which can vary across these comparisons due to some parents reporting a specific domain as not being applicable to their children (or in rare cases due to parents refusing to rate this domain).

The following domains were no longer significant: interactions with mother, interactions with father (p = .082), self-care (p = .058), doing chores (p = .073), follows rules, and interactions with other adults (p = .056). Such findings imply that it is comorbidity with ADHD that may contribute much, though not all, of the impairment associated with ASD. However, a number of other scores remained significant, and in them levels of impairment were of a moderate degree, falling below what had been evident in ADHD cases but higher than more focal disorders such as SLD or DCD. The three summary scores tend to tell the story in that children with ASD have levels of impairment two to four times greater than control children, even in the absence of ADHD comorbidity.

Enough cases existed to study the resulting patterns of impairments for ASD and ADHD alone and for their comorbid occurrence. There were 19 children with ASD only, 108 with ADHD only, and 17 with both disorders (ASD + ADHD) for comparison with the remainder of the sample ($N = 1{,}778$). When the results for the three summary scores were compared for these groups, all omnibus ANOVAs were significant at $p < .001$. The results are portrayed graphically in Figure 7.6. The pairwise contrasts were quite informative. The pattern for all three scores was the same: ADHD + ASD > ADHD only > ASD only > controls. This implies that each disorder produces some unique impairments that are additive when the disorders coexist. The combination of the two disorders, in fact, is the most impairing comorbidity discussed so far in this chapter. Yet it also makes plain that ADHD, whether alone or with ASD, is a more impairing disorder than is ASD—indeed, ADHD is approximately twice as impairing as reflected in both severity and pervasiveness (number of impaired domains). Again, such findings are not just scientifically informative but clearly supportive of the validity of the BFIS-CA scores to discriminate patterns among various learning, developmental, and psychiatric disorders.

ASD is also known to have a significant association with SLD in view of the often impaired, if not bizarre, language development associated with ASD. Is the impairment associated with ASD due to its association with such language delays, or vice versa? Thus yet another informative comparison is possible within this sample, and additional evidence is provided for the validity of the BFIS-CA in differentiating between various disorders that produce some impairment in major life activities. Both disorders are associated with ADHD. Therefore, cases of ADHD were initially removed from any comparisons between these disorders. There were 14

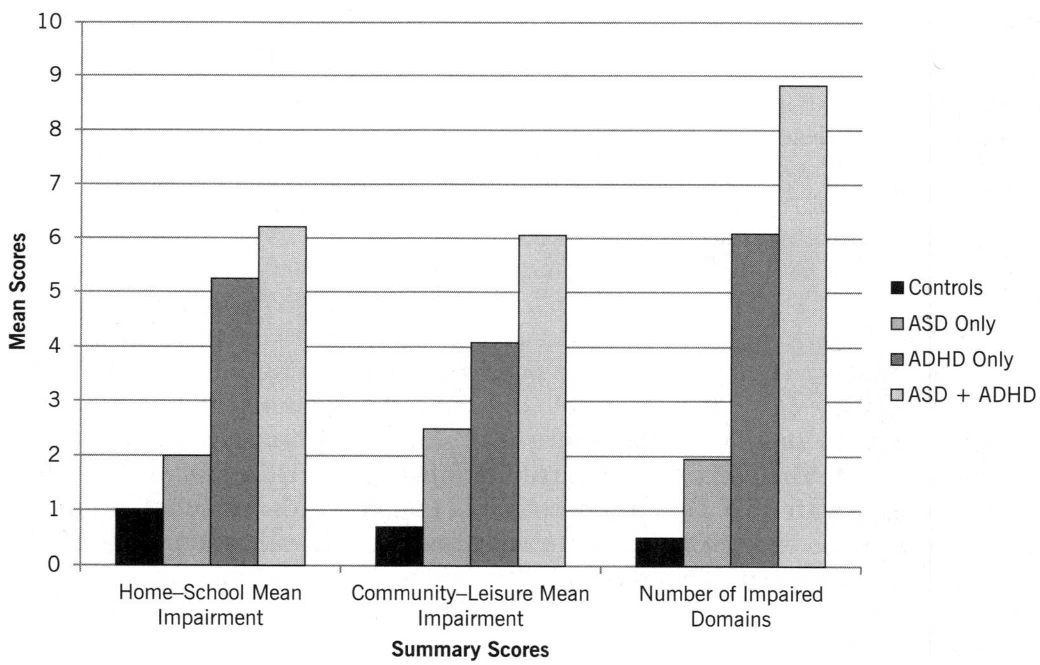

FIGURE 7.6. Comparison of children with ASD only, ADHD only, and ASD + ADHD with control children on the three summary scores from the BFIS-CA. See text for details concerning pairwise comparisons. ADHD diagnosed by research criteria (see text).

cases of ASD only (no ADHD or SLD), 67 cases of SLD only (no ADHD or ASD), and 5 cases of ASD + SLD, all of which were compared with the remainder of the sample (no ADHD; $N = 1{,}711$). All of the ANOVAs were significant at $p < .001$. The comparisons are shown in Figure 7.7. Care must be taken in interpreting results for the comorbid group due to its small sample size and hence low power to detect group differences. Despite such a caveat, pairwise comparisons showed that, for the Home–School mean impairment score, only the ASD + SLD group differed from the control group, with the other two groups falling between these two extremes and not differing from either. In contrast, the pattern for the Community–Leisure mean impairment score was ASD + SLD > ASD only > SLD only, controls, with the latter two groups not being different. For the number of impaired domains score, the pattern was ASD + SLD > SLD only, controls. The ASD-only group did not differ from the SLD-only and controls groups, nor from the comorbid group. All this seems to suggest that ASD (in the absence of ADHD) is still a more impairing disorder in Community-Leisure domains, but it is their comorbidity that stands out as more impairing than either disorder alone and especially than SLD. Once again, validity of the BFIS-CA scores is further established by this capacity to detect differences among various disorders and their comorbid occurrences.

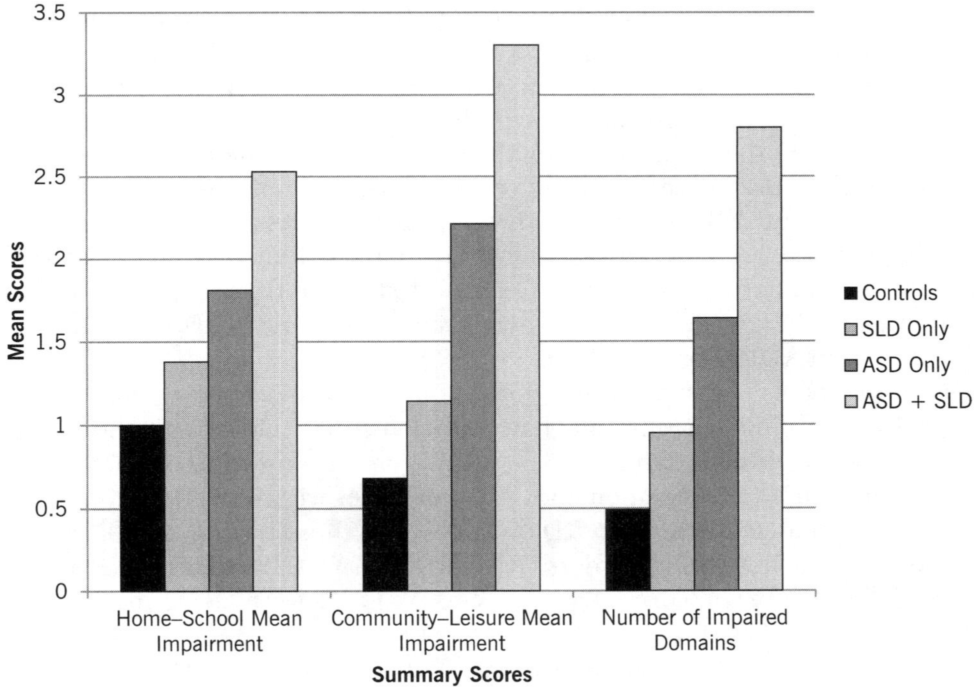

FIGURE 7.7. Comparison of children with ASD only, SLD only, and ASD + SLD with control children on the three summary scores from the BFIS-CA with all cases of ADHD removed from all groups. See text for details concerning pairwise comparisons. ADHD diagnosed by research criteria (see text).

Specific Learning Disabilities

Reading Disorders

Studies suggest that reading disorders (RD) occur in approximately 5–9% of children (Shaywitz, Shaywitz, Fletcher, & Escobar, 1990) and are known to encompass significant problems with language beyond just difficulties with reading. As a consequence, children with RD may also have difficulties with EF, particularly in verbal working memory tasks. But this linkage of RD or dyslexia to EF deficits is complicated by the high comorbidity between RD and ADHD (Germano, Gagliano, & Curatolo, 2010), which often ranges from 15 to 30% of ADHD cases (Barkley, 2006; Del'Homme, Kim, Loo, Yang, & Smalley, 2007). Studies using parent ratings of EF have also found significant deficits in EF in daily life activities in children with RD compared with controls. But these deficits are often significantly milder than the more severe deficits in EF ratings associated with ADHD or ASD (Gioia, Isquith, Kenworthy, & Barton, 2002). Such findings might suggest that a similar pattern would exist among these disorders in their ratings of impairment.

For this manual, comparisons were made between children with professional diagnoses of RD ($N = 77$) and the remainder ($N = 1,845$) on all BFIS-CA scores, and all were significant ($p < .001$). Here again it was important to remove those children with ADHD from these comparisons in view of the substantial impairment associated with it that could be making RD appear to be a more impairing disorder than is actually the case. When this was done and the comparisons were repeated, most comparisons remained significant, but others did not. The results are shown in Table 7.8. Those comparisons that were no longer different from the controls were interactions with mother, interactions with father, playing with other children in the neighborhood, and self-care. Even the remaining significant differences reflected rather small absolute differences from the control group. As might be expected, RD is most impairing in school performance and doing school homework. Its overall level of impairment and pervasiveness, as reflected in the three summary scores, is comparable to other, more focal disorders such as SLD and DCD and is far below the levels seen in ADHD or even ASD.

Greater evidence for such conclusions, however, comes once again from comparing subsets of children who may have either disorder alone with those having it in combination with another disorder with which it is known to often coexist. As noted earlier, ADHD is a common coexisting disorder with RD, and vice versa. For the present manual, children with RD only ($N = 54$), those having ADHD only ($N = 102$), and those having both disorders (RD + ADHD; $N = 23$) were compared on the three BFIS-CA summary scores. The omnibus ANOVAs were all significant (all p's $< .001$). The results are shown in Figure 7.8. The pattern of pairwise comparisons for all three measures was the same: ADHD + RD, ADHD only > RD only > controls. This indicates that it is largely ADHD that is determining the degree and pervasiveness of impairment when the two disorders coexist. The two ADHD groups are the most impaired and pervasively so, and they do not differ from each other in those respects. Although a modest degree of impairment is associated with RD across these measures, it is far less than for either ADHD group. Based on the means,

TABLE 7.8. BFIS-CA Scores for Children in the Entire Sample Having Parent-Reports of a Professional Diagnosis of RD and the Sample Remainder, with ADHD Cases Removed

	No RD (or ADHD) (N = 1,743)		RD (no ADHD) (N = 54)[a]			
Subscale	Mean	*SD*	Mean	*SD*	*F*	*p*
With mother	0.86	1.80	1.23	2.25	1.89	NS
With father	0.98	1.87	1.23	2.14	0.81	NS
School performance	1.06	1.95	2.94	2.96	44.30	< .001
With siblings	1.09	1.89	1.95	2.67	8.34	.004
Playing in neighborhood	0.78	1.61	1.12	1.91	2.11	NS
Community activities	0.66	1.48	1.42	2.11	11.86	.001
Visiting others	0.63	1.39	1.29	1.98	10.97	.001
Playing at school	0.71	1.50	1.37	2.14	8.86	.003
Managing money	0.87	1.69	1.53	2.20	7.32	.007
Self-care	0.63	1.41	1.02	1.92	3.63	NS
Doing chores	1.33	1.92	2.35	2.45	13.73	< .001
School homework	1.21	1.97	3.44	2.76	60.21	< .001
Following rules	0.87	1.70	1.61	2.00	9.07	.003
With other adults	0.61	1.43	1.10	2.03	5.48	.019
Playing sports	0.74	1.58	1.53	2.56	11.00	.001
Home–School mean impairment score	1.00	1.47	1.93	1.85	19.50	< .001
Community–Leisure mean impairment score	0.70	1.35	1.27	1.86	8.57	.003
Number of impaired domains	0.50	1.62	1.35	2.55	13.78	< .001

Note. F, results for the *F*-test; *p*, probability value for the *F*-test if ≤ .05; NS, not significant.
[a]The *N*'s shown here are the maximum sample sizes, which can vary across these comparisons due to some parents reporting a specific domain as not being applicable to their children (or in rare cases due to parents refusing to rate this domain).

ADHD is approximately three times more impairing than is RD in either severity or pervasiveness.

Spelling Disorders

Spelling disorders (SpD) have been far less studied in children than has RD. Such disorders are typically collapsed in children having RD because of a strong relationship between them and because both often share a common association with language problems more generally and phonological awareness and decoding specifically (Lewis, Freebairn, & Taylor, 2002; Warnke, 1999). Initially, children in the original sample having SpD (N = 45) were compared with those without SpD (N = 1,877) on all BFIS-CA scores. As expected, the groups differed significantly on all eight scores from the BDEFS-PF (all p's < .03 and most < .001).

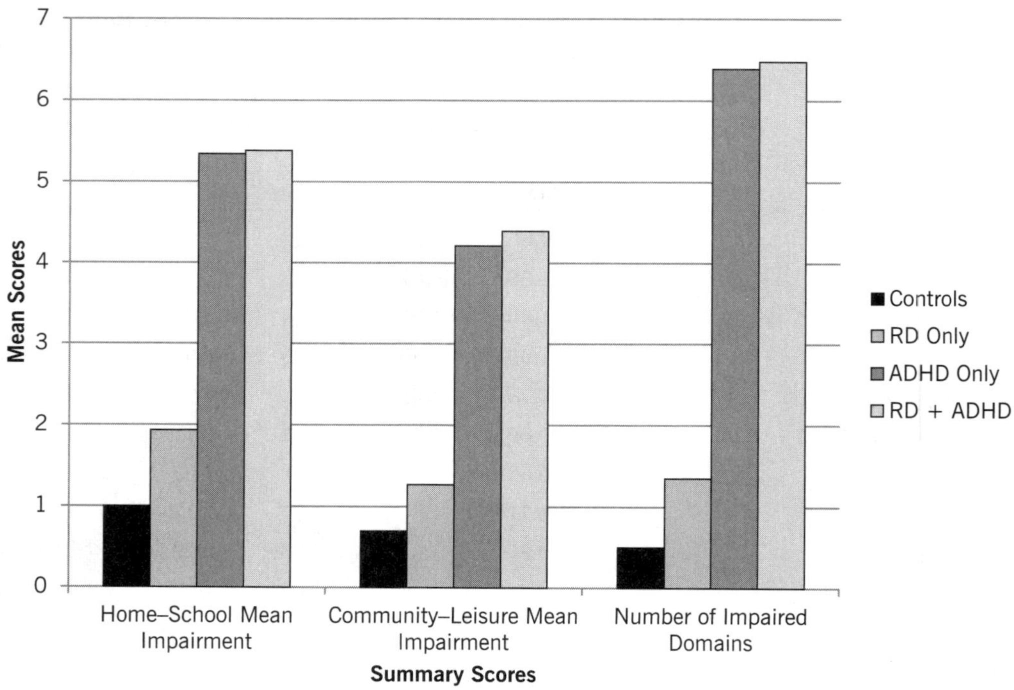

FIGURE 7.8. Comparison of children with RD only, ADHD only, and RD + ADHD with control children on the three summary scores from the BFIS-CA. See text for details concerning pairwise comparisons. ADHD diagnosed by research criteria (see text).

Once again, the specter of comorbidity with ADHD and SpD arises. It has been suggested that 15–25% of children with ADHD may have SpD (Barkley, 2006), though the inverse association has been little studied. Given the high comorbidity of SpD with RD and of RD with ADHD, noted earlier, it is conceivable that ADHD is overrepresented in children with SpD. In the present sample, 12 children with SpD had ADHD, for a comorbidity rate of 27%. Following the same procedure as with the other disabilities noted, the analyses here were repeated with those children having ADHD being removed (reduced *N*'s = 33 and 1,764, respectively). Those results are in Table 7.9. As was evident with RD, the results of these analyses showed that some domain ratings were no longer significantly different between the groups. And once again, those that were nonsignificant were interactions with mother, interactions with father, interactions with siblings (p = .054), playing with other children in the neighborhood, and self-care. The most impaired domains were, as expected, those related to school performance and doing school homework. The differences between groups in the remaining domains, although significant, were fairly modest and similar to those seen for RD. Obviously, SpD is not as impairing a disorder as are some of the more general developmental disorders reviewed here, such as ADHD, ASD, or even DD/MR.

Just as with the other disorders discussed, it is more interesting, informative, and important for determining validity of the BFIS-CA scores that they reveal patterns of impairments between various disorders and not just from a control group. In this

TABLE 7.9. BFIS-CA Scores for Children in the Entire Sample Having Parent-Reports of a Professional Diagnosis of SpD and the Sample Remainder, with ADHD Cases Removed

	No SpD (or ADHD) (N = 1,764)		SpD (no ADHD) (N = 33)[a]			
Subscale	Mean	*SD*	Mean	*SD*	*F*	*p*
With mother	0.87	1.80	1.32	2.12	1.93	NS
With father	0.99	1.88	1.00	1.98	0.01	NS
School performance	1.08	1.97	3.22	2.91	36.31	< .001
With siblings	1.10	1.91	1.81	2.40	3.71	NS
Playing in neighborhood	0.79	1.62	1.13	2.03	1.36	NS
Community activities	0.67	1.49	1.29	2.13	5.18	.023
Visiting others	0.64	1.40	1.22	2.04	5.29	.022
Playing at school	0.72	1.52	1.29	1.95	4.28	.039
Managing money	0.88	1.70	1.55	2.31	4.65	.031
Self-care	0.64	1.43	0.84	1.67	0.64	NS
Doing chores	1.34	1.94	2.38	2.27	8.87	.003
School homework	1.23	1.99	3.59	2.77	43.31	< .001
Following rules	0.88	1.71	1.66	1.86	6.41	.011
With other adults	0.62	1.44	1.25	2.12	5.96	.015
Playing sports	0.74	1.60	1.72	2.48	10.47	.001
Home–School mean impairment score	1.01	1.49	1.95	1.60	12.41	< .001
Community–Leisure mean impairment score	0.71	1.36	1.28	1.88	5.49	.019
Number of impaired domains	0.51	1.65	1.27	1.87	6.78	.009

Note. F, results for the *F*-test; *p*, probability value for the *F*-test if $\leq .05$; NS, not significant.

[a]The *N*'s shown here are the maximum sample sizes, which can vary across these comparisons due to some parents reporting a specific domain as not being applicable to their children (or in rare cases due to parents refusing to rate this domain).

sample, children with SpD only ($N = 33$) were therefore compared to children with ADHD only ($N = 113$) and those having both disorders ($N = 12$; SpD + ADHD), as well as with the control group ($N = 1{,}764$), so as to study such relative patterns. These groups were compared on the three BFIS-CA summary scores, and the omnibus ANOVAs were all significant (all p's $< .001$). The results are shown in Figure 7.9. In all comparisons, the two ADHD groups score worse but do not differ from each other. The pairwise comparisons for the Home–School mean impairment score showed that both ADHD groups were more impaired than the SpD-only and control group. The SpD-only group was more impaired than the control group, but the magnitude of this difference was rather small. For the Community–Leisure mean impairment score, both ADHD groups differed from the SpD-only and control groups, who this time did not differ from each other. That same pattern occurred for the number of impaired domains score. Thus, outside of work-related situations, SpD is not more impairing than what is seen in control children. By these metrics, ADHD is three to four times more impairing, and pervasively so, than is SpD.

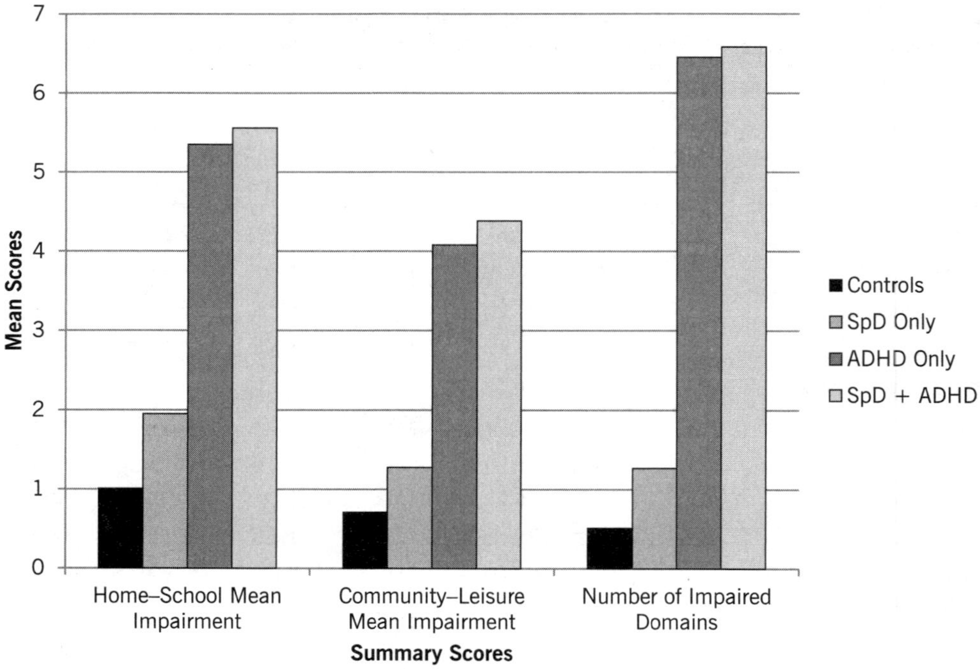

FIGURE 7.9. Comparison of children with SpD only, ADHD only, and SpD + ADHD with control children on the three summary scores from the BFIS-CA. See text for details concerning pairwise comparisons. ADHD diagnosed by research criteria (see text).

Math Disorders

Approximately 3–8% of school-age children have math disorders (MD) (Swanson & Jerman, 2006). As with the other learning disorders discussed, MD may be expected to have some modest effects on impairment ratings, especially for school performance and doing school homework. Approximately 2% of the original sample had a professional diagnosis of MD (N = 44). These children were initially compared with the remainder of the sample (N = 1,878) on all BFIS-CA scores. As seen in the preceding comparable analyses, significant differences were evident on all scores (all p's < .003). However, children with MD may also have ADHD (and vice versa) at higher rates than expected by chance. As discussed, the overlap with ADHD might account for the group differences on the impairment ratings. It has been estimated that 10–18% of children with ADHD may also have MD (Capano, Minden, Chen, Schachar, & Ickowicz, 2008; Del'Homme et al., 2007). Children with ADHD were removed from the groups, and the comparisons were made again between the children with MD only (N = 29) and the remainder (N = 1,768). The results are shown in Table 7.10. Just as with the other learning disabilities discussed herein, the domain ratings for interactions with mother, interactions with father, and self-care were not significantly different between the groups. Again, the more impaired domains were, as anticipated, school performance and doing school homework. But in this instance, relative to SpD, social interactions with others, such as siblings, other chil-

TABLE 7.10. BFIS-CA Scores for Children in the Entire Sample Having Parent-Reports of a Professional Diagnosis of MD and the Sample Remainder, with ADHD Cases Removed

	No MD (or ADHD) (N= 1,768)		MD (no ADHD) (N= 29)[a]			
Subscale	Mean	*SD*	Mean	*SD*	*F*	*p*
With mother	0.87	1.81	1.04	1.86	0.21	NS
With father	0.98	1.87	1.44	2.31	1.45	NS
School performance	1.07	1.96	3.86	3.05	54.45	< .001
With siblings	1.10	1.91	2.05	2.58	4.86	.028
Playing in neighborhood	0.78	1.61	1.39	2.20	3.91	.048
Community activities	0.66	1.49	1.62	2.30	10.20	.001
Visiting others	0.64	1.39	1.54	2.22	11.24	.001
Playing at school	0.72	1.51	1.58	2.14	7.65	.006
Managing money	0.88	1.69	1.85	2.52	8.66	.003
Self-care	0.64	1.44	0.82	1.59	0.44	NS
Doing chores	1.33	1.93	3.11	2.53	23.15	< .001
School homework	1.23	1.98	4.39	2.86	69.45	< .001
Following rules	0.88	1.71	1.89	2.01	9.63	.002
With other adults	0.62	1.44	1.29	2.17	5.82	.016
Playing sports	0.74	1.60	1.79	2.36	9.88	.002
Home–School mean impairment score	1.01	1.48	2.30	1.73	20.79	< .001
Community–Leisure mean impairment score	0.71	1.36	1.46	1.93	8.36	.004
Number of impaired domains	0.51	1.65	1.48	2.15	9.78	.002

Note. F, results for the *F*-test; *p*, probability value for the *F*-test if ≤ .05; NS, not significant.
[a]The *N*'s shown here are the maximum sample sizes, which can vary across these comparisons due to some parents reporting a specific domain as not being applicable to their children (or in rare cases due to parents refusing to rate this domain).

dren, and other adults were somewhat more impaired. Nevertheless, as is seen in the results for the three summary scores, MD is more impairing of work-related domains (Home–School) than of leisure or community domains. And although children with MD are more pervasively impaired than control children, its impact is rather mild compared with the disorders of ADHD, ASD, and DD/MR discussed earlier.

As before, additional analyses were then conducted to evaluate the pattern of impairments in MD relative to ADHD and their comorbid condition. Comparisons were made among those children with MD only (N = 29), those with ADHD only (N = 110), and those having the comorbid condition (MD + ADHD; N = 15); these three groups were also compared with the control group (N = 1,768). The omnibus ANOVAs for the three summary scores were all significant (all p's < .001). The results are shown in Figure 7.10. Here we find from the pairwise contrasts that in Home–School mean impairment scores, both ADHD groups are more impaired than the other two groups and do not differ from each other. The MD only group is

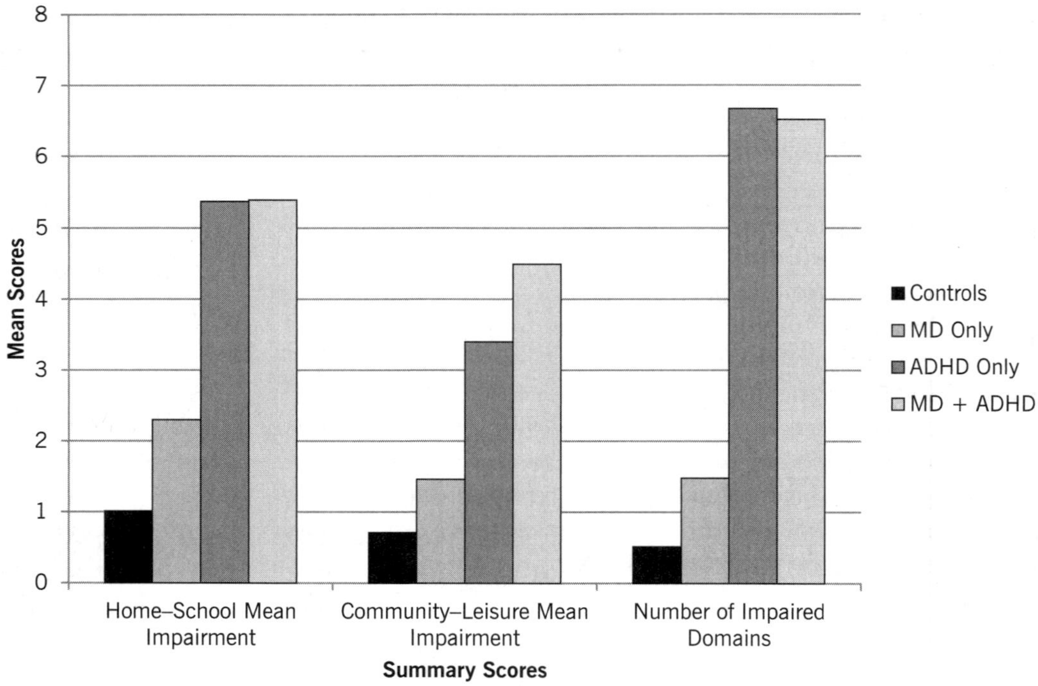

FIGURE 7.10. Comparison of children with MD only, ADHD only, and MD + ADHD with control children on the three summary scores from the BFIS-CA. See text for details concerning pairwise comparisons. ADHD diagnosed by research criteria (see text).

more impaired than the control group but less than half as impaired as the ADHD groups. This same pattern prevailed for the number of impaired domains, on which score ADHD, whether alone or in combination with MD, was more than four times as pervasively impairing as was MD. For the Community–Leisure mean impairment score, the pattern was more distinctive: ADHD only > MD + ADHD > MD only > controls. It is as if the presence of the comorbid MD slightly reduced the impairment in these nonwork domains seen in ADHD alone. Why that might be the case is not easily explained at this time. It could simply reflect the vastly greater number of cases of ADHD only ($N = 109$) relative to their comorbid state ($N = 15$) that might lead some differences between groups to reach significance while other comparisons did not do so.

Here is another instance in which differential patterns of impairment between two different disorders may be of interest, if only for additional evidence of validity of the BFIS-CA scores. Are there differences in impairment between children who have MD only, those who have reading disorders only (RD), and those with both conditions? Typically, these two disorders can coexist at higher rates than expected from their base rates, but they can also occur independently (Swanson & Jerman, 2006). Therefore, children with MD only ($N = 6$) were compared with those with RD only ($N = 31$), those with both disorders (MD + RD, $N = 23$), and the remainder of the sample (control; $N = 1{,}737$). Any children with ADHD were removed from these comparisons given the overrepresentation of that disorder in these conditions (Del'Homme et al., 2007), in case of any differential association of ADHD with these other disorders, and because it is so impairing a disorder in its own right. The limited number of children with MD limits the power of the comparison of that group with the others, and so this analysis is more exploratory than definitive. The omnibus ANOVAs were all significant (all p's < .006). For the Home–School mean impairment score, the pairwise comparisons found that only the MD + RD group was more impaired than the control group, with the other two groups not differing from each other or from the comorbid or control groups. For the Community–Leisure mean impairment score, none of the groups were found to differ from each other; likewise for the number of impaired domains score. This indicates that when ADHD is not present, specific learning disorders such as RD and MD are not especially impairing of most domains, are not very pervasively impairing, and may not differ from each other in these respects. It is their association with ADHD that may increase impairment in comorbid cases. Because there were few differences evident here, the results are not depicted in a graph.

Writing Disorders

Following the same reasoning as for the other learning disabilities, writing disorders (WD) would likewise be expected to be associated with some impairment, such as in school performance and doing school homework, but not to be as impairing or as pervasively so as major disorders such as ADHD, ASD, or DD/MR. For this reason, children with professional diagnoses of WD ($N = 43$) were initially compared with the remainder of the original sample ($N = 1{,}879$) on all BFIS-CA scores. As might be expected, all comparisons were significant (all p's < .003). But, as with the other learning and language disorders, children with WD are at elevated risk for ADHD. Certainly children with ADHD have a significant rate of comorbid WD or, at the very least, difficulties with writing, even if they do not rise to the level of a WD (Barkley, 2006; Re, Pedron, & Cornoldi, 2007). For instance, Del'Homme and colleagues (2007) found that children with ADHD had WD in 16–24% of their cases, which is similar to reports from other studies (Barkley, 2006). In this instance, ADHD occurred in 35% of the cases of WD ($N = 15$). Therefore, the group comparisons were repeated with the ADHD cases once again removed from both groups. The results are shown in Table 7.11. All comparisons remained significant except for interactions with father. This was not the case for the other learning disabilities discussed, in which fewer domains differed significantly from controls. It implies that WD might be associated with more pervasive impairment than these other academically related disorders, even when cases of ADHD are removed from those with WD. Examination of the three summary scores indicates that this may be so given that these scores indicate greater severity of impairment across domains and a somewhat greater number of domains being impaired than was evident for the other learning disorders.

Following the same logic used earlier, it is even more informative to examine the impact of WD alone ($N = 28$), that of ADHD alone ($N = 110$), and the combination

TABLE 7.11. BFIS-CA Scores for Children in the Entire Sample Having Parent-Reports of a Professional Diagnosis of WD and the Sample Remainder, with ADHD Cases Removed

	No WD (or ADHD) (N = 1,769)		WD (no ADHD) (N = 29)[a]			
Subscale	Mean	*SD*	Mean	*SD*	*F*	*p*
With mother	0.86	1.80	1.58	2.42	3.97	.047
With father	0.99	1.87	1.33	2.32	0.81	NS
School performance	1.07	1.96	4.07	2.96	61.35	< .001
With siblings	1.09	1.90	2.48	2.56	11.92	.001
Playing in neighborhood	0.77	1.58	2.36	2.96	24.01	< .001
Community activities	0.65	1.46	2.62	2.71	44.64	< .001
Visiting others	0.63	1.38	2.11	2.45	29.80	< .001
Playing at school	0.70	1.49	2.38	2.56	31.58	< .001
Managing money	0.86	1.67	2.52	2.85	25.13	< .001
Self-care	0.63	1.42	1.44	1.99	8.58	.003
Doing chores	1.33	1.92	3.26	2.65	26.41	< .001
School homework	1.23	1.98	4.56	2.75	74.29	< .001
Following rules	0.88	1.71	1.96	2.05	10.64	.001
With other adults	0.61	1.43	1.96	2.31	23.37	< .001
Playing sports	0.72	1.56	3.28	3.06	63.72	< .001
Home–School mean impairment score	1.00	1.47	2.59	1.75	30.53	< .001
Community–Leisure mean impairment score	0.96	1.34	2.40	2.37	42.06	< .001
Number of impaired domains	0.50	1.63	2.32	2.40	33.72	< .001

Note. F, results for the F-test; p, probability value for the F-test if $\leq .05$; NS, not significant.

[a]The N's shown here are the maximum sample sizes, which can vary across these comparisons due to some parents reporting a specific domain as not being applicable to their children (or in rare cases due to parents refusing to rate this domain).

of the two disorders (WD + ADHD, N = 15) in comparison with the control group (N = 1,769). These comparisons were made on the three BFIS-CA summary scores and, as before, all omnibus ANOVAs were significant (at $p < .001$). The results are shown in Figure 7.11. The pattern was the same for all three scores. Pairwise comparisons showed that the two ADHD groups were always significantly more impaired than the WD-only and control groups, with the two ADHD groups not differing from each other. This indicates that whatever impairment is created by WD may not be unique but associated with degrees of ADHD symptoms, given that, when they are comorbid, the effects are not additive. Specifically, the pattern was: WS + ADHD, ADHD only > WD only > controls. Whatever is the source, WD is a more pervasive and impairing condition than the other learning disorders, as is evident in the fact that the mean scores for the WD-only group were 2.5–4.5 times greater than for the control group and more than twice as high relative to the other learning disorders such as MD. Yet ADHD is approximately twice as impairing as even WD.

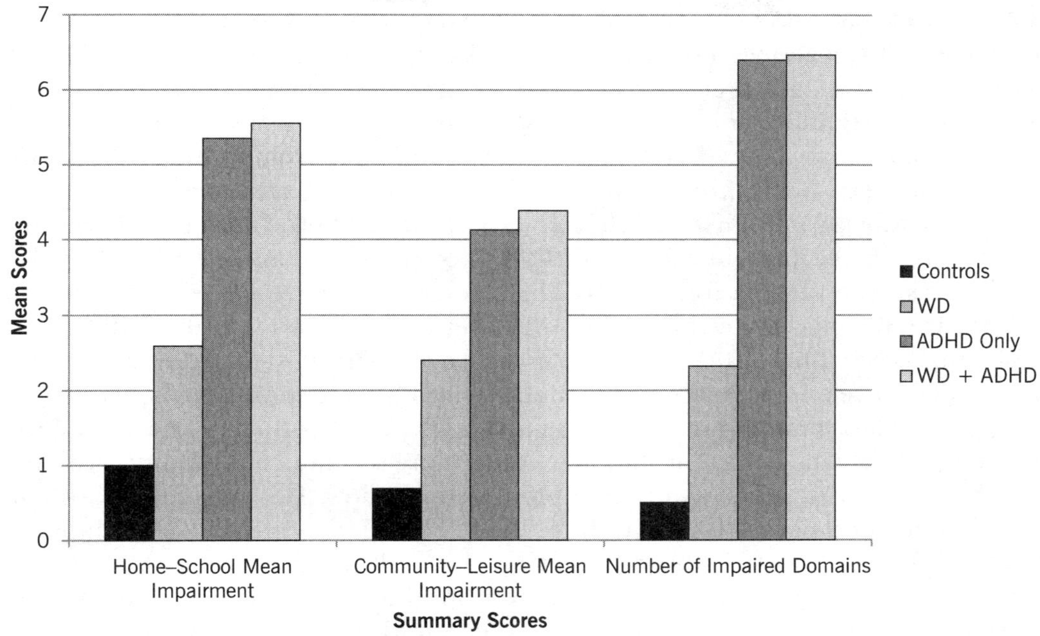

FIGURE 7.11. Comparison of children with WD only, ADHD only, and WD + ADHD with control children on the three summary scores from the BFIS-CA. See text for details concerning pairwise comparisons. ADHD diagnosed by research criteria (see text).

Psychiatric Disorders

Anxiety Disorders

Studies have shown that symptoms of anxiety or fears are commonplace in childhood. The percentage of actual anxiety disorders in childhood varies widely across studies, from 2.6 to 41.2% (Cartwright-Hatton, McNicol, & Doubleday, 2006), and is largely related to diagnostic criteria and ascertainment methods. But the prevalence of children who meet criteria for a diagnosis of an anxiety disorder during any 3- to 6-month period may be closer to 2–11% in children (Costello et al., 1996; Last, Perrin, Hersen, & Kazdin, 1996) and 8–19% in mid-adolescence (Essau, Conradt, & Petermann, 2000; Kashani & Orvaschel, 1988). There is a high rate of remission of anxiety disorders over a 3- to 4-year period in childhood (82%) and a small chance of relapse back to the original anxiety disorder (8%). But some additional risk remains for the development of new psychiatric disorders (30%; Last et al., 1996). Depression is the most common comorbidity (approximately 28%) in conjunction with anxiety disorders by adolescence, but ADHD also exists in a significant minority of cases (Essau et al., 2000).

In the sample, 56 children (2.9%) were reported by parents to have received professional diagnoses of anxiety disorders. This percentage is relatively low compared with the actual prevalence of the disorders in this age range and may have to do with the underdetection and hence underdiagnosis of such disorders by professionals (Pliszka, 2009). Or perhaps it is owing to the low agreement of parent- and child-reports of a child's anxiety and the fact that clinicians are less likely to directly interview children about their anxieties (Pliszka, 2009). Children with and without anxiety disorder diagnoses were compared on all of the BFIS-CA scores. The differences were substantial and significant in all comparisons (all p's < .001).

Once again, however, ADHD can be a common comorbidity in children with anxiety disorders, being present in 17–35% of those children under 12 and in at least 9% of adolescents (Pliszka, 2009; Shatz & Rostain, 2006; Tannock, 2009). This was the case in the present sample, with 39% of cases with anxiety disorders also meeting research criteria for ADHD. The reverse can also arise, with 20–50% of ADHD cases having a comorbid anxiety disorder in childhood (Pliszka, 2009; Shatz & Rostain, 2006; Tannock, 2009). The presence of ADHD often increases the risk for school failure and for additional mental health intervention than is the case in anxiety disorders alone (Hammerness et al., 2010) and may further exacerbate the degree of anxiety in such comorbid cases even more so than comorbidity with ASD and chronic tic disorders (Guttmann-Steinmetz, Gadow, De Vincent, & Crowell, 2010). Yet the presence of anxiety in children with ADHD may reduce their inhibitory (Pliszka, 2009; Tannock, 2009) or attention (Vloet, Konrad, Herpertz-Dahlmann, Polier, & Gunther, 2010) problems. Given the substantial impact of ADHD on parent ratings of impairment, as reported earlier, children having ADHD needed to be removed from the sample to study the independent impact of anxiety disorders on impairment ratings. Reanalyses were then conducted between children with and without diagnoses of anxiety disorders. Thirty-four children had anxiety disorders but did not meet research criteria for ADHD, and they were compared with the remainder of the sample (N = 1,763) after the cases of ADHD were removed from both groups. The comparisons of these two groups are shown in Table 7.12. All remained significant, although the magnitude of the differences was now substantially reduced by removal of the ADHD cases, as would be expected. This makes it clear that anxiety disorders can be associated with impairment in daily life activities, and pervasively so, even absent any overlap with ADHD.

Once again, however, the pattern that may exist between children with anxiety disorders alone (N = 34), those with ADHD alone (N = 103), and those with both disorders (N = 22) is important to examine for any evidence of a unique profile of impairment associated with each disorder and their cooccurrence. Again, the power of such comparisons may be limited given the small sample of cases having both disorders, but robust differences may still be evident. As with the other disorders discussed, the three groups were compared with each other and against the remainder of the sample (N = 1,763) on the three summary scores. All omnibus ANOVAs were significant (all p's < .001). The findings are graphically illustrated in Figure 7.12. In all three instances, the disorders appear to be additive: anxiety + ADHD > ADHD only > anxiety only > controls. This suggests that anxiety disorders are impairing in their own right but only about half as much as ADHD. But they seem to be having a unique impact on impairment. Although ADHD is worse, its combination with anxiety is markedly more so (showing additivity), leading to some of the highest ratings of mean impairment and of pervasiveness of impairment seen among most of the disorders discussed. On average, children with both disorders were impaired (placed at or above the 93rd percentile) in more than half of the domains sampled on the BFIS-CA.

TABLE 7.12. BFIS-CA Scores for Children in the Entire Sample Having Parent-Reports of a Professional Diagnosis of Anxiety Disorder and the Sample Remainder, with ADHD Cases Removed

	No anxiety disorder (or ADHD) (N= 1,763)		Anxiety disorder (no ADHD) (N= 34)[a]			
Subscale	Mean	*SD*	Mean	*SD*	*F*	*p*
With mother	0.85	1.79	1.91	2.47	10.62	.001
With father	0.97	1.87	1.94	2.30	8.30	.004
School performance	1.09	1.99	2.56	2.65	16.98	< .001
With siblings	1.09	1.90	2.17	2.74	9.08	.003
Playing in neighborhood	0.77	1.60	2.14	2.40	19.94	< .001
Community activities	0.65	1.48	2.14	2.29	28.02	< .001
Visiting others	0.63	1.39	1.76	1.85	20.89	< .001
Playing at school	0.70	1.50	2.13	2.38	26.94	< .001
Managing money	0.87	1.69	2.13	2.50	16.20	< .001
Self-care	0.63	1.42	1.16	2.07	4.12	.042
Doing chores	1.34	1.94	2.34	2.19	8.33	.004
School homework	1.25	2.01	2.69	2.57	15.79	< .001
Following rules	0.88	1.70	1.64	2.34	6.27	.012
With other adults	0.60	1.42	1.91	2.39	26.44	< .001
Playing sports	0.74	1.59	2.36	2.75	22.05	< .001
Home–School mean impairment score	1.01	1.48	2.02	1.81	15.05	< .001
Community–Leisure mean impairment score	0.70	1.35	1.96	1.97	27.61	< .001
Number of impaired domains	0.51	1.62	1.65	3.11	15.84	< .001

Note. F, results for the F-test; p, probability value for the F-test if $\leq .05$; NS, not significant.
[a]The N's shown here are the maximum sample sizes, which can vary across these comparisons due to some parents reporting a specific domain as not being applicable to their children (or in rare cases due to parents refusing to rate this domain).

Depression

Evidence indicates that the rate of depression in childhood ranges from 2 to 10% (Fleming, Offord, & Boyle, 1989; Kashani et al., 1983; Lefkowitz & Tesiny, 1985; Lewinsohn, Hops, Roberts, Seeley, & Andrews, 1993; Son & Kirchner, 2000). In adolescents it is higher (5–8%) (Son & Kirchner, 2000). The lifetime prevalence rate by adolescence in some studies was as much as 33% (Lewinsohn et al., 1993). Although depression may occur alone in children, it is typically associated with anxiety in 16–62% of all cases (Kendall, 1992), among other disorders.

In the present sample, the parents of 32 children reported a professional diagnosis of depression for their children (1.6%). This rate is toward the lower end of that found in epidemiological studies noted earlier. Again, as with anxiety disorders, this could result from low rates of agreement between parents and children about a

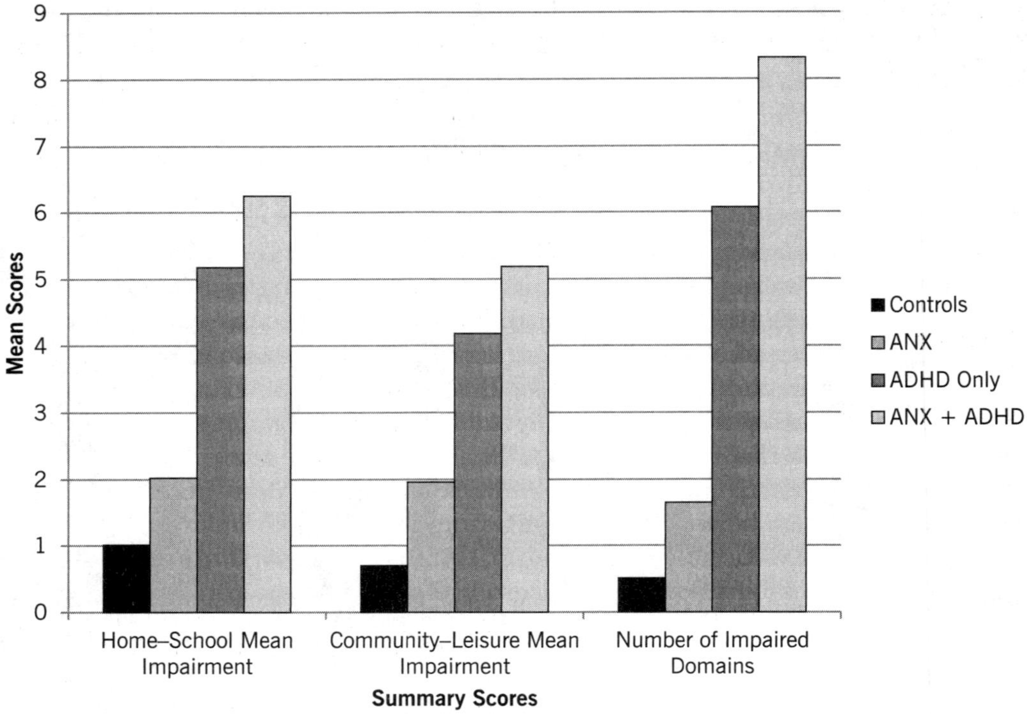

FIGURE 7.12. Comparison of children with anxiety disorders (ANX) only, ADHD only, and ANX + ADHD with control children on the three summary scores from the BFIS-CA. See text for details concerning pairwise comparisons. ADHD diagnosed by research criteria (see text).

child's depressive symptoms or mood states, as well as limited efforts to detect depression in children by professionals. It may also have to do with limitations in the DSM criteria for depression when applied to children (Pliszka, 2009). When the children with depression were compared with the remainder of the sample on all BFIS-CA scores, substantial and significant differences were evident in all comparisons (all p's < .001). Here again, there is a problem with depression overlapping with ADHD. As many as 20–50% of children with depression may have ADHD, and 20–30% or more of children with ADHD may have depression (Carlson & Meyer, 2009; Pliszka, 2009). When the ADHD cases (N = 9) were removed from the depression group and the control group, all differences remained significant. Those analyses are shown in Table 7.13. Even after removing the ADHD cases, depression is associated with substantial levels of impairment, 2.5 to 4 times greater than in the control group. Thus depression in children, even in the absence of comorbid ADHD, is associated with significant and pervasive impairment in daily life.

Of just as much interest is whether this effect shows a unique pattern relative to children with ADHD only or those with both disorders. To evaluate these patterns, children with depression only (N = 23) were compared with those with ADHD only (N = 116) and those with both disorders (depression + ADHD; N = 9), as well as with the remainder of the sample (N = 1,774) on the three summary scores. These

TABLE 7.13. BFIS-CA Scores for Children in the Entire Sample Having Parent-Reports of a Professional Diagnosis of Depression (DEP) and the Sample Remainder, with ADHD Cases Removed

	No DEP (or ADHD) (*N* = 1,774)		DEP (no ADHD) (*N* = 23)[a]			
Subscale	Mean	*SD*	Mean	*SD*	*F*	*p*
With mother	0.85	1.78	3.00	2.96	31.19	< .001
With father	0.97	1.86	2.86	2.53	21.19	< .001
School performance	1.08	1.97	3.95	2.90	45.48	< .001
With siblings	1.08	1.90	3.20	2.63	24.32	< .001
Playing in neighborhood	0.77	1.60	2.68	2.63	26.51	< .001
Community activities	0.66	1.48	2.10	2.47	18.91	< .001
Visiting others	0.63	1.40	1.87	2.07	17.51	< .001
Playing at school	0.71	1.50	2.50	2.58	27.63	< .001
Managing money	0.86	1.68	2.87	2.78	31.70	< .001
Self-care	0.62	1.41	1.95	2.50	18.76	< .001
Doing chores	1.33	1.92	3.74	2.78	35.41	< .001
School homework	1.24	1.99	3.96	2.93	41.38	< .001
Following rules	0.87	1.69	2.65	2.81	24.71	< .001
With other adults	0.60	1.42	2.43	2.55	36.67	< .001
Playing sports	0.74	1.60	2.93	2.63	27.60	< .001
Home–School mean impairment score	1.00	1.46	3.11	2.11	46.48	< .001
Community–Leisure mean impairment score	0.70	1.35	2.36	2.01	33.90	< .001
Number of impaired domains	0.50	1.60	2.65	3.65	38.85	< .001

Note. F, results for the *F*-test; *p*, probability value for the *F*-test if ≤ .05; NS, not significant.
[a]The *N*'s shown here are the maximum sample sizes, which can vary across these comparisons due to some parents reporting a specific domain as not being applicable to their children (or in rare cases due to parents refusing to rate this domain).

results can be seen in Figure 7.13. The power for the comorbid sample is quite low, however, and may obscure group differences that are less than large or robust. For the mean severity scores, the pairwise comparisons showed the following pattern: depression + ADHD, ADHD only > depression only > controls. Here we see that depression only results in a substantial elevation in mean impairment scores but that ADHD is even worse. However, the comorbid condition does not significantly elevate such impairment ratings, as was the case for anxiety disorders. The two ADHD groups do not differ, and so no evidence for additivity of disorder effects is found here. However, when examining the pervasiveness of impairment (number of impaired domains), the impact of the disorders was additive, with depression + ADHD > ADHD only > depression only > controls. The mean score on this measure was as severe as it was for anxiety disorders, with the comorbid condition being in the impaired range in more than half of all 15 BFIS-CA domains. Once more, in all comparisons, ADHD alone is a more impairing disorder than depression alone,

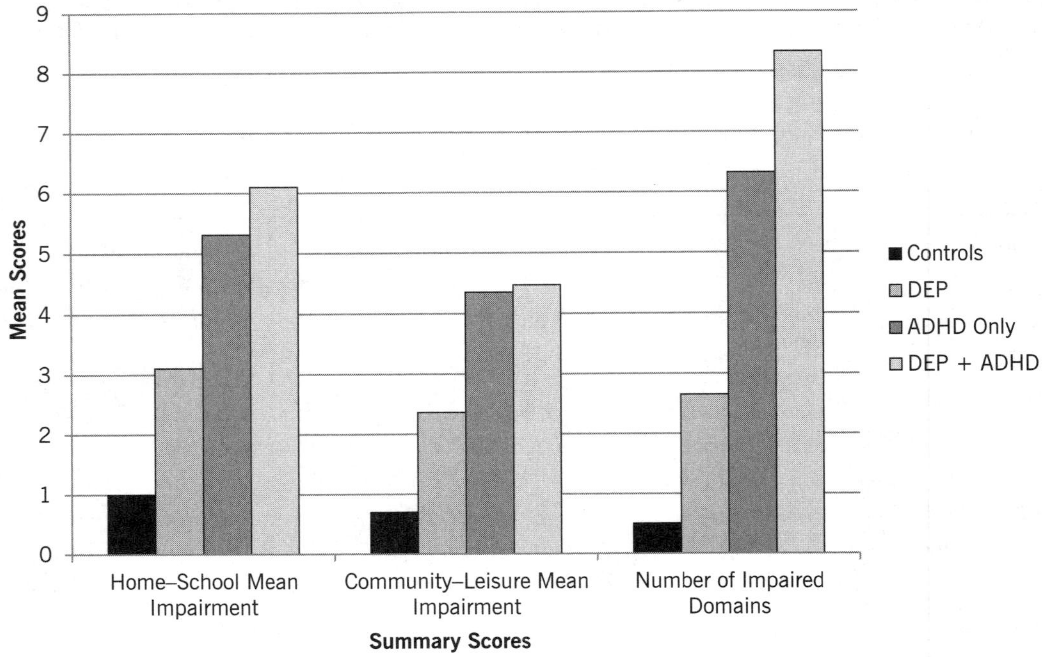

FIGURE 7.13. Comparison of children with depression (DEP) only, ADHD only, and DEP + ADHD with control children on the three summary scores from the BFIS-CA. See text for details concerning pairwise comparisons. ADHD diagnosed by research criteria (see text).

although the latter is considerably more impairing than are the more specific learning disorders or even SLD.

As noted earlier, anxiety is often present in cases of depression and vice versa. It is valuable to see what degrees of impairment are associated with each disorder alone and combined. Of course, the comorbidity of each with ADHD would need to be controlled (removed). Unfortunately, in this sample, just 5 children were comorbid for depression and anxiety when cases of ADHD were removed from the sample. But in 29 cases of anxiety only and 18 cases of depression only no research diagnosis of ADHD was present. These cases were compared against each other and the remainder of the sample ($N = 1,745$) on the three BFIS-CA summary scores. All omnibus ANOVAs were significant at the $p < .001$ level. The results are shown in Figure 7.14. The sample sizes are admittedly small, and thus power to detect group differences is probably restricted to large effect sizes. Nonetheless, some informative patterns emerged in the pairwise comparisons. For the Home–School mean impairment score, the anxiety-only group did not differ from controls. But both depression groups (depression only and depression + anxiety) were more severely impaired, yet did not differ from each other. Hence, in the domains covered by this score, depression is more impairing than anxiety disorders. For the Community–Leisure mean impairment score, again the anxiety-only group did not differ from the control group, nor was it different from the depression-only group, placing between the latter group and the control group in severity. But the depression-only

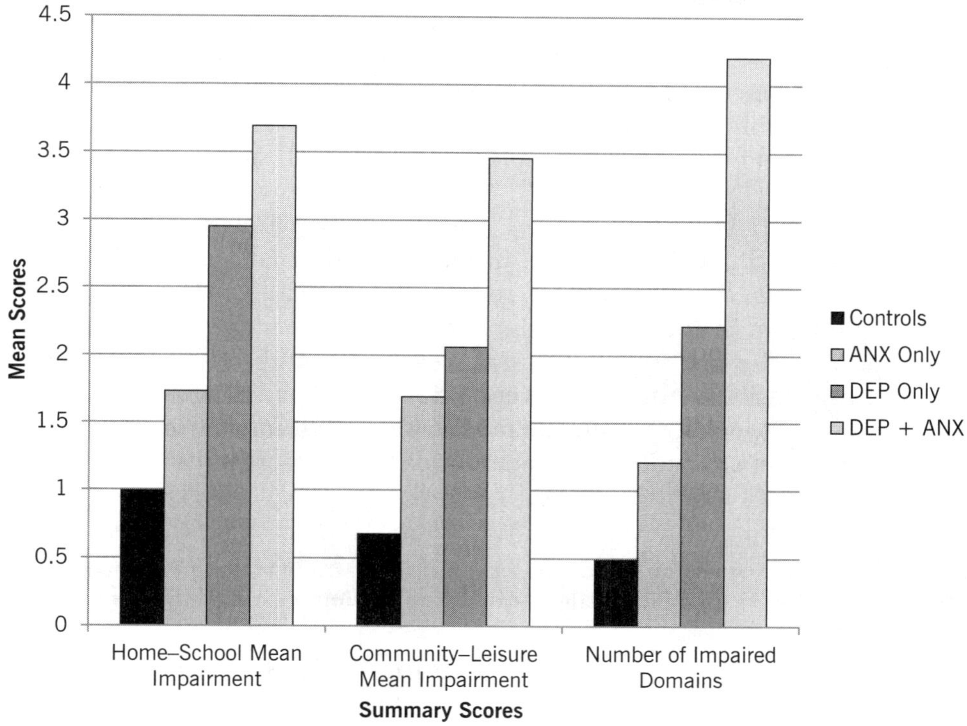

FIGURE 7.14. Comparison of children with anxiety disorders (ANX) only, depression (DEP) only, and DEP + ANX with control children on the three summary scores from the BFIS-CA with all cases of ADHD removed. See text for details concerning pairwise comparisons. ADHD diagnosed by research criteria (see text).

group was more impaired than the control group. The comorbid state was the most impaired, being worse than all other groups, with the pattern being depression + anxiety > depression > controls. This same pattern occurred for the number of impaired domains, indicating again that the comorbidity of the two conditions is worse than depression only or anxiety only. In sum, depression seems to be more impairing than anxiety, but the combination of the two types of disorder is worse than either alone. These findings are not just informative scientifically about the nature of these various disorders and their impairments but provide abundant evidence for the validity of the BFIS-CA scores in being able to distinguish among them.

Bipolar Disorder

Just 14 of the children (0.7%) in the original sample carried a professional diagnosis of bipolar disorder (BPD) or manic–depression, according to parents. This rate is below that found in epidemiological studies, in which up to 6% of children may meet criteria for BPD, averaging about 1.8% (Youngstrom, Arnold, & Frazier, 2010). The results for these 14 children were compared with the rest of the sample. Despite very low power to detect small or moderate effect sizes, all of the comparisons were significant ($p < .001$) and substantial in magnitude. Indeed, the mean differences are among the largest for any disorder other than ADHD. Problematic in research on BPD and in these comparisons is the substantial overlap or comorbidity of BPD with ADHD, averaging 62% (Youngstrom et al., 2010). Consistent with these findings, 7 of the 14 children (50%) having BPD in this small sample also met the criteria for a research diagnosis of ADHD. As with the other disorders discussed, the cases of comorbid ADHD were removed, and the comparisons were redone. These results are shown in Table 7.14. Despite the exceptionally small group with BPD only ($N = 7$), all but two of the comparisons remained significant and were still substantial in magnitude, again approaching the level of impairment seen in ADHD. Those no longer significant were managing money ($p = .053$) and self-care (p = NS). The former could be easily due to low power to detect such small effect sizes. Interactions with others, especially within the family, were substantially impaired in these children given the magnitude of the mean impairment scores in those domains.

TABLE 7.14. BFIS-CA Scores for Children in the Entire Sample Having Parent-Reports of a Professional Diagnosis of BPD to the Sample Remainder, with ADHD Cases Removed

	No BPD (or ADHD) (*N*= 1,790)		BPD (no ADHD) (*N*= 7)[a]			
Subscale	Mean	*SD*	Mean	*SD*	*F*	*p*
With mother	0.86	1.79	4.43	3.78	27.44	< .001
With father	0.98	1.87	4.83	2.40	25.50	< .001
School performance	1.10	1.99	4.57	3.50	20.95	< .001
With siblings	1.09	1.90	5.60	3.13	27.84	< .001
Playing in neighborhood	0.78	1.61	3.71	2.98	23.67	< .001
Community activities	0.67	1.50	2.67	2.66	10.49	.001
Visiting others	0.64	1.41	2.00	2.16	6.43	.011
Playing at school	0.72	1.51	3.33	3.01	17.66	< .001
Managing money	0.89	1.71	2.14	2.12	3.76	NS
Self-care	0.64	1.43	1.29	2.56	1.41	NS
Doing chores	1.35	1.94	4.14	2.73	14.43	< .001
School homework	1.27	2.02	4.14	3.34	14.04	< .001
Following rules	0.89	1.70	3.29	3.04	13.70	< .001
With other adults	0.62	1.45	2.29	2.21	9.16	.003
Playing sports	0.75	1.61	3.00	3.74	9.60	.002
Home–School mean impairment score	1.02	1.48	3.74	2.16	23.51	< .001
Community–Leisure mean impairment score	0.71	1.36	2.80	2.34	16.27	< .001
Number of impaired domains	0.51	1.62	4.28	4.96	36.62	< .001

Note. F, results for the *F*-test; *p*, probability value for the *F*-test if ≤ .05; NS, not significant.

[a]The *N*'s shown here are the maximum sample sizes, which can vary across these comparisons due to some parents reporting a specific domain as not being applicable to their children (or in rare cases due to parents refusing to rate this domain).

Just as with the other disorders, these BPD-only cases were compared with the group with ADHD only and that having BPD + ADHD ($N = 7$) on the three summary scores. All omnibus ANOVAs were significant at $p < .001$. Those findings are portrayed in Figure 7.15. The pairwise contrasts showed that for the Home–School mean impairment score, both ADHD groups were significantly worse than the BPD-only group and did not differ from each other in that respect, although low power may have been a problem in such contrasts. Yet the BPD-only group was still found to be more impaired than the control group, and substantially so. However, for the other two scores, additivity of the disorders is more apparent, with the pattern always being BPD + ADHD > ADHD only > BPD only > controls. Here, in both severity of impairment in Community–Leisure domains and in pervasiveness of impairment across all domains, the comorbid disorders are significantly worse than either disorder alone. Also, comparisons of each disorder with the other show that ADHD is more impairing than BPD. Noteworthy as well is that on the pervasiveness score (number of impaired domains), the comorbid condition is the most severe of any disorders or comorbidities seen here, resulting in impairments in nearly 9 of the 15 domains assessed on the BFIS-CA.

Because of these small sample sizes in such pairwise comparisons, another way to analyze these results to see what the distinct effect of BPD is on impairment is to compare those BPD and control cases while statistically removing (covarying) the

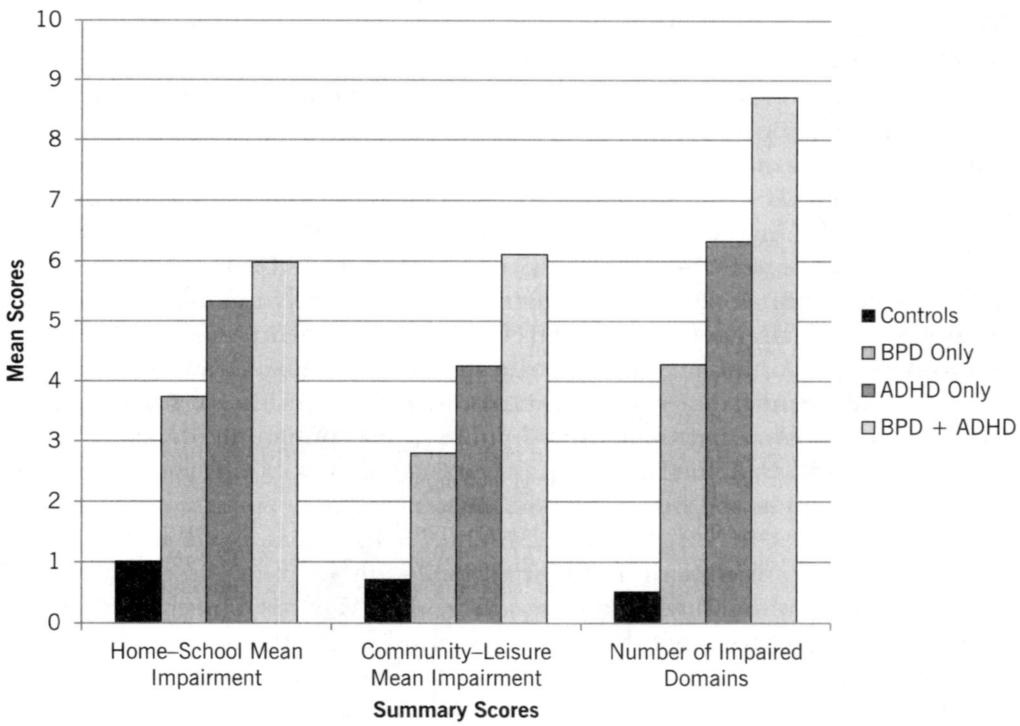

FIGURE 7.15. Comparison of children with BPD only, ADHD only, and BPD + ADHD with control children on the three summary scores from the BFIS-CA. See text for details concerning pairwise comparisons. ADHD diagnosed by research criteria (see text).

severity of ADHD symptoms. When this is done, the effect of BPD on the Home–School mean impairment score remains significant and substantial: control, M = 1.29 (SD = 1.84); BPD M = 4.86 (SD = 2.23; F = 8.91, p = .003). The same is true for the Leisure–Community mean impairment score: Control, M = 0.94 (SD = 1.68); BPD M = 4.45 (SD = 2.52; F = 17.97, p < .001). This was also the case for the number of impaired domains: Control, M = 0.87 (SD = 2.35); BPD, M = 6.50 (SD = 4.89; F = 29.90, p < .001). All of this suggests that BPD has a significant, substantial, and independent adverse impact on these impairment measures in the absence of ADHD symptoms.

Oppositional Defiant Disorder

Prevalence estimates for oppositional defiant disorder (ODD) in the child population range from 2 to 16% (American Psychiatric Association, 2000). But more precise estimates place the number at 4–6% for children and 1–3% for adolescents (Barkley, 1997). ODD is often highly comorbid with ADHD, as it is present in 40–60% of all ODD cases. The inverse is also the case: 40–84% or more of children with ADHD also have ODD (Barkley, 2006; Newcorn, Halperin, & Miller, 2009; Pliszka, 2009). Indeed, some have recently argued that ADHD may cause ODD, or at least contribute substantially to that component of ODD associated with emotional impulsiveness and poor emotional self-regulation (Barkley, 2010). The social conflict component of ODD likely arises from disrupted parenting (Barkley, 2010).

In the present sample, 28 children (1.4%) had received professional diagnoses of ODD, according to parental reports. As noted in Chapter 4, this low rate of diagnosis relative to rates of prevalence of ODD in the population is not uncommon given the reluctance of nonpsychiatric physicians to employ this diagnosis with children, at least in my experience. When the children with ODD were compared with those without ODD on the 18 BFIS-CA scores, all comparisons were significant at p < .001. But the high comorbidity of ADHD with ODD may be contributing to this finding. Seventeen of the children with ODD also had ADHD (61%), consistent with the earlier findings of the high degree of comorbidity among the two disorders. So the comparisons were redone removing the ADHD cases; this left just 11 children having ODD alone. Despite very low power in this analysis for this small ODD group, all results remained significant at p < .001. Those results appear in Table 7.15. The most severely impaired domains are as one would expect given the nature of ODD—in interactions with parents and when work has to be done, such as chores, school homework, or school performance.

As with all of the other disorders discussed herein, it is useful to explore the pattern of findings among children having ODD only (N = 11), those with ADHD only (N = 108), and those having both disorders (N = 17), and the remainder of the sample (N = 1,786). Once more the reader is reminded that the power here to detect small to medium effect sizes is very low. Even so, the comparisons were significant (all p's < .001). The results of these comparisons are illustrated in Figure 7.16. The pairwise comparisons showed that for two of the three summary scores, all groups were distinct from each other, and the disorders were essentially additive in their effects, with ODD + ADHD > ADHD only > ODD only > controls. This pattern occurred on the Home–School mean impairment and the number of impaired domains scores.

TABLE 7.15. BFIS-CA Scores for Children in the Entire Sample Having Parent-Reports of a Professional Diagnosis of ODD and the Sample Remainder, with ADHD Cases Removed

	No ODD (or ADHD) (N= 1,786)		ODD (no ADHD) (N= 11)[a]			
Subscale	Mean	*SD*	Mean	*SD*	F	p
With mother	0.86	1.79	3.70	2.95	24.78	< .001
With father	0.97	1.86	4.36	2.46	36.36	< .001
School performance	1.09	1.98	5.27	2.05	48.55	< .001
With siblings	1.10	1.90	3.75	3.49	15.31	< .001
Playing in neighborhood	0.78	1.61	2.82	2.40	17.41	< .001
Community activities	0.67	1.49	2.88	2.59	17.17	< .001
Visiting others	0.64	1.41	2.09	1.87	11.57	.001
Playing at school	0.71	1.51	3.00	2.26	22.51	< .001
Managing money	0.87	1.68	3.82	3.06	32.97	< .001
Self-care	0.64	1.43	1.73	2.19	6.32	.012
Doing chores	1.34	1.93	3.73	2.80	16.47	< .001
School homework	1.26	2.01	4.64	2.98	30.70	< .001
Following rules	0.88	1.69	4.09	3.08	39.15	< .001
With other adults	0.62	1.44	2.27	2.10	14.24	< .001
Playing sports	0.75	1.60	2.40	3.17	10.32	< .001
Home–School mean impairment score	1.01	1.47	3.94	1.71	43.25	< .001
Community–leisure mean impairment score	0.71	1.36	2.52	2.04	19.21	< .001
Number of impaired domains	0.51	1.64	3.36	2.65	32.78	< .001

Note. F, results for the F-test; p, probability value for the F-test if ≤ .05; NS, not significant.
[a]The N's shown here are the maximum sample sizes, which can vary across these comparisons due to some parents reporting a specific domain as not being applicable to their children (or in rare cases due to parents refusing to rate this domain).

Therefore, in interactions with parents and others when work is to be done, both disorders are pervasively impairing, ADHD is more pervasively impairing, and their combination is even more so. For the Community–Leisure mean impairment score, both ADHD groups scored worse than the ODD-only and control groups, yet the two ADHD groups did not differ from each other. The latter could be due to low power, because the comorbid group was rated as more impaired, if not significantly so. The ODD-only group was more impaired than controls, but not nearly so much in these domains as the ADHD groups. Noteworthy here is that the pervasiveness of the impairments for the comorbid group as indexed through the number of impaired domains score is as high as or higher than that for the comorbidity of BPD + ADHD just discussed.

As with BPD, when small sample sizes exist, as in these instances, these findings can be tested again by a different approach to see if these results still hold true for ODD without as much reduction in the power of the comparisons. That approach is

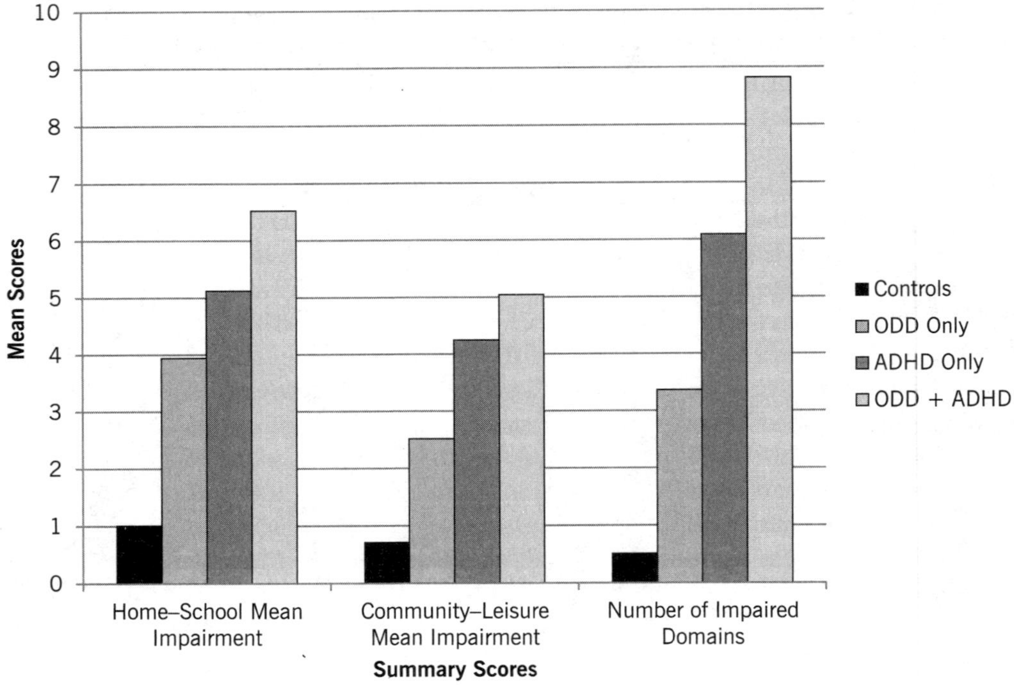

FIGURE 7.16. Comparison of children with ODD only, ADHD only, and ODD + ADHD with control children on the three summary scores from the BFIS-CA. See text for details concerning pairwise comparisons. ADHD diagnosed by research criteria (see text).

to take the entire ODD group and compare it to the remainder of the sample using ANOVA but removing ADHD symptom severity as a covariate. When that was done, the results showed that ODD still contributed significantly and substantially to the Home–School mean impairment score: Control, $M = 1.25$ ($SD = 1.79$); ODD, $M = 5.51$ ($SD = 2.01$; $F = 26.05$, $p < .001$). The same is true for the Leisure–Community mean impairment score: Control, $M = 0.91$ ($SD = 1.66$); ODD, $M = 4.05$ ($SD = 2.40$; $F = 8.23$, $p = .004$). This was also the case for a number of impaired domains: Control, $M = 0.83$ ($SD = 2.28$); ODD, $M = 6.68$ ($SD = 4.35$; $F = 47.66$, $p < .001$). This suggests that ODD, like BPD, has a significant and independent adverse impact on these impairment measures in the absence of ADHD symptoms.

Patterns of Impairments across the Disorders

One can take the results from the tables in this chapter for each disorder and compute effect sizes (ES; Cohen's *d*; Cohen, 1992) to create a common metric on which to compare them. It also allows us to obtain some idea of which disorders are most likely to impair which impairment dimensions (factors) of daily life in children and to what degree relative to the other disorders. This gives a picture of the pattern of impairments across disorders and within each disorder, allowing scores on the three summary scales to be compared directly with each other by this standard metric, ES. An ES here is the difference in the mean raw scores between each disorder and the control group divided by the pooled standard deviation (for both the disorder and control groups). It is therefore the number of standard deviations that separate the mean scores for the disorder from the general population sample not having that disorder. Given that ADHD had such a pervasive and substantial impact on impairment ratings, and because it can be comorbid with each of these disorders in a significant proportion of cases, those comorbid cases involving ADHD are removed from these analyses—except, of course, for the findings for ADHD itself.

The results are shown in Table 7.16. Here one can see the ES differences for each disorder on each of the three BFIS-CA summary scores. For all other disorders except ADHD, of course, all cases having comorbid ADHD (by research criteria) were removed. So the ES reflect just what would likely be associated with each disorder in the absence of empirically diagnosed cases of ADHD. Typically, an ES of 0.20 is considered small, one of 0.50 is medium, and one of 0.80 is large (Cohen, 1992). Perhaps most clinically informative, this table also shows the percentage of cases of each disorder that placed in the clinically impaired range on each of the three BFIS-CA summary scores. These figures are highlighted in bold in the table. The clinically impaired range is defined here (and traditionally) as having a score at or above the 93rd (92.5) percentile for the individual's age group (6–11 or 12–17 years) and sex. Just 7% (approximately) of the population would expect to be in this range, which essentially places the participant 1.5 *SD* above the mean for the general population. Therefore, percentages for each disorder that are higher than 7% indicate that the disorder is associated with an elevation in risk of clinical impairment on that summary score. This table also shows the results for the chi-square tests that compared these percentages with those for the remainder of the sample not having that disorder.

Using the three indicators in the table (ES, its magnitude class, and percentage impaired), one can determine what the impact is of each disorder on these impairment ratings, controlling for (removing) cases of comorbidity with ADHD. To my knowledge, such findings exist nowhere else in the scientific literature on these disorders or on any parent rating scale of impairment. Remember that the absolute ES here is not so important. It might well be different had a more rigorous approach to diagnosing these childhood disorders been used instead of parent reports of a professional diagnosis of their child. It is the *relative* pattern of ES or deficits that is most informative here when comparing disorders with each other, as well as among the impairment scores within and across these disorders.

The first and obvious impression from this table is that ADHD has, by far, the most adverse effect on all domains of daily life activities, regardless of which indicator is used. Whether it is based on parent-reported diagnosis by a professional or on the more rigorous research criteria used in this manual, ADHD results in far more severe impairment ratings and more pervasive impairment across settings than does any other disorder. More children with ADHD fall in the clinically impaired range than those with any other disorder. Using more rigorous research diagnostic criteria to define the disorder appears to result in ES considerably larger than those associated with parent-reported diagnoses, with all ES results placing well above the "large" designation. Using research criteria to define ADHD places

TABLE 7.16. Comparison of BFIS-CA Scores for Children with Various Developmental, Learning, and Psychiatric Disorders

Disorder[a] (*N*)	Home–School mean impairment	Community–Leisure mean impairment	Number of impaired domains
ADHD (171)			
ES	1.51	1.13	1.07
Magnitude[b]	X-large	Large	Large
% Impaired[c]	**43.3**	**39.2**	**43.4**
χ^2 *p*-value	**< .001**	**< .001**	**< .001**
ADHD (research diagnosis) (124)			
ES	2.54	1.92	1.83
Magnitude	X-large	X-large	X-large
% Impaired	**64.5**	**61.3**	**69.6**
χ^2 *p*-value	**< .001**	**< .001**	**< .001**
SLD (71)			
ES	0.28	0.34	0.27
Magnitude	Small	Small	Small
% Impaired	**5.6**	**12.7**	**11.1**
χ^2 *p*-value	NS	.003	.011
DCD (36)			
ES	0.63	0.62	0.43
Magnitude	Medium	Medium	Small
% Impaired	**5.6**	**16.7**	**10.0**
χ^2 *p*-value	NS	.002	NS
DD/MR (9)			
ES	0.85	1.37	0.75
Magnitude	Medium	Large	Medium
% Impaired	**0.0**	**33.3**	**22.2**
χ^2 *p*-value	NS	< .001	.015
Seizures/epilepsy (10)			
ES	0.92	0.80	0.56
Magnitude	Large	Large	Medium
% Impaired	**10.0**	**20.0**	**8.3**
χ^2 *p*-value	NS	.033	NS
TD/TS (8)			
ES	0.39	0.66	0.13
Magnitude	Small	Medium	X-small
% Impaired	**12.5**	**0.0**	**0.0**
χ^2 *p*-value	NS	NS	NS
ASD (19)			
ES	0.62	1.07	0.68
Magnitude	Medium	Large	Medium
% Impaired	**10.5**	**15.8**	**26.3**
χ^2 *p*-value	NS	.035	< .001
RD (51)			
ES	0.56	0.35	0.40
Magnitude	Medium	Small	Small
% Impaired	**11.8**	**11.8**	**13.0**
χ^2 *p*-value	.007	.030	.005

(cont.)

TABLE 7.16. *(cont.)*

Disorder[a] (N)	Home–School mean impairment	Community–Leisure mean impairment	Number of impaired domains
Sp Disorders (32)			
ES	0.61	0.35	0.43
Magnitude	Medium	Small	Small
% Impaired	**9.4**	**12.5**	**12.1**
χ^2 *p*-value	NS	NS	.049
MD (28)			
ES	0.80	0.45	0.51
Magnitude	Large	Small	Medium
% Impaired	**14.3**	**14.3**	**13.8**
χ^2 *p*-value	.008	.027	.024
WD (27)			
ES	0.98	0.75	0.89
Magnitude	Large	Medium	Large
% Impaired	**14.8**	**29.6**	**25.0**
χ^2 *p*-value	.006	< .001	< .001
Anxiety disorders (33)			
ES	0.61	0.75	0.46
Magnitude	Medium	Medium	Small
% Impaired	**12.1**	**18.2**	**11.8**
χ^2 *p*-value	.024	.001	NS
Depression (23)			
ES	1.16	0.97	0.76
Magnitude	Large	Large	Medium
% Impaired	**30.4**	**26.1**	**26.1**
χ^2 *p*-value	< .001	< .001	< .001
ODD (11)			
ES	1.83	1.04	1.29
Magnitude	X-large	Large	Large
% Impaired	**27.3**	**36.4**	**36.4**
χ^2 *p*-value	< .001	< .001	< .001
BPD (7)			
ES	0.93	1.09	1.02
Magnitude	Large	Large	Large
% Impaired	**42.9**	**28.6**	**42.9**
χ^2 *p*-value	< .001	.005	< .001

Note. N, sample size for disorder; ES, Effect Size (Cohen's *d*); research diagnosis, ADHD diagnosed by the research criteria reported in this manual (93rd percentile on ADHD symptom ratings and impairment in at least one domain); χ^2 *p*-value, probability value for the chi-square test if $p < .05$ for comparison of this disorder with the remainder of the sample not having that disorder; NS, not significant.

[a]Except for ADHD, all disorders are based on parent-report of the child having received a professional diagnosis of that disorder. ADHD was also diagnosed by the research criteria presented in this manual (see above). All disorders except ADHD have cases with comorbid ADHD (research diagnosis) removed from these analyses.

[b]Magnitude is graded as < .20 = extra small (X-small), .20+ = small, .50+ = medium, .80+ = large (see Cohen, 1992), and 1.5+ = extra large (X-large).

[c]"% Impaired" means the percentage of children with this disorder who placed at or above the 92.5 percentile for the normative sample (N = 1,800) for their age group (6–11 years, 12–17 years) and sex.

another 20–25% of cases in the impaired range on these summary scores. This is most likely the result of the fact that professional diagnoses included cases of ADD, or the inattentive type of ADHD, and perhaps even those having sluggish cognitive tempo (SCT), which may be a different disorder of attention, as noted in Chapter 4. In virtually every domain, the adverse effect of ADHD (research diagnosis) is approximately 2–2.5 *SD* above the mean for children in the sample without ADHD. Such ESs are not just large by traditional definition (Cohen, 1992) but extra large, indicating that the distributions of the impairment scores for the ADHD group overlap minimally, if at all, with the remaining population of children. Indeed, as measured by ES, the impact of ADHD is 2–10 times greater in each of the summary scores than is the case for any other disorder alone (separate from ADHD).

Not surprisingly, both ODD and BPD are the next most adverse disorders in their effects on impairment in domains of daily life for children as measured by ES. ODD in particular is associated with more substantial impairment in Home–School (work) domains than is the case in Community–Leisure domains, to be expected in a disorder characterized by hostility to and defiance of others, especially authorities and especially when work demands are imposed on the child (Barkley, 1997). ADHD symptom severity correlates strongly with that of ODD and BPD (indeed, some symptoms of ADHD occur on the BPD symptom list). This means it is possible that the remaining variation in ADHD symptoms within these groups—even after removing ADHD cases—may still be driving even these differences between ODD or BPD and the control group, or at least a portion of them. To find out, ADHD symptom severity was covaried out of the group comparisons of the entire ODD group in one of the analyses. Yet significant differences were still evident between the ODD and the control groups. Inspecting the percentage of cases in the clinically impaired range also tells us that although ODD and BPD are associated with significant elevations on each summary score, the majority of children with ODD or BPD are not impaired on these summary scores.

The problem of contamination of each disorder by subclinical levels of ADHD symptoms may even exist for some other disorders with which ADHD has a strong relationship. For instance, as noted, recent research suggests a shared genetic liability for ADHD, ASD, and DCD (not to mention ODD). It is therefore possible that some of the impact of these disorders on impairment, as seen in Table 7.16, apart from ADHD, is still a reflection of variation of ADHD symptoms within these groups, albeit at less clinically significant levels. One should therefore consider even these ESs for the various non-ADHD disorders to be at a maximum, as they can still have some contamination with ADHD severity. That is the reason for the previous cautionary statement that it is the *relative* patterns of ESs here and not their absolute degree that is informative. It is also the reason that it is helpful clinically to study the percentage of cases of each disorder that placed in the clinically impaired range.

There are also good reasons to expect that each of these disorders may have a negative impact on impairment in various domains, as discussed earlier, despite being somewhat contaminated with ADHD symptom severity. It makes perfect sense, for instance, that the various specific learning disabilities discussed earlier would have a detrimental impact on school performance and on doing school homework in their own right absent any overlap they may have with ADHD. The specific nature of each learning disorder and its inherent deficits would translate into some degree of adverse effect on some or all of the 15 domains of daily life on the BFIS-CA most related to it and when independent of ADHD, such as between language and social interactions or motor development and playing sports. That is the reason that the pairwise comparisons reported herein of each disorder alone versus those with comorbid ADHD may be as or more revealing of the impact of that disorder on impairment than are the results for the ESs shown in Table 7.16. Even more clinically informative, again, is that percentage of cases placing in the clinically impaired range on each summary score.

Some patterns here are quite surprising. Consider the case of SLD, in which we find that the extent of impairment associated with children having a history of such disorders is quite small, with only 5–12% of cases being rated as currently impaired. In the case of the Home–School mean impairment score, the percentage of cases placing in the impaired range is actually not significantly different from that in the control group. Ten times more children with ADHD (research diagnosis) are impaired on this score than are children with SLD, as are five times more children with ADHD on the other two summary scores. A similar pattern of results exists with children having motor delays or DCD when comorbidity with ADHD is removed. The impact of that set of disorders on impairment is far less severe than is seen for ADHD, ODD, BPD, or depression disorders occurring alone. This is as it should be given the more generalized nature of these latter disorders. Some disorders, such as the learning disabilities, are quite focal or specific in their effects on child development and therefore should be quite focal and mild in their impairment in children's major life activities. Other disorders, such as ADHD, ODD, BPD, and DEP, by contrast are more generalized across psychological functioning and development and are more severe and persistent in nature. This makes it perfectly reasonable that the latter disorders would have greater impairments in each domain of life activity and a more pervasive effect across more domains than would be evident for very focal disorders, such as the learning disabilities.

Another interesting case is TD/TS. Here one sees a pattern opposite to those in most other disorders. The other disorders tend to have a significantly greater adverse impact on functioning in work-related domains, as indexed by the Home–School mean impairment score (or by the specific domain impairment ratings in most tables in this chapter). In contrast, TD/TS seem to have a greater adverse effect on Community–Leisure settings that involve social interactions with others outside the home, in community activities, and in other public situations in which such a disorder might be more embarrassing, stressful, or incapacitating to the child. And when TD/TS are contrasted against ADHD, which frequently co-occurs with them, the findings make plain that it is the comorbid ADHD that will prove far more impairing for the individual than TD/TS.

Even the patterns of effects within the specific learning disabilities are informative. Despite the fact that they all interfere with academic achievement skills necessary for school success, some are more impairing in each of the remaining nonacademic domains assessed on the BFIS-CA than are others and may be more pervasively impairing across domains. This is evident in contrasting WD against RD and SpD. There we see the former having a more impairing effect than the latter two disorders across all three summary scores as reflected in medium to large effect sizes for the former and just small or medium ones for the latter disorders.

Why this should be the case is not immediately evident and may have to do with the differential likelihood of these disorders coexisting with others that may not have been examined in this manual. It may even have to do with comorbidity with ADHD symptoms even though full ADHD cases were removed from these comparisons. Problems with motor coordination more generally and writing specifically are more closely associated with ADHD symptom severity, and this may contaminate the WD group evaluated here more so than the RD and SD groups. The issue is certainly worthy of further research.

Another interesting finding has to do with ANX. Notice that once ADHD cases have been removed, ANX have only a modest impairing effect. Yet even this is not especially impressive when translated into the percentage of cases that are likely to be clinically impaired on any summary scores, in which the proportion is barely above that expected from the population average of 7% for most scales (12–18%). Children with ANX, in fact, were not more pervasively impaired than those in the control group, as reflected in the number of impaired domains score. In contrast, the adverse impact of DEP on impairment in daily life is significantly greater, resulting in an approximately twofold increase in risk of being clinically impaired in each of the summary scores. That of BPD was even greater. Thus, of these three psychiatric disorders having some effect on emotions, DEP is a more impairing disorder than ANX, and BPD is even more so than the other two.

Although they are incredibly informative about the specific disorders and their differential effects on impairment in various domains of daily life, these findings are also an obvious and strong testament to the criterion validity of the BFIS-CA scores. The scores on the scale have the ability to discern different patterns of adverse effects across different disorders, as one might expect given what is known about the nature of these various disorders. Undoubtedly these results are not definitive given the limitations of this study, which deserve reiteration here: (1) the reliance on parent-reports of diagnoses, except ADHD; (2) the small sample sizes in some cells of the analyses, especially after removing comorbid ADHD cases, thus potentially limiting statistical power to detect less than large effect sizes as significant; and (3) the difficulties in exploring two- and three-way comorbidities for their impact on impairment in daily life. These limitations provide ample justification, if more were needed, to further explore these issues with larger samples of better diagnosed cases than was possible here. Yet this is a reasonable initial step toward doing so. The totality of evidence presented here strongly supports the validity of the BFIS-CA scores as measures of impairment in major domains of children's daily life activities.

Conclusion

The previous two chapters have provided a large body of evidence in support of the validity of the BFIS-CA scores for evaluating the nature, degree, and scope or pervasiveness of impairment in the daily life activities of children. Whether for construct or criterion validity, the evidence is sufficient to validate this measure of impairment in children ages 6–17 years. The most compelling evidence for the utility of the BFIS-CA derives from the preceding comparisons showing that the scores from this scale can readily distinguish various patterns of impairments in daily life across various neurodevelopmental, learning, and psychiatric disorders of childhood. It does so beyond the far easier hurdle of just differentiating between any single disorder group and a control group not having that disorder. Evidence here also makes it clear that ADHD has the most severe and pervasive impact on impairment in daily life activities, adversely affecting all domains to a substantial degree. Therefore, it was important to remove such cases when comparing the disorders without ADHD with each other and with control groups given that ADHD is known to be a significant comorbid condition for the vast majority of the disorders discussed here. When that was done, interesting and distinct patterns of impairment in various domains were evident across the disorders. The BFIS-CA, therefore, has considerable utility both in clinical practice when cases of such disorders must be evaluated and also in research into the nature of impairments in these disorders.

The next chapter reviews another line of evidence for the validity of the BFIS-CA scores. It deals with the relationship of BFIS-CA scores to various forms of treatment that were received by children in this large general population sample. This not only provides more evidence for the criterion validity of the BFIS-CA scores but also speaks to the ecological validity of the scale scores.

CHAPTER 8

Relationship of BFIS-CA Scores to Treatments

This chapter provides further evidence for the criterion and ecological validity of the BFIS-CA scores by examining their relationship to various treatments received in the entire original sample. This chapter examines the relationship of the BFIS-CA impairment ratings to psychiatric, educational, and psychological therapies. Is the receipt of each of these treatments in any way related to the severity of impairments as reflected across the BFIS-CA domain and summary scores?

It is self-evident that the degree of impairment in children should be linked to the extent and types of treatment a child has received. After all, the basic rationale for rendering treatment to patients is that they are experiencing some harm or functional ineffectiveness in their lives that the treatment is expected to improve or ameliorate. Moreover, impairment is found in conjunction with many psychiatric and developmental disorders. Psychiatric medications, for instance, are often used to treat the symptoms and impairments associated with such disorders, especially ADHD. This is not to say that treatments do not work to reduce impairment; only that some impairment would be expected in those children who have received various services compared with those who have never done so.

Psychiatric Medications

Parents in the sample were asked whether their children had ever been treated with psychiatric medications for management of a psychiatric or psychological disorder. Children who had been treated were compared with those not treated on all 18 of the BFIS-CA scores. Table 8.1 shows that all ANOVAs were significant at $p < .001$. A more informative means of studying this relationship is to consider what percentage of children who had placed in the clinically impaired range on the BFIS-CA summary scores were treated with psychiatric medications compared with the remainder of the original sample. Figure 8.1 demonstrates that children falling in the clinically impaired range on any BFIS-CA summary score were six to eight times more likely to have been treated with a psychiatric medication than children not in the impaired range (all χ^2's had p's < .001). This finding is not so surprising when one considers that 41% of individuals who received a research diagnosis of ADHD (and 65% of those with parent-reported professional diagnoses of ADHD or ADD) had been treated with medication and that ADHD has the greatest adverse impact on impairment in daily life activities. The next most likely disorders among those who had received medication were anxiety disorders (23.1%) and depression (10.2%).

TABLE 8.1. BFIS-CA Scores for Children in the Entire Sample Who Received Psychiatric Medication and the Sample Remainder

	No medication (N= 1,766)		Medication (N= 156)[a]			
Subscale	Mean	*SD*	Mean	*SD*	*F*	*p*
With mother	0.89	1.83	3.63	2.97	275.55	< .001
With father	1.01	1.95	3.43	2.76	186.12	< .001
School performance	1.14	2.08	4.88	2.85	426.52	< .001
With siblings	1.14	2.00	4.26	2.89	263.89	< .001
Playing in neighborhood	0.83	1.69	3.51	2.92	274.19	< .001
Community activities	0.70	1.58	3.06	2.76	241.23	< .001
Visiting others	0.68	1.50	2.82	2.61	245.96	< .001
Playing at school	0.78	1.65	3.38	2.91	284.87	< .001
Managing money	0.93	1.80	3.55	3.09	236.36	< .001
Self-care	0.71	1.59	2.87	3.01	209.63	< .001
Doing chores	1.42	2.08	4.60	3.00	307.16	< .001
School homework	1.30	2.10	5.06	3.04	416.33	< .001
Follow rules	0.97	1.87	4.05	3.16	331.85	< .001
With other adults	0.69	1.60	2.83	2.65	221.53	< .001
Playing sports	0.79	1.66	3.17	2.89	182.85	< .001
Home–School mean impairment score	1.07	1.60	4.06	2.30	456.05	< .001
Community–Leisure mean impairment score	0.75	1.47	3.17	2.49	330.82	< .001
Number of impaired domains	0.62	1.94	4.27	4.22	390.78	< .001

Note. F, results for the *F*-test; *p*, probability value for the *F*-test if ≤ .05; NS, not significant.

[a]The *N*'s shown here are the maximum sample sizes, which can vary across these comparisons due to some parents reporting a specific domain as not being applicable to their children (or in rare cases due to parents refusing to rate this domain).

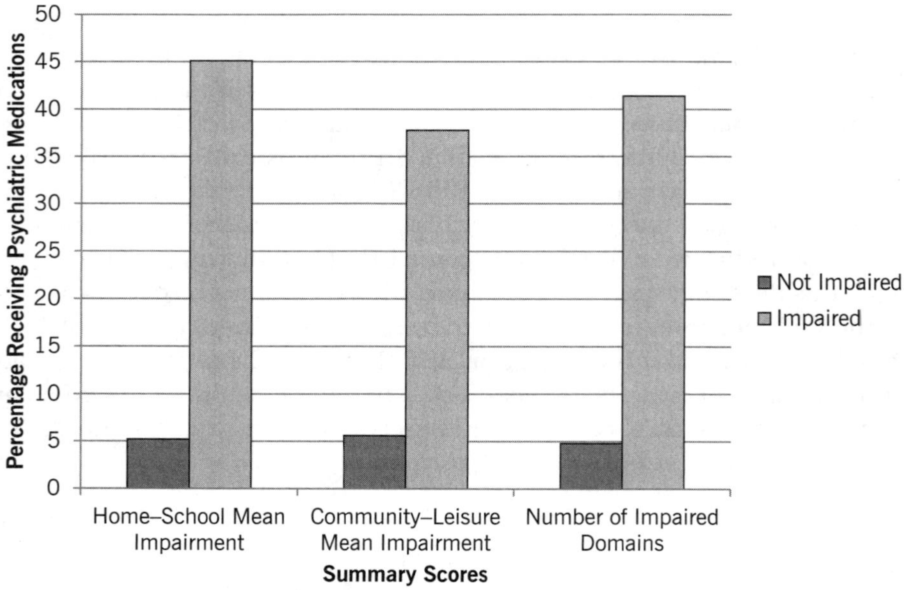

FIGURE 8.1. Percentage of children placing in the clinically impaired (≥ 93rd percentile) and not impaired ranges on each BFIS-CA summary score who had received psychiatric medication. All comparisons are significant at $p < .001$.

Educational Treatments

Academic Tutoring

Parents also reported on the educational treatments their children had received; in this instance, those who had received any type of academic tutoring outside of school. Table 8.2 compares children who had received such treatment and those who had not. All of the comparisons were statistically significant at $p < .001$. Children who had received tutoring had significantly higher scores on all of the BFIS-CA scores; indeed, their scores showed nearly twice the level of impairment as did the scores of those who had not received such tutoring. Yet notice that the impairment ratings in the domains related to school, such as school performance and doing school homework, are much higher than those in nonschool domains. This finding validates the scores on the BFIS-CA generally and on these school-related domains specifically in being able to discern different types of impaired domains from each other. Again, examining the reverse relationship, one can ask whether those who had placed in the clinically impaired range on the summary score ratings on the BFIS-CA were more likely to be receiving such tutoring. The answer is clearly affirmative. Figure 8.2 (page 114) shows that children who placed in that clinical range on the BFIS-CA summary scores were four to six times more likely to have received such services (all χ^2's had p's $< .001$).

Special Education

Academic assistance may also be given in the form of special education services at school. Children who were reported by parents to have received special education

TABLE 8.2. BFIS-CA Scores for Children in the Entire Sample Who Received Academic Tutoring and the Sample Remainder

	No tutoring (N= 1,842)		Tutoring (N= 80)[a]			
Subscale	Mean	*SD*	Mean	*SD*	*F*	*p*
With mother	1.06	2.03	2.40	2.93	30.88	< .001
With father	1.17	2.08	2.12	2.80	14.65	< .001
School performance	1.35	2.31	3.81	3.04	83.26	< .001
With siblings	1.32	2.18	2.95	2.97	34.59	< .001
Playing in neighborhood	0.99	1.89	2.25	2.80	30.45	< .001
Community activities	0.84	1.76	2.04	2.61	30.92	< .001
Visiting others	0.82	1.68	2.04	2.61	27.38	< .001
Playing at school	0.94	1.86	2.29	2.76	36.34	< .001
Managing money	1.10	2.03	2.09	2.87	16.78	< .001
Self-care	0.84	1.79	1.94	2.71	28.39	< .001
Doing chores	1.61	2.28	3.46	2.93	47.98	< .001
School homework	1.51	2.34	4.10	2.94	90.19	< .001
Following rules	1.18	2.13	2.58	2.95	31.13	< .001
With other adults	0.83	1.76	1.80	2.60	21.91	< .001
Playing sports	0.89	1.79	2.32	2.87	39.65	< .001
Home–School mean impairment score	1.25	1.82	2.83	2.38	55.41	< .001
Community–Leisure mean impairment score	0.92	1.66	2.08	2.47	35.36	< .001
Number of impaired domains	0.83	2.29	2.85	4.13	54.46	< .001

Note. F, results for the *F*-test; *p*, probability value for the *F*-test if ≤ .05; NS, not significant.
[a]The *N*'s shown here are the maximum sample sizes, which can vary across these comparisons due to some parents reporting a specific domain as not being applicable to their children (or in rare cases due to parents refusing to rate this domain).

were compared with those who had not on all BFIS-CA scores. Those results appear in Table 8.3. All comparisons were again significant at $p < .001$. As before, the children who had received formal special education had higher subscales than those who did not receive such services. Again, the domains receiving the highest impairment scores were those related to school performance and doing school homework, as would be expected from the nature of this intervention. This finding further validates the BFIS-CA scores, and especially these school-related domain ratings given by parents. Taking the alternative view, one can examine the percentage of children receiving high summary scores that placed them in the clinically impaired range compared with those who did not place in that range and who received such educational services. These results are shown graphically in Figure 8.3. They make it clear that children in the clinically impaired range on the BFIS-CA scores were five to six times more likely to have received special educational services at school (all χ^2's had p's < .001).

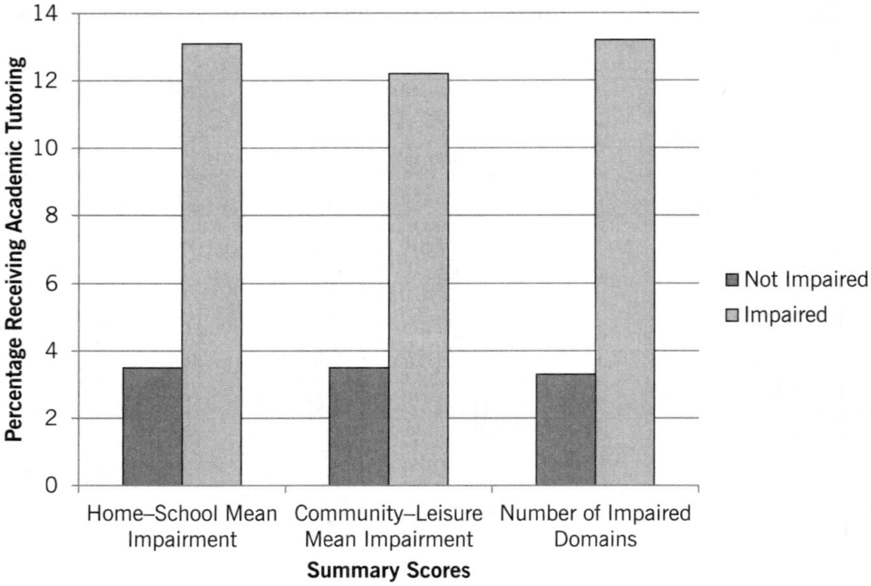

FIGURE 8.2. Percentage of children placing in the clinically impaired (≥ 93rd percentile) and not impaired ranges on each BFIS-CA summary score who had received formal academic tutoring. All comparisons are significant at $p < .001$.

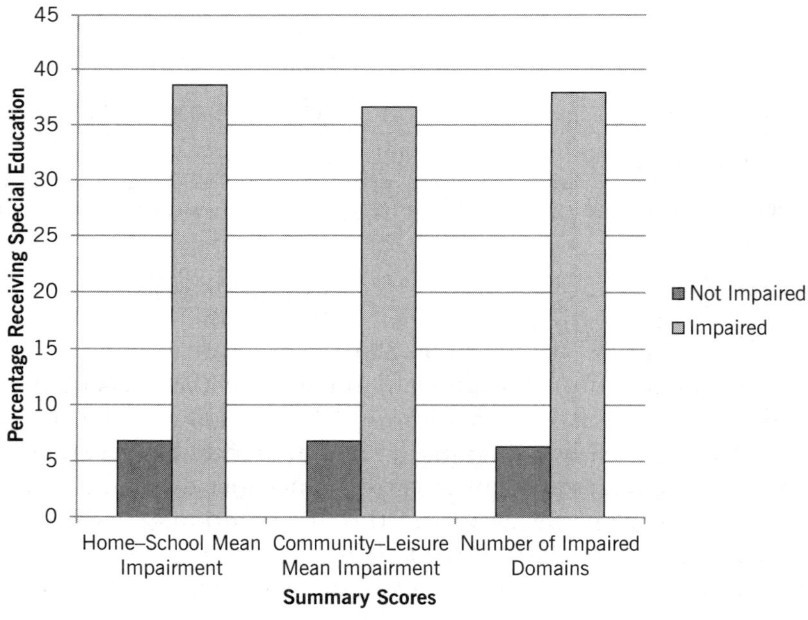

FIGURE 8.3. Percentage of children placing in the clinically impaired (≥ 93rd percentile) and not impaired ranges on each BFIS-CA summary score who had received formal special education services at school. All comparisons are significant at $p < .001$.

TABLE 8.3. BFIS-CA Scores for Children in the Entire Sample Who Received Special Education and the Sample Remainder

	No special education (N = 1,746)		Special education (N = 176)[a]			
Subscale	Mean	*SD*	Mean	*SD*	*F*	*p*
With mother	0.99	1.97	2.31	2.74	63.00	< .001
With father	1.08	2.01	2.42	2.77	59.80	< .001
School performance	1.13	2.08	4.55	2.93	389.99	< .001
With siblings	1.20	2.06	3.35	3.02	124.90	< .001
Playing in neighborhood	0.86	1.74	2.81	2.85	160.16	< .001
Community activities	0.71	1.58	2.71	2.77	188.67	< .001
Visiting others	0.69	1.52	2.51	2.50	192.01	< .001
Playing at school	0.80	1.67	2.96	2.88	210.63	< .001
Managing money	0.98	1.86	2.88	3.01	130.26	< .001
Self-care	0.72	1.59	2.54	3.01	162.33	< .001
Doing chores	1.42	2.10	4.22	2.99	254.53	< .001
School homework	1.29	2.11	4.85	2.93	407.09	< .001
Following rules	1.01	1.94	3.39	3.06	207.99	< .001
With other adults	0.71	1.61	2.40	2.71	145.44	< .001
Playing sports	0.79	1.65	2.78	2.95	147.54	< .001
Home–School mean impairment score	1.10	1.67	3.43	2.31	280.30	< .001
Community–Leisure mean impairment score	0.78	1.50	2.73	2.50	229.56	< .001
Number of impaired domains	0.64	2.03	3.57	4.00	263.86	< .001

Note. F, results for the *F*-test; *p*, probability value for the *F*-test if ≤ .05; NS, not significant.
[a]The *N*'s shown here are the maximum sample sizes, which can vary across these comparisons due to some parents reporting a specific domain as not being applicable to their children (or in rare cases due to parents refusing to rate this domain).

Speech and Language Therapy

Precisely the same pattern of findings was evident for children who had received speech and language therapy at school (N = 219). Those who had received such therapy had significantly higher scores on nearly all of the BFIS-CA scores than did those who had not (N = 1,703; all p's < .003, except interactions with father, .019). And again, the reverse relationship was also significant—those who placed in the clinically elevated range on the BFIS-CA subscales were two to four times more likely to have received such services: Home–School mean impairment score (10.6 vs. 26.1%), Community–Leisure mean impairment score (10.2 vs. 29.3%), number of impaired domains score (9.8 vs. 27.0%; all χ^2's had p's < .001). Similar results were evident for those who had received occupational therapy services (N = 85) compared to those who had not (N = 1,837) in that the former had significantly higher scores on all BFIS-CA scores than those who did not (all p's < .001). Also, those in the clinically impaired range on the BFIS-CA summary scores were five to six times more likely to have had such services: Home–School mean impairment score, 3.3 versus 18.3%; Community–Leisure mean impairment score, 3.1 versus 19.5%; number of impaired domains score, 3.0 versus 18.4% (all χ^2's had p's < .001). The situation was much the same for children who had received physical therapy services (N = 58) compared with those who had not (N= 1,864; all p's < .003). Yet again children in the clinically impaired range were three times more likely to have received such services (all χ^2's had p's < .005).

Psychological Therapy

Parents reported that 187 children had received some type of individual psychological counseling or therapy. Compared with the scores of children who had not received such services, all scores on the BFIS-CA were significant at the $p < .001$ level. Those findings are shown in Table 8.4. As with all of the previous compari-

TABLE 8.4. BFIS-CA Scores for Children in the Entire Sample Who Received Psychological Therapy and the Sample Remainder

	No psychological therapy (N= 1,735)		Psychological therapy (N= 187)[a]			
Subscale	Mean	*SD*	Mean	*SD*	*F*	*p*
With mother	0.89	1.84	3.18	2.93	217.78	< .001
With father	1.00	1.92	3.12	2.88	170.09	< .001
School performance	1.18	2.15	3.86	3.01	235.40	< .001
With siblings	1.15	2.02	3.68	2.91	194.43	< .001
Playing in neighborhood	0.84	1.73	2.93	2.75	190.31	< .001
Community activities	0.71	1.60	2.57	2.63	175.15	< .001
Visiting others	0.72	1.58	2.17	2.31	124.59	< .001
Playing at school	0.79	1.66	2.90	2.88	212.62	< .001
Managing money	0.96	1.85	2.80	2.94	137.62	< .001
Self-care	0.77	1.69	1.99	2.69	73.79	< .001
Doing chores	1.43	2.10	4.04	2.99	233.61	< .001
School homework	1.36	2.19	3.92	3.16	204.27	< .001
Follow rules	0.98	1.90	3.46	3.11	242.22	< .001
With other adults	0.70	1.62	2.40	2.55	158.02	< .001
Playing sports	0.78	1.67	2.66	2.76	139.03	< .001
Home–School mean impairment score	1.09	1.66	3.37	2.32	286.78	< .001
Community–Leisure mean impairment score	0.78	1.53	2.62	2.30	211.93	< .001
Number of impaired domains	0.65	2.04	3.39	3.92	242.12	< .001

Note. F, results for the F-test; p, probability value for the F-test if ≤ .05; NS, not significant.

[a]The N's shown here are the maximum sample sizes, which can vary across these comparisons due to some parents reporting a specific domain as not being applicable to their children (or in rare cases due to parents refusing to rate this domain).

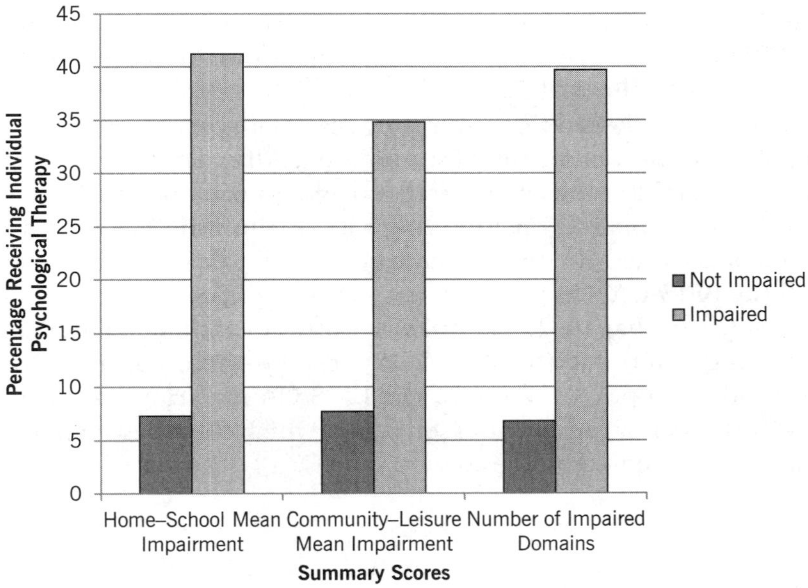

FIGURE 8.4. Percentage of children placing in the clinically impaired (≥ 93rd percentile) and not impaired ranges on each BFIS-CA summary score who had received individual psychological therapy. All comparisons are significant at $p < .001$.

sons, it was also clear that children who placed in the clinically impaired range on the three summary scores were five to seven times more likely to have received such counseling or therapy, as is evident in Figure 8.4. Results were essentially the same for those children who had and had not received family, group, or inpatient psychological treatment. And when comparing children in the clinically impaired range on the BFIS-CA summary scores, those in that range were five to ten times more likely to have received each of these various services. Thus, to the extent that the receipt of treatment can be taken as a marker for impairment in major domains of life activities, numerous lines of evidence here indicate that children receiving such treatments have significantly higher scores on the BFIS-CA and that those having clinically impaired BFIS-CA subscale scores are far more likely to have received such treatments.

Conclusion

The findings presented in this and the previous two chapters provide substantial evidence for the construct, criterion, and ecological validity of the BFIS-CA scores. Differing patterns of domain scores were evident across various neurological, developmental, learning, and psychiatric disorders (see Chapter 7). The scores were also significantly associated with various forms of psychiatric, psychological, and educational treatments in the sense that children receiving such treatment were significantly more likely to be impaired on all BFIS-CA scores than those not receiving that treatment. Moreover, those placing in the clinically impaired range on the BFIS-CA summary scores were significantly more likely to be receiving such services. It is also clear that BFIS-CA scores are related to impairment in major life activities in each of the five domains of the BDEFS-CA. Such findings make the BFIS-CA not only one of the most comprehensive parent rating scales of impairment in children currently available but also one of the best validated. All of these areas are clearly in need of more research, but what research exists supports the validity of the scale. Currently lacking is research on the sensitivity of the BFIS-CA scores to various treatments recommended for the management of the types of impairment documented with the BFIS-CA. Certainly the predecessor scale on which the BFIS-CA is based (the HSQ; see Chapter 2) did prove sensitive to various mental health interventions, implying that the BFIS-CA is likely to do the same. The available evidence concerning validity supports the use of the BFIS-CA in various clinical, scientific, educational, and other organizational settings in which the assessment of children's impairment in daily life is of interest.

CHAPTER 9

Scoring and Interpretation of the BFIS-CA Forms

The BFIS-CA can be used to evaluate parent ratings of the degree of impairment (functional ineffectiveness) that their children may be experiencing in 15 specific domains of major life activities in children ages 6–17 years. The scale can be completed quickly and inexpensively in a clinical practice, research setting, or educational or organizational setting, among others. The BFIS-CA is intended to be used by trained professionals in clinical, research, educational, mental health, or social service organizations who have sufficient educational background and experience in the evaluation of human psychological functioning and psychosocial impairment. Interpreting the BFIS-CA scales, scores, and profiles requires graduate training in a psychological, psychiatric, educational, social service, or medical specialty, including relevant graduate-level training and coursework in the administration and interpretation of psychological measures through an accredited college or university. Besides carefully reviewing and understanding this manual, examiners using the BFIS-CA should be familiar with the *Standards for Educational and Psychological Testing* of the American Psychological Association.

BFIS-CA Materials

The Appendix contains:

- The BFIS-CA Parent Rating Scale.
- A BFIS-CA Score Sheet to be used for all children.

- Four Impairment Profiles, one for each sex within each of two age groups (6–11 years, 12–17 years).
- The BFIS-CA Parent Interview.

The BFIS-CA Parent Rating Scale can be scored to obtain 18 primary scores: There is one score for each of the 15 specific primary domains being rated; two summary scores reflecting the two factors or dimensions of impairment represented by these 15 domains (Home–School mean impairment score, Community–Leisure mean impairment score); and a score for the number of impaired domains. An impaired domain is one on which the child places at or above approximately the 93rd percentile for all children in the sample. The beginning threshold and subsequent range of scores that make up this impairment zone in each domain used for making this determination are indicated on the Impairment Profiles in larger **boldface** type.

All of the 18 primary scores are converted to percentiles by comparing the child with other children of the same age and sex using the appropriate Impairment Profile form for that child's age and sex in the Appendix. Besides the 18 primary scores, 8 secondary impairment questions can be scored relative to the normative population. These deal with more specific questions having to do with (1) number of friends the child has, (2) number of community organizations in which he/she has participated in the past year, (3) number of sports in which he/she has participated in the past year, (4) his/her most recent grade point average, and whether or not he/she (5) has received a report from his/her teacher for behavior or school performance problems in the past school year, (6) has ever been retained in a grade, (7) has ever been suspended or expelled, and (8) has ever received special education services.

With the way the BFIS-CA Impairment Profiles are structured, an examiner can actually make two determinations of impairment for each of the 15 primary domain scores: impairment relative to the entire normative population (6–17 years) and impairment relative to that person's specific age grouping (6–11, 12–17) and sex. The percentiles shown in the top and bottom rows of the Impairment Profiles are associated with each of the raw scores for each age grouping and sex. But the **boldface** larger numbers in each row (for each score) indicate where the impairment range begins for each domain (and the span of scores upward that it comprises) relative *to the entire normative sample.* This allows the examiner to immediately see on the score sheet both (1) if the person being evaluated has a score at the 93rd percentile for his/her age group and sex (percentiles in the top and bottom rows) *and* (2) if that person also surpasses the 93rd to 95th percentile for the entire normative sample (a raw score in the **boldface** larger numbers). The reason that the 93rd–95th percentile range is specified rather than just the 93rd relates to the 0–9 scoring range used for any specific domain. For example, in the normative sample, a score of 5 may place a person at the 90th percentile, whereas the next higher score of 6 is equivalent to the 95th percentile. There is no raw score equivalent to the 93rd percentile exactly because there is no score between 5 and 6. Hence, the score selected to mark the threshold for determining impairment was the whole-number score within the range or closest to either the 93rd to 95th percentile for the entire normative sample.

Besides the BFIS-CA Parent Rating Scale, there is a follow-up Parent Interview provided in the Appendix for obtaining specific information from parents concerning any of their specific domain ratings that are found to fall in the impaired range. The Parent Interview is simply a form that shows the 15 specific domains of major life activity from the BFIS-CA with space underneath each domain to write clinical notes. For instance, imagine that a parent has provided ratings in the domains of school performance and homework that place their child above the 93rd percentile for the entire normative sample. Before accepting this as prima facie evidence of impairment in those domains, the clinician needs to determine more about the veracity of the rating. On what evidence was it based?

If the parent indicated that the child had been retained in a grade, had trouble completing the work during the preceding school year, perhaps was referred for evaluation for special education because of his/her learning or behavior problems, then this event would signal relatively credible evidence of impairment in the school performance and doing school homework domains. That would be especially compelling evidence if the individual's school records further corroborated such claims.

Now consider the possibility that during this interview, the parent reports that his/her rating of the child's school performance problems was based on the fact that his/her child obtained grades of B in science or social studies when the parent felt the child was capable of obtaining an A in those classes. By no stretch of the imagination would this report be considered as indicating "impairment." Relative to the average person or typical child, this is not credible evidence of having significant difficulty functioning effectively in a major life activity. A grade of B in these classes is not functional ineffectiveness relative to the norm of the population, no matter how important the issue may seem to the parent at the time.

Notice here that by itself, the BFIS-CA is not the sole determinant of degree of actual impairment. It is to serve as one source (albeit an important one) of information in making such a determination. However, that source must always be triangulated against other sources in order for the clinician to make a reasonable determination or judgment of impairment (see Chapter 1). Those other sources, as noted in Chapter 1, include (1) the reports of the other parent and of teachers who know this child well, (2) the child's history given by the parent upon subsequent interviewing, and (3) the archival records that may be available for a specific domain, for example, school and medical records, known as the "paper trail" of impairment. Comparison among at least three of these sources should suffice to give the clinician reasonable information on which to make a determination of actual impairment in any particular domain.

For your convenience, the scale, scoring sheets (Impairment Profiles), and interview form may be photocopied by the purchaser of this manual for use in clinical practice or research projects under the limited reproduction license granted by the publisher (see front matter of the book for this limited permission).

Appropriate Purposes and Populations for the BFIS-CA

The BFIS-CA is not intended to replicate or replace other medical, psychological, and psychiatric methods of evaluation and diagnosis in the determination of psychosocial impairment. It provides information that may be important for the ultimate determination of impairment, but it should never serve as the sole source for such a determination. The BFIS-CA is intended to be used for the evaluation of individuals between 6 and 17 years of age, both boys and girls. Typically these will be children or adolescents who reside in the United States, as this country is the source for the normative sample. Use of the BFIS-CA with populations, countries, cultures, or ethnic groups outside of the United States may be inappropriate to the extent that such groups may vary considerably from the normative reference sample described in this manual.

Administration

The BFIS-CA should be given directly to the parent or guardian being asked to complete the rating, along with a clear explanation of the purpose for which the rating is being obtained. The examiner should also clearly explain the instructions for completing the rating scale (see the BFIS-CA Parent Rating Scale in the Appendix), and the parent should have the opportunity to raise concerns or questions about the scale. For greater efficiency in the evaluation process, the BFIS-CA may be mailed out to individuals to complete before the day of the intended evaluation. This mailing should include a cover letter that explains how the scale will be used and the instructions for its completion. This letter should also give the parent a means of contacting the examiner concerning any concerns or questions he/she might have about the scale or its intended purpose.

The BFIS-CA takes an average of 5–7 minutes to complete by the average parent in the general population. If the parent is completing the form in person, the examiner should review the scale for any missed items, then encourage the rater to complete those items, assuming that the item was simply missed and that the rater did not intend to respond "Does not apply" (indicated by a circle around the number 99 on the scale). The failure to complete more than one or two domains on the scale is likely to invalidate the resulting scores and make the use of the normative tables on the Impairment Profiles inappropriate. If the scale has been returned by mail and there is no further opportunity to complete any missed items, these items should be answered with a 0 (*Not at all*) to create a conservative bias to the scores such that the determination of impairment is not unduly exaggerated. Even then, the failure to complete more than two of the domains on any version of the scale should be considered sufficient cause to invalidate the scale. Again, this rule does not apply to specific domains that were answered with circles around the number 99 (*Does not apply*). Those items were in fact addressed by the respondent; they simply do not apply to this child's life at this time.

Scoring the BFIS-CA

Scoring the BFIS-CA Parent Rating Scale is actually very easy. Follow these procedures:

- Using the Score Sheet, transfer all of the raw scores for the 15 primary domains circled by the parent on the Parent Rating Scale onto this Score Sheet.

- For any domain on this Score Sheet with an [HS] beside it, place that raw score in Column 1, labeled "Home–School [HS] Raw Scores."
- For any domain with a [CL] beside it on this Score Sheet, place that raw score in Column 2, labeled "Community [CL] Raw Scores," for the Community–Leisure domains. Notice that some cells or boxes of the Score Sheet are blacked out to assist you in putting the scores in the correct cell or box.
- For any domain that the parent rated as 99, "Does not apply," on the Parent Rating Scale, leave that row blank on the Score Sheet or just draw an X through it.

• Look at each raw score that you entered on the Score Sheet. If that score is equal to or greater than the impairment threshold associated with that specific domain, then place a line underneath it or a circle around this number to highlight it. The impairment threshold for each specific domain score is in parentheses underneath the name of that domain (e.g., "1. With mother" has a threshold ≥ 6).

• Now compute the Home–School mean impairment score. Do this by:

- Adding together all of the raw scores in the Home–School [HS] column.
- Enter this sum in the box on line 16. There are nine domains that make up this score and that have [HS] after the domain name.
- Count the number of domain scores you used to compute that sum in the Home–School [HS] column. This is simply the number of specific-domain raw scores you entered in this column. You added these together to get the sum for the box on line 16. Enter this count in the box on line 17.
- Then divide the sum in the box on line 16 by the number you entered in the box on line 17. You are just dividing the sum of the raw scores in column 1 by the number of raw scores used to compute that sum. You have now computed the Home–School mean impairment score. Place this mean impairment score in the box on line 18.

• Now do the same thing to get the Community–Leisure mean impairment score.

- Add together all of the raw scores in the Community [CL] column (#2).
- Enter this sum in the box on line 19. Six domains make up this sum and have [CL] after the domain name.
- Count the number of domain scores you used to compute that sum in the Community [CL] column. This is simply the number of specific-domain raw scores you entered in this column. You added these together to get the sum for the box on line 19. Enter this count in the box on line 20.
- Then divide the sum in the box on line 19 by the number you entered in the box on line 20. You are just dividing the sum of the raw scores in column 2 by the number of raw scores used to compute that sum. You have now computed the Community–Leisure mean impairment score. Place this mean impairment score in the box on line 21.

• Next, compute the number of impaired domains score. Do this by simply counting the number of raw scores that you placed an underline beneath or a circle around in both columns 1 (Home–School) and 2 (Community–Leisure). Enter this number on line 21 in column 1. This is simply a count of the number of raw scores that met or exceeded the impairment thresholds for the specific domains. Recall that the impairment threshold for each domain is the score that meets or exceeds the 93rd–95th percentile for the entire normative sample of children ages 6–17 years.

• You can now determine the percentiles that go with each of the 15 specific-domain scores, the Home–School mean impairment score, the Community–Leisure mean impairment score, and the number of impaired domains score. To do this,

- Select the Impairment Profile score sheet for that child's sex and age group (6–11 or 12–17).
- Transfer the raw scores from each specific domain from the Score Sheet onto the Impairment Profile. Transfer only the scores circled 0–9 on the Parent Rating Scale to their respective corresponding rows on the Profile. Do this by circling the raw score in that row that matches the rating provided by that parent for that specific domain on his/her rating scale. For any domain that the parent rated as 99, or "Does not apply," on the rating scale, leave that row blank on the Impairment Profile.
- In the row on the Impairment Profile near the bottom labeled "Home–School Mean Impairment Score," find that number that most closely matches the score you just computed for the box on line 18 and circle it. If the score you calculated has two decimal places, round up the second one (hundredth place) to the next highest tenth if it is a 6 or higher. Round it down if that number is a 5 or lower. For instance, a score of 4.27 would be rounded up to 4.3, and a score of 4.25 would be rounded down to 4.2.
- In the row on the Impairment Profile near the bottom labeled "Community–Leisure Mean Impairment Score," find that number that most closely matches the score you just computed in the box on line 21 of the Score Sheet and circle it. Again, if the score you calculated has two decimal places, round up the second one (hundredth place) to the next highest tenth if it is a 6 or higher. Round it down if that number is a 5 or lower. For instance, a score of 4.27 would be rounded up to 4.3, and a score of 4.25 would be rounded down to 4.2.
- Next, in the row labeled "Number of Impaired Domains Score" toward the bottom of the Impairment Profile, circle the number that matches the score you placed in the box on line 22 of the Score Sheet.

• You are now finished scoring the BFIS-CA Impairment Profile. You should have a circled answer in the rows beside each specific domain unless it was answered 99, "Does not apply," in which case you left that row blank. You should have a circled answer beside the two rows marked Home–School Mean Impairment Score and Community–Leisure Mean Impairment Score. Finally, you should have a circled answer next to the Number of Impaired Domains score.

• Now you are ready to determine the percentiles that correspond to each of the scores you have circled on the Impairment Profile. This will tell you how deviant (statistically abnormal or rare) the parent's answers are on the BFIS-CA Parent Rating Scale. To do this, simply look at either the top, or first, row in the table on the Impairment Profile or at the bottom, or last, row. Each of these rows contains the word **Percentiles** in boldface type. To the right of this word, the columns below each score you circled, are the percentiles for that age group and sex from the normative sample that correspond to each of the raw scores you circled on this profile.

- Some percentiles are shown as ranges (i.e., 1–50, 51–75, 76–84) because they are of little or no clinical significance given that they fall in the normal range. Also, the vast majority of children in the sample had such low scores. Indeed, up to 75% or more of the parents in the normative sample rated these domains as having scores of 0, 1, or 2 in most domains.
- Specific percentiles are given starting with the 85th percentile because percentiles at this high range begin to become clinically informative. They mean that the individual is in the top 15% of the population given his/her score.
- Look at each raw score you circled, then look up or down that column at the first or last row of the table to find the corresponding percentile for that raw score. This is the person's percentile in the normative sample for his/her sex and age group for that answer. The higher the percentile, the more deviant the score is relative to the normative sample (general population). Because the examiner is primarily interested in how deviant a score is, especially at the upper percentiles, a more precise percentile score is provided for scores at the 85th–99th+ percentiles. You have now determined the percentile for the child's scores.

• To create a visual profile of the child's total range of impairments (pervasiveness), draw straight lines on the form connecting the circles, starting from the first domain row (Interactions with mother) and continuing downward to the last circle. Do not connect the circles where there is a blank row or gap between them. Draw lines to connect only circles that are adjacent to each other. You have now created a visual profile of the child's impairments.

• Finally, you can write each of the percentile scores from this Impairment Profile back on the Score Sheet. Enter them in Column 3. These are the percentile scores or percentile ranges that correspond to each of the scores that you entered or computed on that Score Sheet for this child. You now have two ways to review the child's percentile scores: (1) using Column 3 of the Score Sheet and (2) looking at the child's Impairment Profile (top or bottom rows marked **Percentiles**). The Impairment Profile can be helpful in explaining these results to the parent or other interested party because it visually demonstrates the child's position (degree of impairment) relative to his/her age group and sex.

Remember that you are determining the child's deviance in two ways. First, you can see his/her deviance *relative to his/her age group and sex* by just looking at the percentiles that correspond to the raw answers you circled on this Impairment Profile. Second, you can determine his/her deviance *relative to the entire normative sample* (ages 6–17) by seeing whether the answer that you circled is in large **boldface** type. If it is, then that score met or exceeded the impairment threshold for that domain, which is at or above the 93rd–95th percentile for the population of 6- to 17-year-olds. This holds regardless of what percentile it represents for that specific age group and sex. In short, you can interpret degree of "impairment" both ways:

relative to the age group and sex and relative to the average person in the entire 6- to 17-year-old population.

Scoring the Secondary Impairment Questions

Besides the 18 primary scores you computed (15 domain ratings and 3 summary scores) from the first part of the BFIS-CA Parent Rating Scale, there are 8 additional and secondary impairment questions in the second part of the scale. Examiners have the option of converting the answers to these questions to their percentages in the population for that child's age and sex on the same Impairment Profile they used above for the child's 18 primary BFIS-CA scores. This might be done to obtain additional information about the extent of psychosocial impairment in that child. These secondary questions involve (1) the number of friends a child has, (2) the number of organized community activities the child participated in in the previous year, (3) the number of organized sports he/she participated in apart from physical education (gym) classes at school, (4) the child's grade point average on his/her last report card, (5) whether or not the parent had received a teacher's report in the most recent school year that the child had trouble with behavior or work performance, (6) whether the child had ever been retained a grade in school, (7) whether the child had ever been suspended or expelled from school, and (8) whether the child had received special education services. Next to each question in the second part of the Impairment Profile are the possible answers, along with the percentiles from the normative sample that correspond to those answers. Examiners may find that the raw answers to these questions and the population percentages associated with them provide further evidence of impairment in that child relative to these domains. To score these questions, simply transfer the answer to each question on the rating scale to the child's Impairment Profile. Do this by circling the raw score answer under that topic on the second part of the Profile. Look above each possible raw score answer in the table under each of these items and you will see either the percentile *or* the percentage in the normative sample that it corresponds to for that child's age group (6–11, 12–17) and sex. Percentiles are provided for the answers to the first three questions that had numerical answers, such as the number of friends, clubs, and sports for that child. But for the remaining questions that had categorical answers (e.g., Was the child retained in a grade?), the tables below each of those questions just indicate the percentage of the normative sample that gave that answer.

Scoring Example

The patient in this example is a 15-year-old male. The parent has completed the BFIS-CA Parent Rating Scale, giving the following raw scores:

With mother	6
With father	99
School performance	8

With siblings	6
Playing in neighborhood	2
Community activities	1
Visiting others	1
Playing at school	2
Managing money	3
Self-care	3
Doing chores	7
School homework	8
Following rules	7
With other adults	2
Playing sports	2

You would then transfer these numbers onto a photocopy of the Score Sheet, like this:

BFIS-CA Score Sheet

Child's name: ____________________ Date: __________

Sex: (Circle one) Male Female Age: __________

BFIS-CA Domain:	1. Home–School [HS] Raw Scores	2. Community [CL] Raw Scores	3. Percentile (from Profile)
1. With mother [HS] (underline score if ≥ 6)	6		95
2. With father [HS] (underline score if ≥ 6)	X		X
3. School performance [HS] (underline score if ≥ 7)	8		95
4. With siblings [HS] (underline score if ≥ 7)	7		94
5. Playing in neighborhood [CL] (underline score if ≥ 6)		2	76–84
6. Community activities [CL] (underline score if ≥ 5)		1	51–75
7. Visiting others [CL] (underline score if ≥ 5)		1	76–84
8. Playing at school [CL] (underline score if ≥ 6)		2	76–84
9. Managing money [HS] (underline score if ≥ 6)	3		76–84
10. Self-care [HS] (underline score if ≥ 5)	3		87
11. Doing chores [HS] (underline score if ≥ 7)	7		92
12. School homework [HS] (underline score if ≥ 7)	8		94
13. Following rules [HS] (underline score if ≥ 7)	7		95
14. With other adults [CL] (underline score if ≥ 5)		2	76–84
15. Playing sports [CL] (underline score if ≥ 5)		2	76–84
16. Sum of Home–School [HS] column scores	48		

17. Number of domain scores used in [HS] sum	8		
18. Home–School mean impairment score (divide #16 by #17)	6.00		94
19. Sum of [CL] column scores		10	
20. Number of domain scores used in [CL] sum		6	
21. Community–Leisure mean impairment score (divide #19 by #20)		1.66	76–84
22. Number of impaired domains (count the number of scores underlined in both the [HS] column and the [CL] column)	6		92

After computing the Home–School mean impairment score, the Community–Leisure impairment score, and the number of impaired domains score, as instructed earlier, you can now transfer all 18 scores over to a photocopy of the Impairment Profile for a Male, Ages 12–17 years, in the Appendix. You would do this by placing a circle around the number in the row next to each of these domains. For instance, in the row marked "With mother," you would circle the number "3." You would not circle any number in the row marked "With father" because this domain did not apply to this teenager according to his mother (i.e., his father no longer has any contact with this teen or is unknown). You can now look at the top or bottom row of the Impairment Profile and see the percentile that corresponds to each of the raw scores that you circle in the rows for each of these 15 specific domains. For instance, notice that for this teenager the score of "3" for the domain of "Self-care" corresponds to the 87th percentile. It is at the higher end of the normal range. However, notice that the score of "8" for the "School performance" domain corresponds to the 95th percentile for this teen's age group and sex. This is a clinically deviant or significant score. Following this procedure, you can obtain a percentile score for each of the teen's 14 specific domain scores that the parent answered (and that were applicable). As a general rule, scores below the 84th percentile should be viewed as *normal, typical,* or *unimpaired.* Those in the 85th–92nd percentiles can be considered *borderline* or of marginal clinical significance. Those between the 93rd and 95th can be considered *mildly impaired,* those between the 95th and 98th percentile can be considered *moderately impaired,* and those at the 99th percentile are considered *severely impaired.* You can now determine the percentile scores (or ranges) for all 18 of the BFIS-CA primary scores and write them back onto the Score Sheet in column 3, if you wish. I have done this in the previous example.

What about those eight secondary impairment questions from the second section of the rating scale? This parent answered them as follows:

Number of friends	6
Number of Clubs or Community Organizations	2
Number of Organized Sports	3
Estimated Grade Point Average	D
Teacher Reported a Behavioral or Learning Problem in the Past School Year	YES

Retained in Grade—Ever	YES
Suspended or Expelled	NO
Ever Received Special Education Services	NO

Look at the second part of the Impairment Profile for this teen. You see tables underneath each of these item topics. The first three questions have percentiles associated with the numbers that were given by the normative sample. In contrast to the first part of the Impairment Profile, on which higher scores for the 15 specific domains indicate higher percentiles and hence abnormality, for these three questions lower scores given by the parent mean a lower percentile or abnormality (impairment). For the number of friends, you can see that having six friends puts this teen at the 60th percentile for the population; this is a quite normal score. Being in two community organizations puts him at the 70th percentile. Again, this is a normal score. This teen participated in three sports last year, which corresponds to the 95th percentile. This is a high but excellent score because higher percentiles in this case are fine.

The next five questions answered by the mother for this teen are categorical in nature, so percentiles are not reported for these answers. Instead, the tables show the *percentage* of the normative sample that gave this answer. The grade point average for this teen was said to have been a D, which just 4% of the population reported. This is a quite abnormal score. The answer of "Yes," that the teacher did give the parent a report of a problem with performing school work last year, was seen in just 32% of the population for this teen's age group and sex; again, this is in the minority. The fact that this teen has been retained in a grade corresponds to just 8% of all teens in this age group and sex. And the fact that this teen was never suspended or expelled places him in with the majority of teens (86%). Just 14% of teens have been suspended or expelled based on the normative sample. Finally, the fact that the teen has not received special education services places him with the majority of teens (86%). The examiner can now write up a report describing these results and using the various percentiles and percentages for these impairment ratings for this teen. Doing this can paint a very detailed portrait of the teen's adjustment. In general, situations at home and involving work (home chores and homework, schoolwork, etc.) are quite problematic for this teen, as are interactions with his mother or siblings. But interactions in the community and participation in other leisure activities appear to be reasonable or normal.

Using the BFIS-CA to Evaluate Response to Treatment

The BFIS-CA can be a valuable tool in evaluating a child's or adolescent's response to treatment, such as rehabilitation of medical disorders, cognitive training as part of neuro-rehabilitation interventions, cognitive-behavioral treatment of children with mental disorders, or medication treatments. Several methods exist for determining how much change should be considered as a positive (or negative) response to treatment. The choice is often arbitrary, such as a change of 20, 30, or 40% from the baseline score. There are statistical approaches to doing so that are better for this purpose. They are better because, unlike such arbitrarily defined thresholds for change, these statistical approaches take into consideration the test–retest reliability of the measure and the variation in change scores in the samples (or general population). One method commonly used for making this determination is the reliable change index (RCI) developed initially by Jacobson and Truax (1991; Jacobson, Roberts, Berns, & McGlinchey, 1999). This approach ensures that the degree of change exceeds that which may result merely from measurement error or unreliability. By calculating the RCI, one can determine whether the degree of change in a score is likely or unlikely to be due to chance or unreliability. For instance, that degree of change is large enough that it would be found by chance just 5% or less of the time, and so it is considered reliable. In other words, the examiner can have confidence that such a change score is not due to unreliability or typical variation within a sample.

An RCI is calculated as $X_1 - X_2/S_{diff}$, where X_1 is the individual's pretest score and X_2 is his/her posttest score. The difference between the two is then divided by the standard error of the difference scores (S_{diff}). S_{diff} can be obtained directly from our results by using this formula and the means and standard deviations for each score in Table 4.1. To do so one needs to also have available the test–retest reliability correlations, as reported in Chapter 6. To save you time, however, the RCI scores needed to be significant have been computed for you and appear in Table 9.1. This table indicates the difference between the pretest and posttest mean scores (S_{diff}) that must be attained for that difference to be considered reliable, which is to say that such a difference would be likely to occur 5% or less of the time by chance alone.

The values for each subscale of the BFIS-CA are shown in Table 9.1 for each age group and sex. To use them, simply take the posttest score of a patient or participant and subtract it from his/her pretest score. Then look in Table 9.1 under the appropriate column for the individual's age group. Look at the line or row that corresponds to the domain or summary score in which you are interested. If the difference in the pre- to posttest scores is equal to or greater than the number shown in this cell of Table 9.1 for that age group and sex, then the change in pre- to posttest scores can be considered to be reliable, or outside the range of error of the measure. Probably the best scores to use in these cases would be the three BFIS-CA summary scores: the Home–School mean impairment score, the Community–Leisure mean impairment score, and the number of impaired domains score. Those scores have higher test–retest reliability correlations than do many of the individual domain ratings and so can be considered more reliable. But the individual domain scores of the BFIS-CA can also be examined for reliable change, if that is of interest.

A change in scores may be reliable, but that does not necessarily make it clinically significant or meaningful. Clinical significance can be determined by assessing whether the person now falls within the normal range following the intervention. That is, does the person's score after treatment allow one to conclude that it likely came from the normal range of scores? This step is often referred to as determining normalization or recovery. For this determination, Jacobson and Truax (1991) recommended that the posttest score now place at or below +2 *SD* of the mean, or approximately the 98th percentile, for the normal population. This is a fairly generous interpretation of normalization. Others might recommend placing below +1.5

SD of the normal mean, or approximately the 93rd percentile, as that is a threshold often used to determine whether someone is clinically impaired. These two percentile demarcations for the normative sample for each age group and sex are provided in Table 9.2. If a child, following treatment, (1) shows a change from pretest score to posttest score that is at least at or above the applicable figure in Table 9.1 (it is a reliable change) and (2) has a final posttest score below the 93rd or 98th percentiles for the normative sample in Table 9.2 (depending on how lenient the definition of recovery is chosen to be), one could conclude that the treatment had resulted not only in reliable change but also in recovery or normalization.

As an example, consider a female child with ADHD or even a closed head injury who is 10 years of age and manifesting significant impairment in her daily life as reflected in a Home–School mean impairment score from the BFIS-CA of 7.2. According to the table of norms in the Appendix for this sex (female) and age group (6–11 years), this parent rating for this child is at the 99th percentile of the population. Following the introduction of treatment for a month with an ADHD medication, the parent completes the BFIS-CA again. The child now has a Home–School mean impairment score of 3.2. According to the norms in that same table in the Appendix, the child now falls at the 88th percentile. Is this degree of change

TABLE 9.1. Differences between Pre- and Posttest Scores from the BFIS-CA Required to Be Considered Reliable Using the RCI

	Sex and age group			
	Males		Females	
Subscale	6–11 years	12–17 years	6–11 years	12–17 years
With mother	1.23	1.20	1.41	1.36
With father	1.45	1.76	1.42	1.68
School performance	1.45	1.71	1.30	1.32
With siblings	1.89	1.85	1.85	1.90
Playing in neighborhood	1.40	1.46	1.34	1.31
Community activities	1.41	1.64	1.29	1.37
Visiting others	1.73	1.77	1.61	1.46
Playing at school	0.97	0.98	0.86	0.78
Managing money	1.84	1.93	1.62	1.78
Self-care	1.33	1.41	1.17	1.13
Doing chores	1.85	2.09	1.59	1.83
School homework	1.74	2.09	1.52	1.63
Following rules	1.44	1.60	1.33	1.36
With other adults	1.18	1.18	1.09	0.97
Playing sports	1.10	1.15	0.85	0.98
Home–School mean impairment score	0.98	1.11	0.92	0.93
Community–Leisure mean impairment score	1.06	1.09	0.94	0.88
Number of impaired domains	1.27	1.41	1.19	1.09

Note. "Reliable" = ocurring 5% or less of the time by chance.

from the medication treatment reliable? That is, is it likely to fall outside the realm of measurement error or unreliability? To find out, compute the degree of change as follows: pretest score (7.2) minus posttest score (3.2) = 4.0 points. Looking at Table 9.1 for females who are 6–11 years old, it can be seen that a change of 0.93 points or greater on the mean impairment score is needed to be considered reliable. The patient's change of 4.0 points from pre- to posttesting clearly exceeds that number and thus can be considered reliable. Thus the clinician can feel confident that the improvement in mean or average impairment is not simply due to measurement error or unreliability and is likely to be a consequence of the treatment. The patient could be considered a treatment responder in this instance (assuming that side effects of the medication are not so annoying as to warrant treatment discontinuation).

Next we wish to know whether the child has been normalized by or has recovered due to the treatment—that is, whether the intervention has brought her to within the normal range. Examine Table 9.2 to see the threshold for the 98th per-

TABLE 9.2. Thresholds for Determining Normalization or Recovery at Posttesting after Treatment

	Sex and age group							
	Males				Females			
	6–11 years		12–17 years		6–11 years		12–17 years	
Subscale	93rd	98th	93rd	98th	93rd	98th	93rd	98th
With mother	5	7	6	8	5	7	6	7
With father	5	7	6	8	5	7	6	8
School performance	6	8	7	8	5	8	6	8
With siblings	6	8	6	8	5	8	6	8
Playing in neighborhood	5	7	5	7	4	7	5	7
Community activities	4	6	5	7	4	6	4	6
Visiting others	4	6	4	6	4	7	4	6
Playing at school	5	7	5	7	4	7	4	6
Managing money	5	7	5	7	5	7	5	8
Self-care	5	7	5	7	4	6	4	7
Doing chores	6	8	7	8	5	7	6	8
School homework	6	8	8	9	5	8	6	8
Following rules	6	8	7	8	5	7	5	7
With other adults	5	7	5	7	4	7	4	6
Playing sports	5	7	5	7	4	6	4	7
Home–School mean impairment	5.0	6.4	5.8	7.4	4.3	7.0	4.7	6.7
Community–Leisure mean impairment	5.2	6.5	4.8	6.8	3.8	6.6	4.0	5.9
Number of domains impaired	6	9	6	11	3	10	4	9

Note. Thresholds are provided for the 93rd and 98th percentiles of the normative sample for each age group for BFIS-CA scores.

centile for females 6–11 years of age (it is 7.0). The patient's posttest score of 3.2 is well below this figure and so could be considered to fall within the broadly defined normal range. As noted earlier, some clinicians and researchers believe that this is too generous a definition of normalcy for determining recovery. Using the criterion of the 93rd percentile above the normal mean may be preferred. In that case, the appropriate column of Table 9.2 shows that this threshold is 4.3. The patient's posttest score of 3.2 is also below this level. By this more conservative definition of normalization, the patient still can be considered to fall within the broadly defined normal range for her age group. This patient therefore may be considered "recovered" or "normalized" by her treatment. In fact, according to the percentiles on the Impairment Profile for girls of this age group, this child's score is at the 88th percentile. By this empirical approach to defining a treatment responder and normalization, the treatment has been successful.

Keep in mind that medications may provide only symptomatic relief in such cases and only when the medication is taken at therapeutic levels. The resulting reliable change (positive response) and normalization therefore refer only to a temporary effect of the medication while in use and not to a permanent alteration of the patient's functioning in the absence of medication management.

Evaluating Change in Impairment Due to Injury

One can use this method for evaluating whether or not an individual has experienced a significant deterioration in his/her adaptive functioning following some form of injury, whether the origin is a traumatic, infectious, cancerous, or vascular event or other causal factor (such as secondary to open heart surgery, cancer treatments such as radiation or chemotherapy, near drowning, or any other hypoxic episode). Here one is asking the question, Has a reliable and significant increase in impairment occurred in this patient? The RCI figures in Table 9.1 can be used as a crude guideline to see whether the deterioration in functioning is reliable (probably outside the realm of measurement error). The child's parent can complete the BFIS-CA on how he/she believes the child is functioning now. He/she can then complete a second version with reference to how well he/she believes the child was functioning prior to the event. This assumes, naturally, that the parent's memory for premorbid functioning is credible. To increase one's clinical confidence in the matter, have someone else who knows the child well also complete the BFIS-CA form concerning the child's premorbid status and again for his/her current postmorbid functioning. This could be the other parent. Then the clinician can compare the child's pre- and postmorbid mean impairment scores from both reports.

Once again, to get the RCI, subtract the postmorbid from the premorbid score, which in this case will be negative. Look at Table 9.1 for the particular mean impairment score and for the patient's age group and sex. If the change in scores is equal to or greater than this number, the patient's deterioration in functioning can be considered to be reliable—that is, the change is probably outside the realm of measurement error or unreliability. The thresholds provided in Table 9.2 for age group and BFIS-CA score can now be used to determine whether this child's scores places him or her outside of the normal range using both the 93rd and 98th percentiles.

That is to say, the child's postmorbid score is now more likely to have been drawn from a distribution of individuals who are impaired than to have been drawn from the general population.

Interpreting the BFIS-CA

Interpretation of the results of the BFIS-CA begins with a competent professional who understands the nature of the construct of psychosocial impairment and of the disorders that may be contributing to it. Chapter 1 can serve as an introduction to the topic of psychosocial impairment, but it is not a substitute for a more thorough grounding in the larger literature on impairment determination (see Goldstein & Naglieri, 2009, for a more thorough discussion of impairment and its assessment). The examiner must have not only a thorough understanding of the introductory chapter of this manual but also a familiarity with the larger scientific and clinical literature on the topic, especially if this is a disability, social security, or special education determination. In brief, the BFIS-CA is intended to measure a child's degree of parent-reported impairment in major domains of daily life activities. Interpretation of the rating scale can be based on the following approaches to understanding the meaning of the scores:

Face Validity

This approach to interpretation is aided by a complete familiarity with the domains contained on the scale. High scores on each domain (typically answers indicating the moderate or severely impaired range) may signal an abnormality in this domain in daily life activities; the domain can be considered to be impaired. One initial means of interpreting each scale in a clinical report is on the basis of the face validity of that domain raw score—Where does it place in the 0–9, Not Impaired to Severely Impaired, range? It is not an impossible occurrence for a single scale to be clinically elevated, but such an occurrence would be cause for further exploration of the reason for such an unusual event. Also in view of the interrelatedness of the scales, computing of interscale differences for additional clinical meaning of disparities across the domain scores is not encouraged, as it has largely not been explored in any research to date. This does not mean, however, that relative fluctuations across the domains will not be evident—only that interpreting the meaning of large disparities between individual domain ratings has little empirical basis at this time. Just interpreting the meaning of each domain separately is likely to be sufficient to convey the meaning of the BFIS-CA scores rather than trying to gain more information from the scale than current research allows. One can also interpret the Home–School mean impairment score as reflecting that range of specific domains (work related) and the Community–Leisure mean impairment score as reflecting its own range of six specific domains (and leisure activities). The score for the number of impaired domains is interpreted as reflecting the pervasiveness of the child's impairment. Given that the scales are moderately to highly intercorrelated, it is quite likely that an individual will produce deviant scores in more than just one or two domains of the BFIS-CA.

Normative Comparison (Percentile Interpretation)

Next, interpretation of each domain and summary score can be done by comparing the individual's scores to that of the normative population using the Impairment Profiles and the equivalent percentiles. This represents the person's relative position in comparison with the general population of children of his/her age and sex. Using the percentile score, the child or teen is said to place at or above this percentage of individuals in the general population of his/her age group and sex in his/her degree of parent-rated impairment in daily life activities. The examiner can actually select the domains on which the respondent has answered with a response that occurs in **boldface** type on the Impairment Profile and directly interpret this score as an abnormality based on the parent's report relative to all children between 6 and 17 years. Or, to be even more accurate, the examiner can inspect the specific percentile provided in the top or bottom row of the Impairment Profile for this child's age and sex and use those as a guide to judging impairment.

Risk Analysis (Using the Evidence on Criterion Validity)

As discussed in Chapter 6, high scores on the BFIS-CA subscales were associated with a variety of difficulties in various domains of major life activities. Therefore, the higher the scores observed on the BFIS-CA, the more likely is the participant to be at risk for problems in these same domains of life activities. These risks should be noted in the clinical interpretation of the larger meaning of the BFIS-CA scores beyond their simply reflecting the two dimensions of impairment for which two of the summary scores are named. Difficulties can be expected for individuals having high scores on the scale in social, academic (or other work-related), community, or other domains. The scores deserve the notice of the examiner and probably should be conveyed to the participant where appropriate and applicable. Such information can also be linked to what is already known about the child or teen from the larger evaluation in which the BFIS-CA serves as simply one component when used for a clinical evaluation of a patient. The examiner will have information on the history of the child or teen with regard to these and other major domains of life activity that can serve to place the findings from the BFIS-CA in this larger context. Risk analysis concerning impairments can be further aided by using the BDEFS-CA (Barkley, 2012), on which national norms are available for parent ratings of potential problems with self-regulation in five dimensions of EF deficits in daily life activities: Self-Management to Time, Self-Organization/Problem Solving, Self-Discipline, Self-Motivation, and Self-Regulation of Emotion.

Pre- to Postinjury Status

As already noted, another approach to interpreting the BFIS-CA exists when the scale has been used to assess possible changes in an individual secondary to a neurological injury or in conjunction with the onset of an acute adverse psychiatric or psychological event. The BFIS-CA can be given twice to the parent of a child or adolescent, with instructions to complete one version for preinjury and the other for postinjury status. These comparisons can be interpreted with appropriate caution for the information they may provide on the impact of the event on impairment in that child's or teen's daily life activities. The information on reliable change and normalization provided in Tables 9.1 and 9.2, respectively, can assist with this interpretation, as discussed before.

Pre- to Posttreatment Change

As noted, the BFIS-CA can also be used to evaluate possible response to intervention by having a parent complete the scale before and after an intervention has been implemented with their child or teen. Guidelines were given earlier and in Tables 9.1 and 9.2 on how to interpret a change in scores as reflecting reliable change and recovery or normalization. This information can be included in the interpretation of the meaning of the BFIS-CA scores so obtained.

Conclusion

The BFIS-CA provides a clinically informative means of evaluating parent-rated psychosocial impairment in 15 major domains of daily life activities in children and teenagers ages 6–17 years. It constitutes one of the most comprehensive parent rating scales of impairment yet developed and normed on a general population of children 6–17 years of age. Further research on and clinical experience with the BFIS-CA is strongly encouraged. Meanwhile, substantial evidence to date shows the BFIS-CA to be reasonably reliable, valid, and useful in assessing multiple dimensions of psychosocial impairment in daily life activities in children and adolescents. It does so by a means that is efficient and cost-effective and also yields valuable information on the potential risks that such impairment(s) may contain in a variety of domains of major life activities. The significance of the BFIS-CA scores is documented in its association with impairment in a variety of domains of children's major life activities and in conjunction with various psychiatric, neurological, and learning disorders. The scale can be used in clinical practice, research, and educational or organizational settings or in other such venues in which the evaluation of potential impairments in a child's or teen's daily life activities is of interest. It can also serve as a basis for evaluating change in psychosocial impairment, whether as a consequence of treatment or secondary to the occurrence of various neurological and psychiatric disorders or even transient psychological events believed to potentially adversely affect an individual's performance of daily life activities. We hope you find the BFIS-CA to be useful in your evaluation of psychosocial impairment in children and adolescents.

APPENDIX

BFIS-CA Forms, Score Sheet, and Impairment Profiles

BFIS-CA Parent Rating Scale 139

BFIS-CA Parent Interview 142

BFIS-CA Score Sheet 145

BFIS-CA Impairment Profile (Ages 6–11, Males Only) 146

BFIS-CA Impairment Profile (Ages 12–17, Males Only) 148

BFIS-CA Impairment Profile (Ages 6–11, Females Only) 150

BFIS-CA Impairment Profile (Ages 12–17, Females Only) 152

BFIS-CA Parent Rating Scale

Child's name: ______________________________ Date: ____________

Sex: (Circle one) Male Female Age: ____________

Name of person completing this form: ______________________________

Relationship to this child: Mother Father Stepmother Stepfather Other (specify): ____________

Part I—Instructions

How much difficulty does your child have functioning effectively in each of these major life activities compared with other children of the same age? That is, to what degree is he/she impaired in each of these life domains? Please circle the number next to each item that best describes his/her degree of difficulty in functioning in that domain **DURING THE PAST 6 MONTHS**. If that situation does not apply to your child (for instance, if he/she has no siblings), please circle the 99 in the last column (under "Does not apply"). If your child is currently taking medication for any psychiatric or psychological disorder, please rate his/her functioning based on how he/she functions while **OFF** of his/her medication.

Major Life Activities	Not at all	Somewhat		Mild		Moderate			Severe		Does not apply
1. In his/her interactions with his/her mother	0	1	2	3	4	5	6	7	8	9	99
2. In his/her interactions with his/her father	0	1	2	3	4	5	6	7	8	9	99
3. In his/her school performance	0	1	2	3	4	5	6	7	8	9	99
4. In his/her social interactions with brothers or sisters	0	1	2	3	4	5	6	7	8	9	99
5. When playing with other children in the neighborhood	0	1	2	3	4	5	6	7	8	9	99
6. In his/her activities in the community (e.g., church, clubs, Scouts, social groups, organizations)	0	1	2	3	4	5	6	7	8	9	99
7. When he/she is visiting other people's homes	0	1	2	3	4	5	6	7	8	9	99
8. When playing with other children at school	0	1	2	3	4	5	6	7	8	9	99

(cont.)

Major Life Activities	Not at all	Somewhat		Mild		Moderate			Severe		Does not apply
9. Managing any money he/she may earn or be given as an allowance	0	1	2	3	4	5	6	7	8	9	99
10. Caring for him/herself daily (dressing, bathing, and hygiene)	0	1	2	3	4	5	6	7	8	9	99
11. Getting chores or other assigned tasks completed at home	0	1	2	3	4	5	6	7	8	9	99
12. Doing school homework	0	1	2	3	4	5	6	7	8	9	99
13. In his/her ability to follow rules	0	1	2	3	4	5	6	7	8	9	99
14. In his/her interactions with other adults (e.g., visitors who come to your home, when visiting others, in other community settings)	0	1	2	3	4	5	6	7	8	9	99
15. Playing sports	0	1	2	3	4	5	6	7	8	9	99

Part II—Instructions

Please answer the following questions about your child's current activities.

16. How many friends does your child have? ________

(NOTE: A friend is someone your child plays or interacts with frequently)

17. In the past year, in how many clubs or community organizations did your child participate (Scouts, church groups, hobby groups, etc.)? ________

18. In the past year, in how many *organized* sports did your child participate at school and in your community? ________

(NOTE: Do not count or include his/her regular physical education classes at school)

19. During the most recent grading period at school, what was your child's average grade across all his/her subjects on his/her report card?

____ A average (90–100%)

____ B average (80–89%)

____ C average (70–79%)

(cont.)

____ D average (60–69%)

____ E or F average (50–59% or failing)

____ Don't know

20. During the past school year, did any of your child's teachers tell you that your child was having problems with his/her behavior or with doing his/her schoolwork?

    NO YES

21. Has your child ever been retained in a grade or held back a grade after he/she started school?

    NO YES

22. Has your child ever been suspended or expelled from school?

    NO YES

23. Has your child ever received special education services?

    NO YES

BFIS-CA Parent Interview

Child's name: ______________________________

Sex: (Circle one) Male Female Age: ______________

Name of person being interviewed: ______________________________

Relationship to this child: Mother Father Stepmother Stepfather Other (specify): ________

Name of interviewer ______________________________ Date ____________

Instructions

Use this form as part of a follow-up interview after the BFIS-CA rating scale has been completed by the parent and scored by the examiner. This form is for purposes of gathering additional information about those domains that the parent has rated as being impaired in his/her child (falling at or above the 93rd percentile). The interviewer should question the parent about the specific reasons for and basis of his/her reporting that his/her child was moderately to severely impaired in that specific domain of major life activity. Ask the parent just what adverse events or consequences have occurred in this domain that would lead him/her to believe that his/her child is functioning so ineffectively in this domain. Record his/her answers below and then use his/her responses to further evaluate the credibility, veracity, or appropriateness or inappropriateness of his/her ratings.

Interactions with mother:

Interactions with father:

School performance:

(cont.)

Interactions with brothers and sisters:

Playing with other children in the neighborhood:

In community organizations (e.g., Scouts, clubs, church)

When visiting other people's homes:

Playing at school with other children:

Managing any money he/she may earn or be given as an allowance:

(cont.)

Caring for him/herself (e.g., dressing, bathing, hygiene):

Getting chores or other assigned tasks completed at home:

Doing school homework:

In his/her ability to follow rules:

In his/her interactions with other adults:

In playing sports:

BFIS-CA Score Sheet

Child's name: ______________________________ Date: ____________________

Sex: (Circle one) Male Female Age: ____________________

BFIS-CA Domain:	**1. Home–School [HS] Raw Scores**	**2. Community [CL] Raw Scores**	**3. Percentile** (from Profile)
1. With mother [HS] (underline score if ≥ 6)			
2. With father [HS] (underline score if ≥ 6)			
3. School performance [HS] (underline score if ≥ 7)			
4. With siblings [HS] (underline score if ≥ 7)			
5. Playing in neighborhood [CL] (underline score if ≥ 6)			
6. Community activities [CL] (underline score if ≥ 5)			
7. Visiting others [CL] (underline score if ≥ 5)			
8. Playing at school [CL] (underline score if ≥ 6)			
9. Managing money [HS] (underline score if ≥ 6)			
10. Self-care [HS] (underline score if ≥ 5)			
11. Doing chores [HS] (underline score if ≥ 7)			
12. School homework [HS] (underline score if ≥ 7)			
13. Following rules [HS] (underline score if ≥ 7)			
14. With other adults [CL] (underline score if ≥ 5)			
15. Playing sports [CL] (underline score if ≥ 5)			
16. Sum of Home–School [HS] column scores			
17. Number of domain scores used in [HS] sum			
18. Home–School mean impairment score (divide #16 by #17)			
19. Sum of [CL] column scores			
20. Number of domain scores used in [CL] sum			
21. Community–Leisure mean impairment score (divide #19 by #20)			
22. Number of impaired domains (count the number of scores underlined in both the [HS] column and the [CL] column)			

BFIS-CA Impairment Profile (Ages 6–11, Males Only)

Child's name: ______________________ Age: ____________ Sex: _____ Date: __________

Instructions: Circle the raw score in each row that corresponds to the answers provided on the BFIS-CA Parent Rating Scale and that you entered or computed on the BFIS-CA Scoring Sheet. Then look up or down the column at the top or bottom row labeled **Percentiles** to determine the percentile in the normative sample that corresponds to that raw score.

Raw Score Percentiles

Percentiles	1–50	51–75	76–84	85	86	87	88	89	90	91	92	93	94	95	96	97	98	99+
With mother [HS]	—	0	1	2	—	—	3	—	—	4	—	5	—	—	**6**	—	**7**	**8–9**
With Father [HS]	—	0	1–2	—	—	—	3	—	—	4	—	—	5	—	**6**	—	**7**	**8–9**
School performance [HS]	0	1–2	3	4	—	—	—	5	—	—	6	—	—	—	—	**7**	**8**	**9**
With siblings [HS]	0	1	2–3	—	—	4	—	—	5	—	—	6	—	—	**7**	—	**8**	**9**
Play—neighborhood [CL]	—	0–1	2	—	—	3	—	—	4	—	—	—	5	—	**6**	—	**7**	**8–9**
Community [CL]	—	0	1–2	—	—	—	—	3	—	—	4	—	—	**5**	—	**6**	—	**7–9**
Visiting others [CL]	—	0	1	2	—	—	—	3	—	—	4	—	—	**5**	—	**6**	**7**	**8–9**
Play—school [CL]	—	0	1–2	—	—	3	—	4	—	—	—	—	5	**6**	—	**7**	**8**	**9**
Managing money [HS]	—	0–1	2	—	3	—	—	4	—	—	5	—	—	**6**	—	**7**	**8**	**9**
Self-care [HS]	—	0	1	2	—	—	—	3	—	—	4	—	**5**	—	**6**	**7**	**8**	**9**
Doing chores [HS]	0	1–2	3	—	4	—	—	5	—	—	6	—	—	**7**	—	**8**	—	**9**
School homework [HS]	0	1–2	3–4	—	—	—	5	—	—	—	6	—	—	—	**7**	—	**8**	**9**
Following rules [HS]	0	1	2–3	—	—	—	4	—	—	—	5	6	—	—	**7**	—	**8**	**9**
With other adults [CL]	—	0	1–2	—	—	—	3	—	—	—	4	—	—	**5**	**6**	—	**7–8**	**9**
Playing sports [CL]	—	—	1–2	—	—	3	—	—	4	—	—	—	**5**	—	**6**	**7**	**8**	**9**
Home–School mean impairment score	0.0–0.5	0.6–2.1	2.2–3.1	3.2–3.3	3.4–3.6	3.7–3.8	3.9–4.0	4.1–4.2	4.3–4.5	4.6–4.7	4.8–4.9	5.0–5.2	5.3–5.6	5.7–5.8	5.9	6.0–6.3	6.4–7.4	7.5+
Community–Leisure mean impairment score	0.0–0.1	0.2–1.4	1.5–2.5	2.6–2.7	2.8–2.9	3.0–3.4	3.5–3.6	3.7–3.8	3.9–4.3	4.4–4.7	4.8–5.0	5.1–5.2	5.3	5.4–5.6	5.7–5.8	5.9–6.4	6.5–7.5	7.6+
Number of impaired domains score	—	0	1	—	—	2	—	3	—	4	5	6	—	—	7	8–9	10–11	12+
Percentiles	1–50	51–75	76–84	85	86	87	88	89	90	91	92	93	94	95	96	97	98	99+

*Enlarged numbers in **boldface** type in each row (representing a specific domain) indicate the start of the range of impairment for that domain (93rd–95th percentiles) compared with the *entire* normative sample. Scores at or above this number are considered "impaired" for purposes of contributing to the computation of the number of impaired domains score.

BFIS-CA Impairment Profile—Secondary Impairment Questions (Ages 6–11, Males Only)

Number of Friends

Percentiles	3	7	14	26	39	56	66	70	77	78	88	89	92	94	95	97	98	99+
Raw Score	0	1	2	3	4	5	6	7	8	9	10	11	12	13–14	15–17	18–24	25–29	30+

Number of Clubs or Community Organizations

Percentiles	21	42	68	83	89	96	98	99+
Raw Score	0	1	2	3	4	5	6	7+

Number of Organized Sports

Percentiles	34	58	80	92	97	98	99+
Raw Score	0	1	2	3	4	5	6+

[*Note*. The following tables show percentages endorsing each answer, *not* percentiles.]

Estimated Grade Point Average:

Percentages:	≤ 1	1	9	29	60
Raw Score	E–F	D	C	B	A

Teacher-Reported Behavioral or Learning Problem in the Past School Year

Percentages:	33	67
Raw Score	YES	NO

Retained in Grade—Ever

Percentages:	4	96
Raw Score	YES	NO

Suspended or Expelled

Percentages	5	95
Raw Score	YES	NO

Ever Received Special Education Services

Percentages:	13	87
Raw Score	YES	NO

BFIS-CA Impairment Profile (Ages 12–17, Males Only)

Child's name: Age: ______________________ Sex: ______________ Date: ______________

Instructions: Circle the raw score in each row that corresponds to the answers provided on the BFIS-CA Parent Rating Scale and that you entered or computed on the BFIS-CA Score Sheet. Then look up or down the column at the top or bottom row labeled **Percentiles** to determine the percentile in the normative sample that corresponds to that raw score.

Raw Score Percentiles

Percentiles	1–50	51–75	76–84	85	86	87	88	89	90	91	92	93	94	95	96	97	98	99+
With mother [HS]	—	0–1	2–3	—	—	4	—	5	—	—	—	—	—	**6**	—	**7**	**8**	**9**
With father [HS]	—	0–1	2–3	—	4	—	—	5	—	—	—	**6**	—	**7**	—	—	**8**	**9**
School performance [HS]	0	1–3	4–5	—	—	6	—	—	—	—	**7**	—	—	**8**	—	—	—	**9**
With siblings [HS]	0	1	2–3	—	—	—	4	—	—	—	5	—	6	—	**7**	**8**	—	**9**
Play—neighborhood [CL]	—	0	1–2	3	—	—	—	—	4	—	—	5	—	**6**	—	—	**7**	**8–9**
Community [CL]	—	0–1	2	3	—	—	—	—	4	—	**5**	—	—	**6**	—	**7**	**8**	**9**
Visiting others [CL]	—	0	1–2	—	—	3	—	—	—	—	4	—	**5**	—	—	**6**	—	**7–9**
Play—school [CL]	—	0	1–2	3	—	—	—	4	—	—	5	—	—	**6**	—	—	**7**	**8–9**
Managing money [HS]	—	0–1	2–3	—	—	—	—	4	—	5	—	—	**6**	—	**7**	—	**8**	**9**
Self-care [HS]	—	0	1–2	—	—	3	—	—	—	4	—	**5**	—	**6**	—	**7**	**8**	**9**
Doing chores [HS]	0	1–2	3–5	—	—	—	—	6	—	—	**7**	—	—	**8**	—	—	—	**9**
School homework [HS]	0	1–3	4–5	6	—	—	—	—	**7**	—	—	—	**8**	—	—	—	—	**9**
Following rules [HS]	0	1	2–3	—	4	—	—	5	—	6	—	—	—	**7**	**8**	—	—	**9**
With other adults [CL]	—	0	1–2	—	3	—	—	—	—	—	4	—	**5**	—	**6**	—	**7**	**8–9**
Playing sports [CL]	—	0	1–2	—	3	—	—	—	—	4	**5**	—	**6**	—	—	**7**	**8**	**9**
Home–School mean impairment score	0.0–0.5	0.6–2.6	2.7–3.9	4.0	4.1–4.5	4.6	4.7	4.8–5.0	5.1–5.3	5.4–5.5	5.6	5.7–5.9	6.0–6.1	6.2–6.6	6.7–6.9	7.0–7.3	7.4–7.7	7.8+
Community–Leisure mean impairment score	0.0–0.1	0.2–1.0	1.1–3.2	3.3–3.5	3.6	3.7–3.8	3.9	4.0–4.1	4.2	4.3	4.4–4.7	4.8–5.0	5.1–5.4	5.5–5.6	5.7–5.9	6.0–6.5	6.6–7.2	7.3+
Number of impaired domains score	—	0	1–2	—	—	3	4	—	5	—	6	—	7	8	—	9–10	11–12	13+
Percentiles	1–50	51–75	76–84	85	86	87	88	89	90	91	92	93	94	95	96	97	98	99+

Note. Enlarged numbers in **boldface** type in each row (representing a specific domain) indicate the start of the range of impairment for that domain (93rd–95th percentiles) compared with the *entire* normative sample. Scores at or above this number are considered "impaired" for purposes of contributing to the computation of the number of impaired domains score.

BFIS-CA Impairment Profile—Secondary Impairment Questions (Ages 12–17, Males Only)

Number of Friends

Percentiles	2	7	16	27	36	52	60	63	70	82	88	91	96	98	99+
Raw Score	0	1	2	3	4	5	6	**7**	8–9	10–11	12–14	15–19	20–29	30–40	41+

Number of Clubs or Community Organizations

Percentiles	28	47	70	84	91	96	98	99+
Raw Score	0	1	2	3	4	5	6–7	8+

Number of Organized Sports

Percentiles	41	66	86	95	98	99
Raw Score	0	1	2	3	4–5	6+

[*Note:* The following tables show percentages endorsing each answer, *not* percentiles.]

Estimated Grade Point Average

Percentages	< 2	4	17	37	40
Raw Score	E–F	D	C	B	A

Teacher-Reported Behavioral or Learning Problem in the Past School Year

Percentages	32	68
Raw Score	YES	NO

Retained in Grade—Ever

Percentages	8	92
Raw Score	YES	NO

Suspended or Expelled

Percentages	14	86
Raw Score	YES	NO

Ever Received Special Education Services

Percentages	14	86
Raw Score	YES	NO

BFIS-CA Impairment Profile (Ages 6–11, Females Only)

Child's name: ______________________ Age: ______________ Sex: ______ Date: ______________

Instructions: Circle the raw score in each row that corresponds to the answers provided on the BFIS-CA Parent Rating Scale and that you entered or computed on the BFIS-CA Score Sheet. Then look up or down the column at the top or bottom row labeled **Percentiles** to determine the percentile in the normative sample that corresponds to that raw score.

Raw Score Percentiles

Percentiles	1–50	51–75	76–84	85	86	87	88	89	90	91	92	93	94	95	96	97	98	99+
With mother [HS]	—	0	1–2	—	—	3	—	—	—	4	—	—	5	—	—	**6**	**7**	**8–9**
With father [HS]	—	0	1	2	—	—	—	3	—	—	4	—	5	—	**6**	—	**7**	**8–9**
School performance [HS]	—	0	1–2	—	—	3	—	—	4	—	5	—	—	6	**7**	—	**8**	**9**
With siblings [HS]	—	0–1	2–3	—	—	—	4	—	—	—	5	—	6	—	**7**	—	**8**	**9**
Play—neighborhood [CL]	—	0	1	2	—	—	—	3	—	—	4	—	5	—	**6**	**7**	**8**	**9**
Community [CL]	—	0	1	—	—	—	—	—	2	—	3	—	4	**5**	—	—	**6–7**	**8–9**
Visiting others [CL]	—	0	1	—	—	—	2	—	—	3	—	4	—	**5**	—	**6**	**7**	**8–9**
Play—school [CL]	—	0	1	—	2	—	—	—	—	3	—	4	5	—	**6**	**7**	—	**8–9**
Managing money [HS]	—	0	1	2	—	—	—	3	—	—	4	—	5	—	—	**6**	**7**	**8–9**
Self-care [HS]	—	0	—	1	—	—	2	—	—	3	—	4	—	**5**	—	**6**	**7**	**8–9**
Doing chores [HS]	0	1	2	—	3	—	—	4	—	—	5	—	—	—	—	6	**7–8**	**9**
School homework [HS]	0	1	2	—	—	—	3	—	4	—	5	—	—	6	**7**	—	**8**	**9**
Following rules [HS]	—	0	1	—	2	—	—	3	—	4	—	5	—	6	**7**	—	**8**	**9**
With other adults [CL]	—	0	—	1	—	—	2	—	—	—	3	4	—	**5**	**6**	**7**	—	**8–9**
Playing sports [CL]	—	0	1	—	—	—	2	—	—	—	3	—	—	4	—	**5**	—	**6–9**
Home–School mean impairment score	0.0–0.2	0.3–1.1	1.2–2.4	2.5	2.6–2.7	2.8–2.9	3.0–3.2	3.3–3.6	3.7	3.8–3.9	4.0–4.2	4.3–4.8	4.9–5.5	5.6–5.9	6.0–6.1	6.2–6.8	6.9–7.1	7.2+
Community–Leisure mean impairment score	0.0–0.1	0.2–0.8	0.9–1.5	1.6–1.7	1.8–1.9	2.0–2.1	2.2	2.3–2.5	2.6–2.8	2.9–3.3	3.4–3.5	3.6–4.0	4.1–4.7	4.8–5.7	5.8–6.2	6.3–6.6	6.7–7.2	7.3+
Number of impaired domains score	—	—	0	—	—	—	—	1	—	—	2	3	4–5	6	7–9	10	11–12	13+
Percentiles	1–50	51–75	76–84	85	86	87	88	89	90	91	92	93	94	95	96	97	98	99+

Note. Enlarged numbers in **boldface** type in each row (representing a specific domain) indicate the start of the range of impairment for that domain (93rd–95th percentiles) compared with the *entire* normative sample. Scores at or above this number are considered "impaired" for purposes of contributing to the computation of the number of impaired domains score.

BFIS-CA Impairment Profile—Secondary Impairment Questions (Ages 6–11, Females Only)

Number of Friends

Percentiles	1	4	12	24	34	51	60	66	72	86	89	93	95	97	98	99+
Raw Score	0	1	2	3	4	5	6	7	8–9	10–11	12–14	15–16	17–19	20–24	25–39	40+

Number of Clubs or Community Organizations

Percentiles	17	36	63	83	91	96	98	99+
Raw Score	0	1	2	3	4	5	6–7	8+

Number of Organized Sports

Percentiles	34	71	89	95	98	99
Raw Score	0	1	2	3	4	5+

[*Note:* The following tables show percentages endorsing each answer, *not* percentiles.]

Estimated Grade Point Average

Percentages	≤ 1	≤ 1	8	27	61
Raw Score	E–F	D	C	B	A

Teacher-Reported Behavioral or Learning Problem in the Past School Year

Percentages	21	79
Raw Score	YES	NO

Retained in Grade—Ever

Percentages	3	97
Raw Score	YES	NO

Suspended or Expelled

Percentages	7	93
Raw Score	YES	NO

Ever Received Special Education Services

Percentages	5	95
Raw Score	YES	NO

BFIS-CA Impairment Profile (Ages 12–17, Females Only)

Child's name: ______________________ Age: ____________ Sex: ______ Date: ____________

Instructions. Circle the raw score in each row that corresponds to the answers provided on the BFIS-CA Parent Rating Scale and that you entered or computed on the BFIS-CA Score Sheet. Then look up or down the column at the top or bottom row labeled **Percentiles** to determine the percentile in the normative sample that corresponds to that raw score.

Raw Score Percentiles

Percentiles	1–50	51–75	76–84	85	86	87	88	89	90	91	92	93	94	95	96	97	98	99+
With mother [HS]	—	0	1–3	—	—	—	4	—	—	5	—	—	**6**	—	—	**7**	—	**8–9**
With father [HS]	0	1	2–3	—	4	—	—	—	5	—	—	—	**6**	—	**7**	—	**8**	**9**
School performance [HS]	—	0–1	2–3	—	—	—	4	—	5	—	—	—	—	6	**7**	—	—	**8–9**
With siblings [HS]	0	1	2–3	—	—	—	4	—	5	—	—	6	—	—	**7**	—	**8**	**9**
Playing—neighborhood [CL]	—	0	1	2	—	—	3	—	—	—	4	—	5	—	**6**	—	**7**	**8–9**
Community [CL]	—	0	1	2	—	—	—	—	3	—	—	4	**5**	—	—	—	**6**	**7–9**
Visiting others [CL]	—	0	1	—	—	—	2	—	—	—	3	—	4	—	—	**5**	**6**	**7–9**
Play—school [CL]	—	0	1	—	2	—	—	—	—	3	—	—	4	—	5	—	**6**	**7–9**
Managing money [HS]	—	0	1–2	—	—	—	—	3	4	—	—	5	—	**6**	—	**7**	**8**	**9**
Self-care [HS]	—	—	0	—	1	—	—	2	—	—	3	—	4	—	**5**	**6**	**7**	**8–9**
Doing chores [HS]	0	1–2	3	4	—	—	—	—	5	—	—	6	—	—	**7**	—	**8**	**9**
School homework [HS]	0	1	2–3	—	—	4	—	—	5	—	—	—	6	—	**7**	—	**8**	**9**
Following rules [HS]	—	0	1–2	—	3	—	—	4	—	—	—	5	—	6	**7**	—	—	**8–9**
With other adults [CL]	—	0	1	—	—	2	—	—	—	3	—	—	4	—	**5**	—	**6**	**7–9**
Playing sports [CL]	—	0	1	—	2	—	—	—	3	—	—	4	—	**5**	**6**	—	**7**	**8–9**
Home–School mean impairment score	0.0–0.3	0.4–1.9	2.0–3.0	3.1–3.2	3.3–3.5	3.6	3.7–3.8	3.9–4.0	4.1–4.3	4.4	4.5–4.6	4.7–4.8	4.9–5.1	5.2–5.3	5.4–5.8	5.9–6.5	6.6–7.1	7.2+
Community–Leisure mean impairment score	0.0	0.1–0.8	0.9–2.2	2.3	2.4	2.5	2.6–2.7	2.8–2.9	3.0–3.1	3.2–3.7	3.8–3.9	4.0–4.1	4.2–4.5	4.6–4.8	4.9–5.3	5.4–5.6	5.7–6.2	6.3+
Number of impaired domains score	—	0	—	1	—	—	2	—	—	—	3	4	—	5	6	7–8	9–10	11+
Percentiles	1–50	51–75	76–84	85	86	87	88	89	90	91	92	93	94	95	96	97	98	99+

Note. Enlarged numbers in **boldface** type in each row (representing a specific domain) indicate the start of the range of impairment for that domain (93rd–95th percentiles) compared with the *entire* normative sample. Scores at or above this number are considered "impaired" for purposes of contributing to the computation of the number of impaired domains score.

BFIS-CA Impairment Profile—Secondary Impairment Questions (Ages 12–17, Females Only)

Number of Friends

Percentiles	1	5	11	21	32	51	61	64	69	82	91	94	97	98	99+
Raw Score	0	1	2	3	4	5	6	7	8–9	10–14	15–19	20–29	30–34	35–49	50+

Number of Clubs or Community Organizations

Percentiles	20	41	57	74	85	93	96	97	98	99+
Raw Score	0	1	2	3	4	5	6	7–8	9	10+

Number of Organized Sports

Percentiles	46	72	88	95	98	99+
Raw Score	0	1	2	3	4	5+

[*Note:* The following tables show percentages endorsing each answer, *not* percentiles.]

Estimated Grade Point Average

Percentages	≤ 1	2	12	34	50
Raw Score	E–F	D	C	B	A

Teacher-Reported Behavioral or Learning Problem in the Past School Year

Percentages	19	81
Raw Score	YES	NO

Retained in Grade—Ever

Percentages	6	93
Raw Score	YES	NO

Suspended or Expelled

Percentages	6	94
Raw Score	YES	NO

Ever Received Special Education Services

Percentages	6	97
Raw Score	YES	NO

References

Abikoff, A., Hechtman, L., Klein, R. G., Weiss, G., Fleiss, K., Etcovitch, J., et al. (2004). Symptomatic improvement in children with ADHD treated with long-term methylphenidate and multimodal psychosocial treatment. *Journal of the American Academy of Child and Adolescent Psychiatry, 43*, 802–811.

Achenbach, T. M. (2001). *Manual for the Child Behavior Checklist/4–18 and 1991 Profile.* Burlington, VT: Author.

Adams, C. D., McCarthy, M., & Kelly, M. L. (1995). Adolescent versions of the Home and School Situations Questionnaires: Initial psychometric properties. *Journal of Clinical Child Psychology, 24*, 377–385.

Altepeter, T. S., & Breen, M. (1992). Situational variation in problem behavior at home and at school in attention-deficit disorder with hyperactivity. *Journal of Child Psychology and Psychiatry, 33*, 741–748.

Aman, M. G., McDougle, C. J., Scahill, L., Handen, B., Arnold, L. E., Johnson, C., et al. (2010). Medication and parent training in children with pervasive developmental disorders and serious behavior problems: Results from a randomized clinical trial. *Journal of the American Academy of Child and Adolescent Psychiatry, 49*, 727.

American Heritage Dictionary of the English Language. (2000). New York: Houghton Mifflin.

American Heritage Medical Dictionary. (2009). New York: Houghton Mifflin.

American Medical Association. (2008). *American Medical Association guide to the assessment of permanent impairment.* Washington, DC: Author.

American Psychiatric Association. (2000). *Diagnostic and statistical manual of mental disorders* (4th ed., text rev.). Washington, DC: Author.

Americans with Disabilities Act. (1990). United States Public Law 101-336, Title 42, Chapter 126. Washington, DC.

Banaschewski, T., Neale, B. M., Rothenberger, A., & Roessner, V. (2007). Comorbidity of tic disorders and ADHD: Conceptual and methodological considerations. *European Child and Adolescent Psychiatry, 16*(Suppl. 1), 5–14.

Barkley, R. A. (1981). *Hyperactive children: A handbook for diagnosis and treatment.* New York: Guilford Press.

Barkley, R. A. (1997). *Defiant children: A clinician's manual for assessment and parent training* (2nd ed.). New York: Guilford Press.

Barkley, R. A. (2006). *Attention-deficit hyperactivity disorder: A handbook for diagnosis and treatment* (3rd ed.). New York: Guilford Press.

Barkley, R. A. (2010). Deficient emotional self-regulation is a core component of ADHD. *Journal of ADHD and Related Disorders, 1,* 5–37.

Barkley, R. A. (2011a). *Barkley Deficits in Executive Functioning Scale (BDEFS).* New York: Guilford Press.

Barkley, R. A. (2011b). *Barkley Functional Impairment Scale (BFIS).* New York: Guilford Press.

Barkley, R. A. (2012). *Barkley Deficits in Executive Functioning Scale—Children and Adolescents (BDEFS-CA).* New York: Guilford Press.

Barkley, R. A., & Edelbrock, C. S. (1987). Assessing situational variation in children's problem behaviors: The Home and School Situations Questionnaire. In R. J. Prinz (Ed.), *Advances in behavioral assessment of children and families* (Vol. 3, pp. 157–176). Greenwich, CT: JAI Press.

Barkley, R., Fischer, M., Newby, R. F., & Breen, M. J. (1988). Development of a multi-method clinical protocol for assessing stimulant drug responding in ADD children. *Journal of Clinical Child Psychology, 17,* 14–24.

Barkley, R. A., & Murphy, K. R. (1998). *Attention-deficit hyperactivity disorder: A clinical workbook* (2nd ed.). New York: Guilford Press.

Barkley, R. A., & Murphy, K. R. (2006). *Attention-deficit hyperactivity disorder: A clinical workbook* (3rd ed.). New York: Guilford Press.

Barry, T. D., Pinard, F. A., Barry, C. T., Garland, B. H., & Lyman, R. D. (2011). The utility of home problem pervasiveness and severity in classifying children identified with attention-deficit/hyperactivity disorder. *Child Psychiatry and Human Development, 42,* 152–165.

Bird, H. R., Canino, G., Rubio-Stipec, M., & Ribera, J. C. (1987). Further measures of the psychometric properties of the Children's Global Assessment Scale. *Archives of General Psychiatry, 44,* 821–844.

Blaskewitz, N., Werten, T., & Kathmann, N. (2008). Performance of children on symptom validity tests: TOMM, MSVT, and FIT. *Archives of Clinical Neuropsychology, 23,* 379–391.

Boyle, C. A., Decoufle, P., & Yeargin-Allsop, M. (1994). Prevalence and health impact of developmental disabilities in U.S. children. *Pediatrics, 93,* 399–403.

Brandenburg, N. A., Friedman, R. M., & Silver, S. E. (1990). The epidemiology of childhood psychiatric disorders: Prevalence findings from recent studies. *Journal of the American Academy of Child and Adolescent Psychiatry, 29,* 76–83.

Breen, M., & Barkley, R. A. (1983). The Personality Inventory for Children (PIC): Its clinical utility with hyperactive children. *Journal of Pediatric Psychology, 8,* 359–366.

Breen, M., & Barkley, R. A. (1988). Child psychopathology and parenting stress in girls and boys with attention-deficit disorder with hyperactivity. *Journal of Pediatric Psychology, 13,* 265–280.

Bryant, F. B. (2000). Assessing the validity of measurement. In L. G. Grim & P. R. Yarnold (Eds.), *Reading and understanding more multivariate statistics* (pp. 99–146). Washington, DC: American Psychological Association.

Capano, L., Minden, D., Chen, S. X., Schachar, R. J., & Ickowicz, A. (2008). Mathematical learning disorder in school-age children with attention-deficit hyperactivity disorder. *Canadian Journal of Psychiatry, 53,* 392–399.

Carlson, G. A., & Meyer, S. E. (2009). ADHD with mood disorders. In T. E. Brown (Ed.), *ADHD comorbidities: Handbook for ADHD complications in children and adults* (pp. 97–130). Washington, DC: American Psychiatric Publishing.

Cartwright-Hatton, S., McNicol, K., & Doubleday, K. (2006). Anxiety in a neglected population: Prevalence of anxiety disorders in pre-adolescent children. *Clinical Psychology Review, 26,* 817–833.

Cohen, J. (1992). A power primer. *Psychological Bulletin, 112,* 155–159.

Constantinou, M., & McCaffrey, R. J. (2003). Use of the TOMM for evaluating children's effort to perform optimally on neuropsychological measures. *Child Neuropsychology, 9,* 81–90.

Cook, T. D., & Campbell, D. T. (1979). *Quasi-experimentation: Design and analysis issues for field settings.* Chicago: Rand McNally.

Costello, E. J., Angold, A., Burns, B. J., Stangl, D. K., Tweed, D. L., Erkanli, A., et al. (1996). The Great Smoky Mountains Study of Youth: Goals, design, methods, and the prevalence of DSM-III-R disorders. *Archives of General Psychiatry, 53,* 1129–1136.

Costello, E. J., Egger, H., & Angold, A. (2005). 10-year research update review: The epidemiology of child and adolescent psychiatric disorders: I. Methods and public health burden. *Journal of the American Academy of Child and Adolescent Psychiatry, 49,* 972–986.

Costello, E. J., Mustillo, S., Erkanli, A., Keeler, G., & Angold, A. (2003). Prevalence and development of psychiatric disorders in childhood and adolescence. *Archives of General Psychiatry, 60,* 837–844.

Crowe, L. M., Beauchamp, M. H., Catroppa, C., & Anderson, V. (2011). Social function assessment tools for children and adolescents: A systematic review from 1988 to 2010. *Clinical Psychology Review, 31,* 767–785.

Danforth, J. S., Harvey, E., Ulaszek, W. R., & McKee, T. E. (2006). The outcome of group parent training for families of children with attention-deficit hyperactivity disorder and defiant/aggressive behavior. *Journal of Behavior Therapy and Experimental Psychiatry, 37,* 188–205.

Del'Homme, M., Kim, T. S., Loo, S. K., Yang, M. H., & Smalley, S. L. (2007). Familial association and frequency of learning disabilities in ADHD sibling pair families. *Journal of Abnormal Child Psychology, 35,* 35–55.

Donders, J. (2005). Performance on the Test of Memory Malingering in a mixed pediatric sample. *Child Neuropsychology, 11,* 221–227.

DuPaul, G. J., & Barkley, R. A. (1992). Situational variability of attention problems: Psychometric properties of the Revised Home and School Situations Questionnaires. *Journal of Clinical Child Psychology, 21,* 178–188.

DuPaul, G. J., Power, T. J., Anastopoulos, A. D., & Reid, R. (1998). *The ADHD Rating Scale—IV.* New York: Guilford Press.

Essau, C. A., Conradt, J., & Petermann, F. (2000). Frequency, comorbidity, and psychosocial impairment of anxiety disorders in German adolescents. *Journal of Anxiety Disorders, 14,* 263–279.

Fabiano, G. A., Pelham, W. E., Jr., Waschbusch, D. A., Gnagy, E. M., Lahey, B. B., Chronis, A. M., et al. (2006). A practical measure of impairment: Psychometric properties of the Impairment Rating Scale in samples of children with attention-deficit hyperactivity disorder and two school-based samples. *Journal of Clinical Child and Adolescent Psychology, 35,* 369–385.

Faust, D., Hart, K., & Guilmette, T. J. (1988). Pediatric malingering: The capacity of children to fake believable deficits on neuropsychological testing. *Journal of Consulting and Clinical Psychology, 56,* 578–582.

Faust, D., Hart, K., Guilmette, T. J., & Arkes, H. R. (1988). Neuropsychologists' capacity to detect adolescent malingerers. *Professional Psychology: Research and Practice, 19,* 508–515.

Flanagan, R. (1995). A review of the Behavior Assessment System for Children (BASC):

Assessment consistent with the requirements for the Individuals with Disabilities Education Act (IDEA). *Journal of School Psychology, 33,* 177–186.

Fleming, J. E., Offord, D. R., & Boyle, M. H. (1989). Prevalence of childhood and adolescent depression in the community: The Ontario Child Health Study. *British Journal of Psychiatry, 155,* 647–654.

Gathje, R. A., Lewandowski, L. J., & Gordon, M. (2008). The role of impairment in the diagnosis of ADHD. *Journal of Attention Disorders, 11,* 529–537.

Germano, E., Gagliano, A., & Curatolo, P. (2010). Comorbidity of ADHD and dyslexia. *Developmental Neuropsychology, 35,* 475–493.

Gioia, G. A., Isquith, P. K., Guy, S. C., & Kenworthy, L. (2000). *BRIEF: Behavior Rating Inventory of Executive Function—Professional manual.* Odessa, FL: Psychological Assessment Resources.

Gioia, G. A., Isquith, P. K., Kenworthy, L., & Barton, R. M. (2002). Profiles of everyday executive function in acquired and developmental disorders. *Child Neuropsychology, 8,* 121–137.

Gladman, M., & Lancaster, S. (2003). A review of the Behavior Assessment System for Children. *School Psychology International, 24,* 276–291.

Goldstein, S., & Naglieri, J. A. (Eds.). (2009). *Assessment of impairment: From theory to practice.* New York: Springer.

Gordon, M., Antshel, K., Faraone, S., Barkley, R., Lewandowski, L., Hudziak, J., et al. (2006). Symptoms versus impairment: The case for respecting DSM-IV's Criterion D. *Journal of Attention Disorders, 9,* 465–475.

Gordon, M., & Keiser, S. (Eds.). (1998). *Accommodations in higher education under the Americans with Disabilities Act (ADA): A no-nonsense guide for clinicians, educators, administrators, and lawyers.* New York: Guilford Press and GSI Publications.

Groot, C. M. de, Yeates, K. O., Baker, G. B., & Bornstein, R. A. (1997). Impaired neuropsychological functioning in Tourette's syndrome subjects with co-occurring obsessive–compulsive and attention-deficit symptoms. *Journal of Neuropsychiatry and Clinical Neuroscience, 9,* 267–272.

Guttmann-Steinmetz, S., Gadow, K. D., De Vincent, C. J., & Crowell, J. (2010). Anxiety symptoms in boys with autism spectrum disorder, attention-deficit hyperactivity disorder, or chronic tic disorder and community controls. *Journal of Autism and Developmental Disorders, 40,* 1006–1016.

Hammerness, P., Geller, D., Petty, C., Lamb, A., Bristol, E., & Biederman, J. (2010). Does ADHD moderate the manifestation of anxiety disorders in children? *European Child and Adolescent Psychiatry, 19,* 107–112.

Harris, E. L., Schuerholz, L. J., Singer, H. S., Reader, M., Brown, J. E., Cox, C., et al. (1995). Executive function in children with Tourette syndrome and/or attention deficit hyperactivity disorder. *Journal of the International Neuropsychological Society, 1,* 511–516.

Hesdorffer, D. C., Ludvigsson, P., Olafsson, E., Gudmundsson, G., Kjartansson, O., & Hauser, A. (2004). ADHD as a risk factor for incident unprovoked seizures and epilepsy in children. *Archives of General Psychiatry, 61,* 731–736.

Hodges, K., & Kim, C. (2000). Psychometric study of the Child and Adolescent Functional Assessment Scale: Prediction of contact with the law and poor school attendance. *Journal of Abnormal Child Psychology, 28,* 287–297.

Hodges, K., & Wong, M. M. (1996). Psychometric characteristics of a multidimensional measure to assess impairment: The Child and Adolescent Functional Assessment Scale. *Journal of Child and Family Studies, 5,* 445–467.

Jacobson, N. S., Roberts, L. J., Berns, S. B., & McGlinchey, J. B. (1999). Methods for defining and determining the clinical significance of treatment effects: Description, application, and alternatives. *Journal of Consulting and Clinical Psychology, 67,* 300–307.

Jacobson, N. S., & Truax, P. (1991). Clinical significance: A statistical approach to defining meaningful change in psychotherapy research. *Journal of Consulting and Clinical Psychology, 59,* 12–19.

Kaplan, B., Crawford, S., Cantell, M., Kooistra, L., & Dewey, D. (2006). Comorbidity, co-occurrence, continuum: What's in a name? *Child Care, Health, and Development, 32,* 723–731.

Kashani, J. H., McGee, R. O., Clarkson, S. E., Anderson, J. C., Walton, L. A., Williams, S., et al. (1983). Depression in a sample of 9-year-old children: Prevalence and associated characteristics. *Archives of General Psychiatry, 40,* 1217–1223.

Kashani, J. H., & Orvaschel, H. (1988). Anxiety disorders in mid-adolescence: A community sample. *American Journal of Psychiatry, 145,* 960–964.

Kaufmann, R., Goldberg-Stern, H., & Shuper, A. (2009). Attention-deficit disorders and epilepsy in childhood: Incidence, causative relations and treatment possibilities. *Journal of Child Neurology, 24,* 727–733.

Kendall, P. C. (1992). Anxiety and depression in children and adolescents. *Psychological Bulletin, 111,* 244–255.

Khalifa, N., & Knorring, A. von (2007). Prevalence of tic disorders and Tourette syndrome in a Swedish school population. *Developmental Medicine and Child Neurology, 45*(5), 315–319.

Ku, P. H., & Boone, K. B. (2002). Suspect cognitive symptoms in a 9-year-old child: Malingering by proxy. *Clinical Neuropsychologist, 16,* 90–96.

Kurlan, R., Como, P. G., Miller, B., Palumbo, D., Deeley, C., Andersen, E. M., et al. (2002). The behavioral spectrum of tic disorders: A community-based study. *Neurology, 59*(3), 414–420.

Last, C. A., Perrin, S., Hersen, M., & Kazdin, A. E. (1996). Prospective study of childhood anxiety disorders. *Journal of the American Academy of Child and Adolescent Psychiatry, 35,* 1502–1510.

Lauth, G. W., Otte, T. A., & Heubeck, B. G. (2009). Effectiveness of a competence training programme for parents of socially disruptive children. *Emotional and Behavioural Difficulties, 14,* 117–126.

Leckman, J. F. (2004). Phenomenology of tics and natural history of tic disorders. *Brain and Development, 25*(Suppl. 1), S24–S28.

Leclair, N., Leclair, S., & Brigham, C. R. (2009). The medical model of impairment. In S. Goldstein & J. A. Naglieri (Eds.), *Assessment of impairment: From theory to practice* (pp. 59–75). New York: Springer.

Lefkowitz, M. M., & Tesiny, E. P. (1985). Depression in children: Prevalence and correlates. *Journal of Consulting and Clinical Psychology, 53,* 647–656.

Lewandowski, L. J., Lovett, B. J., & Gordon, M. (2009). Measurement of symptom severity and impairment. In S. Goldstein & J. A. Naglieri (Eds.), *Assessment of impairment: From theory to practice* (pp. 5–14). New York: Springer.

Lewinsohn, P. M., Hops, H., Roberts, R. E., Seeley, J. R., & Andrews, J. A. (1993). Adolescent psychopathology: I. Prevalence and incidence of depression and other DSM-III-R disorders in high school students. *Journal of Abnormal Psychology, 102,* 133–144.

Lewis, B. A., Freebairn, L. A., & Taylor, H. G. (2002). Correlates of spelling abilities in children with early speech sound disorders. *Reading and Writing: An Interdisciplinary Journal, 15,* 389–407.

Lovett, B. J., Gordon, M., & Lewandowski, L. J. (2009). Measuring impairment in a legal context: Practical considerations in the evaluation of psychiatric and learning disabilities. In S. Goldstein & J. A. Naglieri (Eds.), *Assessment of impairment: From theory to practice* (pp. 93–103). New York: Springer.

Mahone, M. E., Cirino, P. T., Cutting, L. E., Cerrone, P. M., Hogelthorn, K. M., Hiemenz, J. R., et al. (2002). Validity of behavior rating inventory of executive function in children with ADHD and/or Tourette syndrome. *Archives of Clinical Neuropsychology, 17*(7), 643–663.

Mash, E. J., & Barkley, R. A. (Eds.). (2003). *Assessment of childhood disorders* (2nd ed.). New York: Guilford Press.

McGrath, L. M., Hutaff-Lee, C., Scott, A., Boada, R., Shriberg, L. D., & Pennington, B. F. (2008). Children with comorbid speech sound disorder and specific language impairment are at increased risk for attention-deficit/hyperactivity disorder. *Journal of Abnormal Child Psychology, 36,* 151–163.

McKinzey, R. M., Prieler, J., & Raven, J. (2003). Detection of children's malingering on Raven's Standard Progressive Matrices. *British Journal of Clinical Psychology, 42,* 95–99.

Merriam-Webster's Medical Dictionary. (2007). New York: Merriam-Webster.

Morgan, J. E., & Sweet, J. J. (2008). *Neuropsychology of malingering casebook.* London: Psychology Press.

Mosby's Medical Dictionary. (2009). New York: Elsevier.

Mulligan, A., Anney, R. J. L., O'Regan, M., Chen, W., Butler, L., Fitzgerald, M., et al. (2009). Autism symptoms in attention-deficit/hyperactivity disorder: A familial trait which correlates with conduct, oppositional defiant, language, and motor disorders. *Journal of Autism and Developmental Disorders, 39,* 197–209.

Nagle, A. M., Everhart, D. R., Durham, T. W., McCammon, S. L., & Walker, M. (2006). Deception strategies in children: Examination of forced choice recognition and verbal learning and memory techniques. *Archives of Clinical Neuropsychology, 21,* 777–785.

Naglieri, J. A., Goldstein, S., & LeBuffe, P. (2010). Resilience and impairment: An exploratory study of resilience factors and situational impairment. *Journal of Psychoeducational Assessment, 28,* 349–356.

Newcorn, J. H., Halperin, J. M., & Miller, C. J. (2009). ADHD with oppositionality and aggression. In T. E. Brown (Ed.), *ADHD comorbidities: Handbook for ADHD complications in children and adults* (pp. 157–176). Washington, DC: American Psychiatric Publishing.

Olfson, M., Marcus, S. C., Weissman, M. M., & Jensen, P. S. (2002). National trends in the use of psychotropic medications by children. *Journal of the American Academy of Child and Adolescent Psychiatry, 41,* 514–521.

Piek, J. P., Dyck, M. J., Francis, M., & Conwell, A. (2007). Working memory, processing speed, and set-shifting in children with developmental coordination disorder and attention-deficit hyperactivity disorder. *Developmental Medicine and Child Neurology, 49,* 678–683.

Pliszka, S. R. (2009). *Treating ADHD and comorbid disorders: Psychosocial and psychopharmacological interventions.* New York: Guilford Press.

Re, A. M., Pedron, M., & Cornoldi, C. (2007). Expressive writing difficulties in children described as exhibiting ADHD symptoms. *Journal of Learning Disabilities, 40,* 244–255.

Reiersen, A. M., Constantino, J. N., Volk, H. E., & Todd, R. D. (2007). Autistic traits in a population-based ADHD twin sample. *Journal of Child Psychology and Psychiatry, 48,* 464–472.

Reynolds, C., & Kamphaus, R. (2004). *Behavior Assessment System for Children–2.* Circle Pines, MN: American Guidance Service.

Riley, A. W., Coghill, D., Forrest, C. B., Lorenzo, M. J., Ralston, S. J., Spiel, G., et al. (2006). Validity of the health-related quality of life assessment in the ADORE study: Parent report form of the CHIP—Child Edition. *European Child and Adolescent Psychiatry, 15*(Suppl. 1), I/63–I/71.

Roberts, R. E., Attkinsson, C. C., & Rosenblatt, A. (1998). Prevalence of psychopathology among children and adolescents. *American Journal of Psychiatry, 155,* 715–725.

Roessner, V., Becker, A., Banaschewski, T., & Rothenberger, A. (2007). Executive functions in children with chronic tic disorders and ADHD: New insights. *European Child and Adolescent Psychiatry, 16*(Suppl. 1), 36–44.

Schorre, B. E., & Vandvik, I. H. (2004). Global assessment of psychosocial functioning in child and adolescent psychiatry. *European Child and Adolescent Psychiatry, 13,* 273–286.

Shaffer, D., Gould, M. S., Brasic, J., Ambrosini, P., Fisher, P., Bird, H., et al. (1983). A children's global assessment scale (CGAS). *Archives of General Psychiatry, 40,* 1228–1231.

Shatz, D. B., & Rostain, A. (2006). ADHD with comorbid anxiety: A review of the current literature. *Journal of Attention Disorders, 10,* 141–149.

Shaywitz, S. E., Shaywitz, B. A., Fletcher, J. M., & Escobar, M. D. (1990). Prevalence of reading disability in boys and girls: Results of the Connecticut Longitudinal Study. *Journal of the American Medical Association, 264,* 998–1002.

Simonoff, E., Pickles, A., Charman, T., Chandler, S., Loucas, T., & Baird, G. (2008). Psychiatric disorders in children with autism spectrum disorders: Prevalence, comorbidity, and associated factors in a population-derived sample. *Journal of the American Academy of Child and Adolescent Psychiatry, 47,* 921–929.

Singer, H. S., & Walkup, J. T. (1991). Tourette syndrome and other tic disorders: Diagnosis, pathophysiology, and treatment. *Medicine (Baltimore), 70,* 15–32.

Sinzig, J., Walter, D., & Doepfner, M. (2009). Attention-deficit/hyperactivity disorder in children and adolescents with autism spectrum disorder: Symptom or syndrome? *Journal of Attention Disorders, 13,* 117–126.

Slick, D. J., Tan, J. E., Strauss, E. H., & Hultsch, D. F. (2004). Detecting malingering: A survey of experts' practices. *Archives of Clinical Neuropsychology, 19,* 465–473.

Son, S. E., & Kirchner, J. T. (2000). Depression in children and adolescents. *American Family Physician, 62,* 2297–2308, 2311–2312.

Spencer, T., Biederman, J., Coffey, B., Geller, D., Wilens, T., & Faraone, S. (1999). The 4-year course of tic disorders in boys with attention-deficit/hyperactivity disorder. *Archives of General Psychiatry, 56,* 842–847.

Sukhodolsky, D. G., Vitulano, L. A., Carroll, D. H., McGuire, J., Leckman, J. F., & Scahill, L. (2009). Randomized trial of anger control training for adolescents with Tourette's syndrome and disruptive behavior. *Journal of the American Academy of Child and Adolescent Psychiatry, 48,* 413–421.

Swanson, H. L., & Jerman, O. (2006). Math disabilities: A selective meta-analysis of the literature. *Review of Educational Research, 76,* 249–274.

Tannock, R. (2009). ADHD with anxiety disorders. In T. E. Brown (Ed.), *ADHD comorbidities: Handbook for ADHD complications in children and adults* (pp. 131–155). Washington, DC: American Psychiatric Publishing.

Thomas, C. P., Conrad, P., Casler, R., & Goodman, E. (2006). Trends in the use of psychotropic medications among adolescents, 1994–2001. *Psychiatric Services, 57,* 63–69.

Tombaugh, T. N. (2004). *Test of Memory Malingering.* North Tonawanda, NY: MultiHealth Systems.

Vloet, T. D., Konrad, K., Herpertz-Dahlmann, B., Polier, G. G., & Gunther, T. (2010). Impact of anxiety disorders on attentional functions in children with ADHD. *Journal of Affective Disorders, 124,* 283–290.

Wakefield, J. C. (1992). The concept of mental disorder: On the boundary between biological facts and social values. *American Psychologist, 47,* 373–388.

Wakefield, J. C. (1997). Normal inability versus pathological disability: Why Ossorio's definition of mental disorder is not sufficient. *Clinical Psychology: Science and Practice, 4,* 249–258.

Walker, J. S. (2011, July). Malingering in children: Fibs and faking. *Child and Adolescent Psychiatric Clinics of North America, 20*(3), 547–556.

Warnke, A. (1999). Reading and spelling disorders: Clinical features and causes. *European Child and Adolescent Psychiatry, 8*(Suppl. 3), III2–III12.

Welsh, M. C., & Pennington, B. F. (1988). Assessing frontal lobe functioning in children: Views from developmental psychology. *Developmental Neuropsychology, 4,* 199–230.

World Health Organization. (2001). *International classification of diseases* (10th ed.). Geneva, Switzerland: Author.

Youngstrom, E. A., Arnold, L. E., & Frazier, T. W. (2010). Bipolar disorder and ADHD comorbidity: Both artifact and outgrowth of shared mechanisms. *Clinical Psychology: Science and Practice, 17,* 350–359.

Zito, J. M., Safer, D. J., DosReis, S., Gardner, J. F., Magder, L., Soeken, K., et al. (2003). Psychotropic practice patterns for youth: A 10-year perspective. *Archives of Pediatric and Adolescent Medicine, 157,* 17–25.

Index

Page numbers followed by *f* indicate figure, *t* indicate table

Academic tutoring, BFIS-CA scores and, 112, 113*t*, 114*f*
Adaptation, evolved, 6–7
ADHD Rating Scale—IV, 63
Age, relationship to BFIS-CA scores, 37–39, 38*f*
American Academy of Child and Adolescent Psychiatry, assessment guidelines of, 9
American Academy of Pediatrics, assessment guidelines of, 9
American Medical Association, guidelines of, 9–10
Americans with Disabilities Act (ADA), disability defined by, 8–9
Anxiety disorders
- ADHD and, 108
- BFIS scores and, 91–92, 93*t*, 94*f*
- BFIS-CA scores and, 105*t*
- medications for, 111

Attention-deficit disorder (ADD), 65, 66*t*, 70, 106, 111
Attention-deficit/hyperactivity disorder (ADHD)
- anxiety disorders and, 91–92, 108
- autism spectrum disorders and, 78–81, 79*t*, 80*f*, 81*f*
- BFIS-CA scores and, 63, 64–65, 65*f*, 66*t*, 104*t*
- bipolar disorder and, 98–100
- delayed motor development/coordination and, 69–73, 107
- depression and, 94–96
- developmental delay/mental retardation and, 73
- disorder contamination by, 106
- genetic liability for, 106
- HSQ scores and, 21
- math disorders and, 86–89
- medications for, 111
- oppositional defiant disorder and, 100–102
- reading disorders and, 82–83
- seizure disorders/epilepsy and, 74–75, 76*t*
- speech and language disorders and, 66–69, 107
- spelling disorders and, 84–85
- tic disorders/Tourette syndrome and, 75–78, 77*t*
- writing disorders and, 89–90

Autism spectrum disorders
- BFIS-CA scores and, 72–82, 79*t*, 80*f*, 81*f*, 104*t*
- genetic liability for, 106

Barkley Deficits in Executive Functioning Scale—Children and Adolescents, BFIS-CA and, 60–63, 61*t*, 62*f*
Barkley Functional Impairment Scale—Children and Adolescents
- administration of, 122
- appropriate purposes and populations for, 121–122
- BDEFS-CA ratings and, 60–63, 61*t*, 62*f*
- construct measured by, 51. *See also* Psychosocial impairment
- deficit measurement method of, 23
- development of, 20–30
- Home Situations Questionnaire and, 22
- Impairment Profiles for. *See* Impairment Profiles
- interpreting
  - using face validity, 134
  - using normative comparison (percentile interpretation), 135
  - using pre- to postinjury status, 135–136
  - using pre- to posttreatment change, 136
  - using risk analysis, 135
- materials for, 119
- Parent Interview for, 120
- Parent Rating Scale and, 119–120
- parent-report version of, 24
- research supporting, 2
- scale items of, 23
- scores for. *See* BFIS-CA scores
- scoring procedures for, 122–126. *See also* Score Sheet; Scoring
- supplementary sources of information and, 121
- treatments and, 110–118

Barkley Functional Impairment Scale—Children and Adolescents—Interview, form for, 23
Behavior Assessment System for Children—2, 14, 15, 16, 52

Behavior problems, teacher-reported, 46. *See also* School performance/adjustment
Behavior Rating Inventory of Executive Functioning (BRIEF), 62
BFIS-CA scores
effect size of, 102–103, 104t–105t
learning disabilities and, 82–91
math disorders, 86–89, 87*t*, 88*f*
reading disorders, 82–83, 83*t*, 84*f*
spelling disorders, 83–85, 85*t*, 86*f*
writing disorders, 89–90, 90*t*, 91*f*
neurodevelopmental disorders and, 64–81
ADHD, 64–65, 65*f*, 66*t*
autism spectrum disorders, 78–82, 79*t*, 80*f*, 81*f*
delayed motor development/coordination, 66–69, 67*t*, 68*f*, 69–73, 70*t*, 71*f*, 72*f*
developmental delay/mental retardation, 73, 74*t*, 75*f*
seizure disorders/epilepsy, 74–75
speech and language disorders, 66–69, 67*t*, 68*f*
tic disorders/Tourette syndrome, 75–78, 76t, 77t
psychiatric disorders and, 91–102
anxiety disorders, 91–92, 93*t*, 94*f*
bipolar disorder, 97–100, 98*t*, 99*f*
depression, 93–97, 95*t*, 96*f*, 97*f*
oppositional defiant disorder, 100–102, 101*t*, 102*f*
psychiatric medications and, 110–111, 111*t*, 112*f*
relationship to demographic factors, 37–47
Bipolar disorder
ADHD and, 106
BFIS-CA scores and, 97–100, 98*t*, 99*f*, 105*t*
daily life domains and, 106

CGAS. *See* Children's Global Assessment Scale (CGAS)
Child Behavior Checklist, 13, 15, 16, 52
Children's Global Assessment Scale (CGAS), 11–13
Clinician ratings, 11–13
Community involvement
impairment ratings for, 54–55, 54*f*
questions pertaining to, 44
Community–Leisure domains
BFIS-CA and BRIEF scores for, 62
calculating impairment scores for, 123
calculating mean impairment scores for, 124
impairment scores for, 36, 40*f*, 61, 61*f*
TD/TS and, 107
Construct validity, 51–60
face validity and, 51–52
factor analysis and, 52
other measures of impairment and, 52–60
community involvement, 54–55, 54*f*
school performance/adjustment, 56–58, 56*f*, 59*f*, 60
sports participation, 55–56, 55*f*
unpopularity, 52–54, 53*f*
Criterion validity, 60–63
ADHD symptom ratings and, 63
EF ratings and, 60–63, 62*f*, 62*t*
treatments and, 110. *See also* Treatment; *specific treatments*

Daily life activities
EF and, 62–63, 62*f*
See also Major life activities
Deficit measurement, 23
Delayed motor development/coordination
ADHD and, 107
BFIS-CA scores and, 66–69, 67*t*, 68*f*, 69–73, 70*t*, 71*f*, 72*f*, 104*t*–105*t*
genetic liability for, 106
Demographic factors, 25–30
age, sex, biological relationship, 25–26
children's developmental and psychiatric diagnoses, 28–29
ethnicity, 27
geographic region, 26–27
household income, 27–28
parent education, 26
parental employment status, 28
parental marital status, 28
relationship to BFIS-CA scores, 37–47
Depression
BFIS-CA scores and, 93–97, 95*t*, 96*f*, 97*f*, 105*t*
medications for, 111
Developmental delay/mental retardation, BFIS-CA scores and, 73, 74*t*, 75*f*, 104*t*
Diagnostic and Statistical Manual of Mental Disorders (DSM-IV-TR)
Global Assessment of Functioning Scale in, 1
malingering defined by, 18
psychosocial impairment in major life activities and, 1
Disability
ADA definition of, 8–9
guidelines for assessing, 9
Disability status, functional impairment and, 1
Disorder(s)
ADHD contamination of, 106
impairment and, 6
impairment patterns and, 102–109
See also specific disorders
Domain ratings, internal consistency of, 48–50
Domain responses, frequency of, 32–33, 34*t*, 35–36, 35*f*
Domains
abnormality thresholds for, 36
See also Community–Leisure domains; Home–School domains

Educational treatments
BFIS-CA scores and, 112–117
See also Academic tutoring; Special education services
Effect size (ES), of disorders on BFIS-CA, 102–103, 104*t*–105*t*, 106
Epilepsy, BFIS scores and, 74–75
Equal Employment Opportunity Commission (EEOC), ADA definition of impairment and, 8
Ethnic group, relationship to BFIS-CA scores, 42–43
Executive functioning
BFIS-CA validity and, 60–63, 61*t*, 62*f*
daily life activities and, 62–63, 62*f*

Face validity
defined, 51–52
for interpreting BFIS-CA, 134
Factor analysis, 31–32
for BFIS-CA domains, 31–32, 33*t*
construct validity and, 52
Frequency of domain responses, 32–33, 34t, 35–36, 35*f*

Friendships
  impairment ratings for, 52–54, 53*f*
  questions pertaining to, 44
Functional impairment. *See* Psychosocial impairment

GAF Scale. *See* Global Assessment of Functioning (GAF) Scale in DSM-IV-TR
Geographic region, relationship to BFIS-CA scores, 43
Global Assessment of Functioning (GAF) Scale in DSM-IV-TR, 1, 11, 13
Grade point average, 45–46
Grade retention, 46, 58, 59*f*

Harm, definitions of, 7–8
Home Situations Questionnaire, 2
  development of BFIS-CA and, 20–22
Home–School domains
  BFIS and BRIEF scores for, 62
  calculating impairment score for, 123
  calculating mean impairment score for, 124
  effect size of, 102–103, 104*t*–105*t*
  impairment scores for, 36, 40*f*, 61, 61*t*
  ODD and, 106

Impairment
  definitions of, 1–2, 5, 8, 51
  guidelines for assessing, 9
  hierarchical concept of, 8–9
  injury-related, evaluating change from, 133–134
  patterns of, across disorders, 102–108
  severity of, 7
  supplementary information sources and, 121
  See also Psychosocial impairment
Impairment Profiles, 2–3, 119–120
  creation of, 47
  female
    ages 6–11, 150–151
    ages 12–17, 152–153
  male
    ages 6–11, 146–147
    ages 12–17, 148–149
  structure of, 120
Impairment Rating Scale, 14
Impairment scores
  calculating for Community–Leisure Domains, 123
  calculating for Home–School Domains, 123
  creating visual profile of, 125
  mean, calculating, 124
Impairment-related questions
  scoring, 126
  secondary, 43–47, 52–63
Individuals with Disabilities Education Act (IDEA), 1
Injury, pre- and poststatus for interpreting BFIS-CA, 135
Injury-related impairment, evaluating change from, 133–134

Knowledge Networks, 24–25

Learning disabilities, BFIS scores and, 82–91

Major life activities
  examples of, 7–8
  functional impairment in, 7
  psychosocial impairment in, DSM-IV-TR and, 1
Malingering, assessment of, 18–19
Math disorders, BFIS-CA scores and, 86–89, 87*t*, 88*f*, 105*t*
Medical disorder, defined, 66
Mental disorders of childhood, psychosocial impairment and, 5–6

Neurodevelopmental disorders
  BFIS scores and, 64–81
  See also specific disorders
Normative comparison, for interpreting BFIS-CA, 135
Normative sample
  absence of, 2
  demographic characteristics of, 25–30. *See also* Demographic factors
  methods of collecting, 24–25

Oppositional defiant disorder
  ADHD and, 106
  BFIS-CA scores and, 100–102, 101*t*, 102*f*, 105*t*
  daily life domains and, 106

Parent Interview, 2, 120
  domains in, 120–121
  form for, 142–144
Parent Rating Scale, 119–120
  form for, 139–141
  primary scores for, 120
Parent ratings, 13–15
Parenting Rating Scale, 2
  secondary impairment-related questions on, 43–47
Parents, instructions to, 22, 23–24
Percentile interpretation, for interpreting BFIS-CA, 135
Percentile scores, determining, 124–125
Psychiatric disorders, BFIS scores and, 91–102
  for anxiety disorders, 91–92, 93*t*
  for bipolar disorder, 97–100, 98*t*, 99*f*
  for depression, 93–97, 94*f*, 95*t*, 96*f*
  for oppositional defiant disorder, 100–102, 101*t*, 102*f*
Psychiatric medications, BFIS-CA scores and, 110–111, 111*t*, 112*f*
Psychological therapy, BFIS-CA scores and, 116–117, 116*t*, 117*f*
Psychosocial impairment
  adult, assessment sources for, 10
  assessment of
    AMA guidelines for, 9–10, 16
    information sources for, 17
    malingering and, 18–19
    SSA guidelines for, 11, 16
    suggestions for, 15–19
    and triangulation among sources, 17–18
  definitions of, 22–23
  evaluation of, 11–15
    with clinician ratings, 11–13
    with parent ratings, 13–15
  instruments for measuring, 1–2
  See also Impairment

Quality of life scales, 14–15
Questions, impairment-related. *See* Impairment-related questions

Rating scales, permission for photocopying, 2
Reading disorders
  BFIS-CA scores and, 82–83, 83*t*, 84*f*, 104*t*
  versus SpD and WD, 107–108
Reliability, test–retest, 48–50, 50*t*
Reliable change index (RCI), calculating
  for change after treatment, 130–132, 131*t*, 132*t*
  for change due to injury, 133–134
Response to treatment
  BFIS-CA for evaluating, 129–133, 131*t*, 132*t*
  RCI and, 130–132, 131*t*, 132*t*
Risk analysis, for interpreting BFIS-CA, 135

School performance/adjustment
impairment ratings for, 56–58, 56*f*, 58*f*, 59*f*, 60
questions pertaining to, 45–47
School suspension, 58, 59*f*
Schoolwork problems, teacher-reported, 46
Score Sheet, 119
example of, 127–128
form for, 145
permission for photocopying, 2
Scoring, 119–136
example of, 126–129
materials for, 119–121
primary, 120
procedures for, 122–126
of secondary impairment questions, 126
Seizure disorders/epilepsy, BFIS-CA scores and, 74–75, 104*t*
Self-reports, 10
Sex, relationship to BFIS-CA scores, 39, 40*f*, 41*t*–42*t*
Sluggish cognitive tempo (SCT), 106
Social Security Administration, assessment guidelines of, 10–11, 16
Special education services, 47
BFIS-CA scores and, 112–113, 114*f*, 115*t*
Speech and language disorders
ADHD and, 107
BFIS-CA scores and, 66–69, 67*t*, 68*f*, 104*t*
Speech and language therapy, BFIS-CA scores and, 115–116
Spelling disorders
BFIS-CA scores and, 83–85, 85*t*, 86*f*, 105*t*
versus RD and WD, 107–108
Sports participation
impairment ratings for, 55–56, 55*f*
questions pertaining to, 45
Suspension/expulsion, 46–47
Symptoms
definitions of, 6
severity of, 7

Test of Memory Malingering, 18
Test–retest reliability, 48–50, 50*t*
Tic disorders/Tourette syndrome
BFIS-CA scores and, 75–78, 76*t*, 77*t*, 104*t*
Community–Leisure domains and, 107
Treatment
BFIS-CA scores and, 110–118
pre- and poststatus for interpreting BFIS-CA, 135
response to. *See* Response to treatment
See also specific treatments
Tutoring, BFIS-CA scores and, 112, 113t, 114*f*

Unpopularity, impairment ratings of, 52–54, 53*f*

Validity, 51–63. *See also* Construct validity; Criterion validity

Web-enabled Knowledge Panel, 24
Writing disorders
BFIS-CA scores and, 89–90, 90*t*, 91*f*, 105*t*
versus RD and SpD, 107–108